A Matter of Taste

Lucy Waverman   James Chatto

A MATTER OF TASTE

Inspired Seasonal Menus
with Wines and Spirits
to Match

HarperCollins Publishers Ltd

A Matter of Taste
© 2004 by Lucy Waverman and James Chatto. All rights reserved.

Published by HarperCollins Publishers Ltd

First Edition

HarperCollins books may be purchased for educational, business, or sales promotional use through our Special Markets Department.

HarperCollins Publishers Ltd
2 Bloor Street East, 20th Floor
Toronto, Ontario, Canada
M4W 1A8

www.harpercollins.ca

Library and Archives Canada Cataloguing in Publication

Waverman, Lucy
A matter of taste : inspired seasonal menus with wines and spirits to match / Lucy Waverman, James Chatto.

Includes index.
ISBN 0-00-200672-3

1. Cookery. 2. Alcoholic beverages. 3. Menus. I. Chatto, James II. Title.

TX728.W38 2004   641.5   C2004-903332-8

9 8 7 6 5 4 3 2 1

Printed and bound in Belgium by Proost NV, Turnhout
Jacket design by Alan Jones   Text design by Carol Moskot
Composition by Roy Nicol
Set in DIN and Scala

Contents

Introduction

THIS IS A BOOK ABOUT PLEASURE—the pleasure we find in cooking and eating wonderful food paired with well-chosen wines and spirits. It might be the seductive rendezvous of slow-roasted shoulder and rack of lamb with a dashing Italian cult red Sagrantino. It could be the way a juicy fillet of cod with Romesco sauce dances so elegantly with a fragrant, fruity Spanish rosado.

When the dish and the drink are truly in harmony, the result far surpasses the sum of the parts.

We have discussed these matters many times over the past ten years, sitting side by side at *Food & Drink* magazine's editorial meetings, braiding ideas about menus and recipes with wines and cocktails, spirits and beers. We often talked about writing a book together. When the magazine received two nominations as Best Food Magazine and Best Drink Magazine at the 2003 Jacob's Creek World Food Media Awards in Australia, we felt the time had come.

But what sort of book would it be?

Our first decision was to use the seasons as a frame. Lucy's cooking has always been profoundly inspired by seasonal ingredients and by the different ways in which we think about food from one time of year to another. The same is true of wines and cocktails. Some drinks are perfect for winter evenings curled up by the fire; others only come into their own on a hot summer's day.

Within each season, Lucy's menus run the gamut from sophisticated dinner parties to hearty family feasts to quick and easy midweek meals. Some reflect traditional celebrations like Thanksgiving, New Year's Eve or a family brunch; others have more unexpected themes—a wine-tasting shower, a book club gathering, a dinner with a theme of lemons. James finds wine or spirits matches for every course as well as before-dinner cocktails, aperitifs and occasional suggestions for something delicious to sip after the guests have gone. All sorts of careful harmonies run through the matched menus, but the individual recipes and wine pairings also work beautifully on their own. We urge you to play around with them. Take charge! Experiment! Put your favorite recipes together to create menus that suit your own taste.

The index may be a handy part of that exercise; we hope it will also serve as a more general tool when you want to match food and drink. If you're blessed with a bumper crop of tomatoes, for instance, use the index to find all of Lucy's tomato recipes; each one comes with suggested wine pairings. Or turn the whole process around and start from the wine's point of view. If you find yourself with a gorgeous bottle of British Columbian Chardonnay and want to cook something to flatter the wine, seek it out in the index and check out the recipes we feel it matches.

Another important criterion was to write a book that people could actually read. Stirred in among the menus are Food Tech tips on cooking techniques and ingredients, short essays on different aspects of wine and spirits and the tall tales that lie behind every cocktail worth its salt. We offer no apology if they sometimes sound a tad opinionated: eating and drinking is a very personal business! So, Lucy's recipes reflect her passion for pears and ginger, green vegetables and fish, and also her love of food that is simple, organic, easy to prepare and vibrant with flavor. Meanwhile, James indulges his affection for whisky and fortified wines, devises cocktails to showcase his beloved Plymouth gin, but cruelly neglects vodka. Beer, too, is conspicuous by its absence—a subject so rich and varied that it deserves a volume of its own.

Every close relationship has its ups and downs. In the course of planning this book we fought and argued, sulked, laughed but always came to terms in the end, finding food and drink matches that delighted us both. Some of them may seem unconventional, such as single malt Scotch served straight from the freezer to accompany Lucy's delectable Triple Chocolate Truffle Tart, but we urge you to try them. And, yes, there were times when challenges led to compromise. Lucy reluctantly cut back on the tartly dressed salad garnishes that she likes to serve with some appetizers (wine is too easily unmanned by a vinaigrette). But she insisted on keeping her gorgeous soups (notoriously tricky matches for vino), forcing James to rise to the occasion with such pairings as chilled dry vermouth for Scallop and Fennel Soup.

A cookbook, a food book, a primer on wine and spirits, an introduction to the casual art of bringing all these elements together, this book is first and foremost a personal celebration of the things we most love to eat and drink.

LUCY WAVERMAN   JAMES CHATTO

June 2004

Food Basics

FOR ME, FOOD IS A PASSION. I love to prepare it, eat it and share it with my family and friends. Taste, of course, is always paramount, and I believe the best taste comes from using high-quality, seasonal ingredients and preparing them simply and properly. Recipes do not need to be complicated, expensive, time-consuming or rigid. Most of the recipes in this book are forgiving, and many can be made ahead. We all taste differently, so trust your own palate, adapt or vary the recipes according to your own tastes and adjust seasonings as you see fit, especially at the end of the cooking.

Some things do, however, make a real difference in cooking. Here are some of the most important ingredients and equipment that I believe truly affect the quality of the end result.

Organic Ingredients A growing number of consumers today are buying organic foods. For reasons of health and flavor, I try to buy naturally raised or organic meat and poultry and organic fruits and vegetables. Now most supermarkets have an organic section; there are also home delivery companies that will deliver organic foods to your door.

Stock The quality of a finished dish is often directly related to the quality of the stock used in it. I find it very therapeutic to make my own stock. To make chicken stock, for instance, follow the recipe for chicken soup (page 64), but use lots of bones instead of a whole chicken. If you shudder at the thought of making your own stock, look for the many excellent storebought stocks that are available. Buy low-salt products if possible, because stock is often reduced down in recipes, intensifying the saltiness. I like the stock sold in Tetra Paks, especially the organic versions, and I always read the labels. If you are buying chicken stock, for example, make sure that chicken is the first ingredient listed and look for stocks that do not contain MSG. Good-quality beef, veal and chicken stock are often available frozen at butcher shops.

Butter I use unsalted butter in cooking. The water content is lower than that of salted butter, making it better for baking and cooking, and I prefer the taste. Unsalted butter can also be heated to a higher temperature without burning.

In general I prefer not to use shortening because it is full of trans fat. However, in pastry, a small amount added to the butter results in a flakier crust. If you don't want to use shortening, you can use lard or a trans fat–free margarine, or increase the butter.

Herbs I use fresh herbs whenever possible in cooking, as their flavor is much superior to dried. However, if you must substitute dried herbs, use only one-third the amount of fresh. When using parsley (which is always available fresh), I prefer the superior flavor and look of flat-leaf Italian parsley rather than curly parsley.

Onions I use several kinds of onions in recipes. Cooking onions are strongly flavored, and I use them only in long-simmered dishes. Spanish onions are milder than cooking onions, but stronger than sweet onions, and I find they are the best all-purpose onions to have around. When sweet onions such as Vidalia are on the market, they are excellent eaten raw or caramelized.

Gingerroot I really like ginger, though for some people it is an acquired taste. It comes in so many forms that sometimes it can be difficult to know which one to use. I use grated or chopped fresh gingerroot in cooking. Look for firm, smooth tubers that feel heavy for their size. Ground ginger tastes nothing like fresh, though it is used in baking and in some Eastern Mediterranean dishes. Preserved ginger and candied ginger are often confused. Preserved ginger is ginger that has been preserved in syrup. Candied ginger has been cooked, sugared and dried. It is used in baking and is wonderful coated with chocolate. Pickled ginger is served as a condiment with sushi.

Vanilla I always use real vanilla, even though it is expensive. Other vanilla flavorings taste artificial.

Equipment I use a food processor, blender, hand blender and mini chop in the kitchen. Blenders are best when you want smooth purees for soups; the food processor usually gives you a chunkier texture. Hand blenders are invaluable for making quick purees, and they are easy to wash. I also use them to combine salad dressings or other liquid ingredients. The mini chop can chop a large amount of garlic or ginger, which you can store to use for a week's worth of cooking by covering it with oil and refrigerating. I also use the mini chop to chop fresh herbs and nuts and to grind spices.

Some of the recipes in this book call for foods to be very thinly sliced or shredded. The mandolin makes this much easier. Today there are many inexpensive versions available.

I always use metal baking sheets and pans for roasting and baking. They hold the heat better than china or glass and do a better job of browning.

Wine Tech

Wine and Food Matching

A GREAT MANY PEOPLE ARE PERFECTLY CONTENT to cook a delicious meal and open a bottle of their favorite wine without giving much thought to how the food and the wine will get on together. It's like introducing one of your friends to another. You love them both: why shouldn't they hit it off? More often than not, everything will be okay—but okay is not good enough in our book. We want more.

Finding a wine that works beautifully with a specific dish enhances the pleasure we take in eating and drinking. The food actually tastes better and so does the wine. And sometimes that enhancement soars to epiphanic heights. That is the ultimate goal, the reason why we think about matching food and wine in the first place.

And thinking is central to the process. The best way to match wine to food is by trial and error—an invaluable learning experience when you're on your own but risky when entertaining. Better to spread a tablecloth in your imagination, picture the dishes and try to work out which wines you might pour. Think about the richness, weight and textures of each course, the way it was cooked, the flavors and aromas of everything on the plate. Now think about wines in the same way, beginning with their weight or body.

One time-tested rule of thumb holds that rich, heavy food fares best with full-bodied wines and lightweight dishes with light-bodied wines. Another concerns acidity: a tart vinaigrette on a salad, a generous squeeze of lemon over a piece of barbecued chicken or a tangy tomato sauce narrow your wine options to something with plenty of acidity of its own. Sweetness, too, plays a role. If the dessert is sweeter than the wine, the wine will taste thin and diminished. Dramatic saltiness can make the tannins in a big red wine taste bitter. It's also a good idea to check for any potential dangers among the ingredients. Certain foods can knock many wines for six—ice cream, chocolate, horseradish, fresh grapefruit and artichokes are among the most notorious threats—while the oils in some very oily fish can react with the tannins in red wine to create a metallic effect in your mouth.

It sounds like a minefield, but in practice such pitfalls are rare. Far more often, food seems to bring out interesting and attractive new sides of a wine's personality, just as wine does with people. Here's a demure Ontario rosé, closed and unforthcoming on its own, that suddenly tastes like wild strawberries when served with a lightly dressed green salad. There's a sober, joyless young Bordeaux swathed in a dark cloak of tannins. Drink it with lamb and you suddenly taste ripe black currants. At least, you may do. The effect may seem different in your mouth than it does in mine, for matching food and wine is a highly subjective matter. The way we experience a wine is influenced by umpteen variables, from deep-rooted prejudices to what we each had for breakfast, from physical sensitivities to the mood of the moment.

That is why the whole food-and-wine matching process really is a matter of taste. The pairings suggested in this book are simply the wines, aperitifs and cocktails that I think work best with Lucy's wonderful menus. I have tried to explain why they work for me and to sketch the thinking behind each choice. Serving several wines with each course and tasting how differently they behave is all part of the fun.

This book does not recommend particular wine producers or vintages. Bottles that are familiar in one part of the world may well be unavailable in others. Instead, I've tried to identify wines by region, grape variety and style, which shifts the final responsibility for selection onto you and your liquor store. Cultivate a relationship with a well-informed, imaginative sales person, someone who will know precisely which wine to reach for when you go in and ask for a juicy, lightly oaked Sonoma Chardonnay, or who can suggest a couple of dazzling alternatives. Bring the wines home, cook up a storm, pull a few corks and let the pleasure begin.

Lucy and I agree that one example is worth a thousand words of theory. The following First Principles menu, while delicious in its own right, serves as a blueprint for matching wine to food and explains many of the precepts to be found in the rest of the book.

First Principles

Salmon Rillettes
Classic Roast Chicken with a Twist
Mashed Potatoes with Garlic
Green Beans
Crème Brûlée with Roasted Pears and Lemongrass
SERVES 4

I DEVELOPED THIS SIMPLE MENU of classic tastes as a framework for James to outline the basic principles of how wine works with food. I love his food and drink logic and the way he assesses the flavors, textures and weight of the food to find just the right wine, producing taste sensations I never thought possible. In this menu he suggests a number of accompaniments for the rich flavors of the roast chicken and the earthy, rustic mashed potatoes, and you can follow his logic to make your own choice. I do, and I have to admit my own preference for a luscious, mouth-filling Pinot Noir from the Central Otago region of New Zealand!

Salmon Rillettes

SERVES 4

A true rillette is a type of pork pâté, where the pork is cooked slowly with lots of lard and then pounded together with the fat. In these fish rillettes, fresh and smoked salmon are combined with butter, and the result is much lighter.

Serve the rillettes with hot toast.

8 oz salmon fillet, skin removed

¼ cup white wine

8 oz smoked salmon, coarsely chopped

¼ cup chopped green onions

1 tbsp chopped fresh dill

½ cup butter, at room temperature

⅓ cup mayonnaise

Salt and freshly ground pepper

1 tbsp lemon juice

Garnish

2 cups mache or other soft lettuce

1 tbsp extra-virgin olive oil

Salt and freshly ground pepper

2 tbsp salmon caviar

Place salmon fillet in a small skillet. Pour wine over salmon. Turn heat to medium and heat until you see steam. Cover and cook for 3 minutes (salmon will not be quite cooked through).

Remove salmon from skillet and flake. Reduce liquid in skillet if needed until 2 tbsp remain.

Add salmon and liquid to a food processor with smoked salmon, green onions, dill, butter and mayonnaise. Puree until combined but not quite smooth. Season with salt, pepper and lemon juice. Chill for 3 hours or overnight.

Toss mache with olive oil, salt and pepper.

Place 3 small oval-shaped scoops of salmon on each plate. Garnish with mache and top with a sprinkle of salmon caviar.

And to drink . . .

AS A WINE THAT WORKS deliciously well with Lucy's opulent salmon rillettes, I recommend a dry Gewürztraminer from the French region of Alsace. The first reason has to do with weight. A dish with the silky, buttery weight of the rillettes needs a wine with weight of its own, otherwise the wine will seem too thin by comparison. Alsatian Gewürztraminer has a voluptuous viscosity that slides like satin over your tongue.

Now consider acidity. This isn't an acidic wine at all, but that's okay—there is little sense of acidity in the dish. That trace of lemon juice in the rillettes only serves to refresh them, and Lucy has not included lemon juice or vinegar in the dressing for the garnish of salad leaves.

What about saltiness? There is some in the dish from the smoked salmon and the salmon caviar, but salt is only really a problem with the tannins in a big red wine, accentuating their bitterness.

Sweetness? With such a rich dish you could consider a sweet wine—even a late harvest Gewürztraminer from the same region—but I think it might prove too cloying. A dry Alsatian Gewürztraminer actually gives the initial illusion of sweetness—part of the flavor of this particular grape—but finishes refreshingly dry.

Surprisingly, perhaps, we come to the flavor and aroma of the wine last. Alsatian Gewürz' has a gorgeously exotic aroma like litchis or rose petals, but beneath it you can often detect a smoky, gingery note that reaches out to the smokiness of the smoked salmon in the rillettes and forms a sort of bridge between wine and food. With all the "technical" issues dealt with, such aesthetic connections are what these matchmaking games are all about.

Classic Roast Chicken
with a Twist

SERVES 4

James wanted very simple seasonings for this main course, to let the chicken flavor soar and the wine shine. Have your butcher remove the backbone and breastbone of the chicken so it will lie flat, or do it yourself. Butterflied chicken allows for easier carving and quicker cooking.

2 tbsp butter, melted	Gravy
1 4-lb chicken, butterflied	2 cups chicken stock
1 tbsp chopped fresh tarragon	1 tsp tomato paste
1 tsp grated lemon zest	1/2 tsp chopped fresh tarragon
2 tsp kosher salt	2 tbsp butter, diced
2 tsp cracked black pepper	Salt and freshly ground pepper

Preheat oven to 400°F.

Brush melted butter over chicken skin. Season both sides of chicken with tarragon, lemon zest, salt and pepper. Lay chicken on a rack in a roasting pan, skin side up.

Bake for one hour, or until skin is crisp and juices run clear. Transfer chicken to a carving board to rest for 10 minutes while you make gravy.

Remove all fat from roasting pan. Add stock, tomato paste and tarragon to pan, scraping up any bits from bottom of pan.

Bring gravy to a boil over medium heat and boil for 3 to 4 minutes, or until slightly thickened. Remove from heat and stir in butter until absorbed. Season with salt and pepper.

Cut chicken into 4 pieces and serve with gravy.

And to drink . . .

IT'S TRUE, I DID ASK LUCY to keep this demonstration menu simple, but simplicity tends to broaden, not narrow, the field of opportunity for the person choosing the wine. The rillettes offered relatively few choices—smoked salmon is a difficult match. A roast chicken, seasoned but otherwise served as nature intended, happily straddles the divide between red and white wines and opens up all sorts of possibilities.

You can start by ruling out the extremes. A great big powerhouse of a red would overwhelm the natural textures and flavors of the dish. A crisp, lightweight white might be an interesting contrast (especially to the rich mashed potatoes) but would ultimately contribute little but refreshment. So, we've narrowed the field to full-bodied whites and medium-bodied reds.

Although there are many regional anomalies, the grape varieties used to make a wine are a good clue to its weight. Chardonnay, for example, is usually more full bodied than Sauvignon Blanc, which is more full bodied than dry Riesling. Cabernet Sauvignon is usually weightier than Pinot Noir. Forsaking all others, therefore, let's think about Chardonnay and Pinot Noir for our chicken.

The other things on the plate are also a vital part of the wine-matching process. Often a sauce turns out to be the most pungent and flavorful element of a dish and so determines the choice of wine. This time, however, Lucy's demure reduction takes a back seat to the chicken. The green beans are also passengers, quietly along for the ride. But those buttery, garlic-flecked mashed potatoes do play a role, adding richness and weight. You could meet that richness head to head with a ripe, oaky Chardonnay from California or Australia, though that soft, sweet oak tends to blur flavors in the clinch. Better, perhaps, to look for an unoaked version or else a more elegant Burgundian Chardonnay, like a Mâcon, to freshen your palate. For the Pinot, try something good from Burgundy if it suits your budget (cheap Burgundy is so often disappointing), or look for something with better value from Ontario, Oregon, Tasmania or New Zealand's dramatically impressive Martinborough and Central Otago regions. Open the red and the white and let your guests decide which they prefer.

Mashed Potatoes with Garlic

SERVES 4

The combination of floury Yukon Gold potatoes and waxy red potatoes gives an unusual but delightful texture and color to this homey and sophisticated mash. Sauté the garlic ahead of time and beat the butter and potatoes together just before serving.

1½ lbs Yukon gold potatoes, peeled	½ cup butter
8 oz red potatoes, unpeeled and scrubbed	4 cloves garlic, thinly sliced
	Salt and freshly ground pepper

Cut potatoes into even-sized chunks and place in a pot. Cover with cold salted water and bring to a boil over high heat. Reduce heat and simmer for 10 to 15 minutes, or until potatoes are tender.

Heat butter in a skillet over low heat while potatoes are cooking. Add garlic to skillet and sauté for 5 minutes, or until golden.

Drain potatoes well. Return pot to turned-off burner and shake to dry out potatoes. Mash with a potato masher, leaving some texture in potatoes. Season with salt and pepper.

Strain garlic-flavored butter over potatoes and combine gently. Taste and adjust seasonings if necessary. Pile into a buttered serving dish and scatter fried garlic over potatoes.

Green Beans

SERVES 4

Boil the green beans ahead of time. Once they are cooked, run cold water over them (or shock them, as it is known in kitchen-speak) until the beans are cold, then drain and reserve. Sauté the beans just before serving.

8 oz green beans, topped and tailed	Salt and pepper to taste
1 tbsp butter	2 tsp lemon juice

Bring a pot of salted water to a boil over high heat. Add green beans and boil for 3 to 4 minutes, or until crisp-tender. Drain and shock in cold water.

Heat butter in a skillet over medium heat. Add beans and sauté until hot, 2 to 3 minutes. Season with salt, pepper and lemon juice.

Crème Brûlée with Roasted Pears
and Lemongrass

SERVES 4

You can make this in a large gratin dish, but it looks more attractive served in individual dishes. Use large ramekins, about 4 inches across and 1 to 1½ inches deep.

Roasted Pears	Crème Brûlée
2 Bartlett pears	1 stalk lemongrass
2 tsp granulated sugar	2 cups whipping cream
	5 egg yolks
	½ cup granulated sugar

Preheat oven to 425°F and butter 4 ramekins.

Peel, halve and core pears. Place half a pear flat side down in each ramekin. Sprinkle each pear half with ½ tsp sugar. Roast pears for 25 minutes, or until soft and slightly golden at edges. Remove ramekins from oven and set aside to cool. Reduce oven temperature to 325°F.

Discard top 2 inches of lemongrass stalk. Smash stalk with back of a knife and chop coarsely.

Place cream and lemongrass in a pot while pears are roasting and bring to a boil over high heat. Remove from heat and cool for 15 minutes. Strain and discard lemongrass.

Combine egg yolks and ¼ cup sugar in a bowl and whisk until thick and lemon-yellow. Whisk cream into egg yolk mixture and pour into ramekins, covering roasted pears and any juice that has formed.

Place ramekins in a larger pan and fill pan with enough hot water to come halfway up sides of ramekins. Bake for 35 to 40 minutes, or until custards are set but still have a slight wobble in center. Chill.

Sprinkle 1 tbsp sugar over each ramekin. Place ramekins under broiler and, watching carefully, broil until sugar is melted and golden. Remove immediately and cool for 30 minutes before serving.

And to drink . . .

I LOVE DESSERT WINES. Bringing out a new treat in the late innings of dinner revivifies the evening and rejuvenates the conversation, especially since most dessert wines are a little eccentric and have their own tales to tell.

Matching a wine to dessert isn't particularly complicated. The main thing to remember is that the wine should be as sweet or a little sweeter than the food—if not, it will taste weak and inadequate, however delicious it might be when enjoyed on its own. Acidity is important, too, especially with a fruit dessert. A lemon tart, for example, is certainly sweet but it's also sour enough to demand a wine that also has good acidity—a late harvest Riesling, perhaps.

Acid isn't the issue with this rich crème brûlée, fragrant with lemongrass and juicy poached pear: the heavy, silky texture is much more important, together with the chance to enhance the flavor of those pears. There is something pear-like about the grapy flavor of Muscat grapes and a smooth, well-chilled, fortified Muscat from France (Rivesaltes or Beaume-de-Venises, for example) would be a deliciously easy option. Approaching from a different direction, sweet, frothy, foamy Moscato d'Asti is as light as laughter, a contrast rather than a compliment to the weight of the dessert. But Muscat de Rivesaltes remains my number one choice, lifting the exotic perfume of the lemongrass and holding hands with the pear. Or you could enter into the spirit of the fruit with a small glass of pear eau-de-vie, served very cold indeed.

Wine Tech

Cellaring and Service

I WISH I POSSESSED A WINE CELLAR, but I have never had the budget or the patience to amass a collection of age-worthy favorites. I have never spent weeks converting a cupboard or corner of the basement into a perfect nursery for the future brood—a space free of bright light, vibration, pungent odors and sudden changes in temperature. I have never felt the fierce parental pride at seeing some cherished Cabernet, bought at a bargain price in its gangly adolescence, mature into the full flower of winehood. These joys are denied me. So, too, is the carefree trip to the cellar to fetch up two or three different bottles that might or might not prove superb when my wife suddenly decides tonight is the night to create the world's best paella. Nowhere to store a case of vintage port against my newborn godson's twenty-first birthday. Nowhere to hide a trophy bottle from a pair of thirsty eyes.

If I did have a cellar, I would treat it like a laboratory and stock it with consummate care. Most wines are made to be drunk soon after they're sold, not laid down for years. My bins would hold the exceptions: red and white Burgundies, red Bordeaux and stars from the northern Rhône, sweet Sauternes and Vouvrays; barolos, brunellos and amarones from Italy; vintage Champagnes to taste in their decadent maturity; ports and Madeiras and Spanish Tempranillos from renowned houses; fine German Rieslings with aromas that change from lime and slate to petrol; macho reds from California, Washington State and Australia, and a host of obscure curiosities. I would open examples of each with every passing year, taking nerdly note of their evolution, watching them grow old with me.

The ideal ambient temperature for a wine cellar is somewhere between 52 and 60 degrees Fahrenheit, with good humidity. I remember being shown around the vaulted, dungeon-like *caves* of a French château and learning they naturally stayed at 58 degrees, day or night, winter or summer—an enviable cool rarely achieved in a North American home, unless your storage area has its own air-conditioner. This, incidentally, is pretty much the perfect temperature at which to serve dry white, rosé and light red wines. Sparkling and sweet white wines are best slightly cooler—around 50 degrees—partly because they seem more refreshing and partly because chilling lowers our perception of sweetness. If you don't use a wine thermometer (I don't know anyone who does), there's no need to fret. Put your Champagne or late harvest Vidal in the refrigerator for an hour or in a bucket of ice and water for 20 minutes.

Especially when served with food, wine—even full-bodied red wine—has an obligation to refresh. Medium- and full-bodied reds are often served too warm in our overheated homes, and that can make them seem dull and flabby. A couple of minutes in a bucket of ice and water will drop the temperature a notch or two.

Drinking wine from a beautiful glass is good for the soul and also good for the wine. If I were a millionaire with cooks and bottle-washers and several temperate wine cellars, I would explore the extraordinary range of stemware created by such firms as Riedel and Spiegelau to showcase every kind of wine at its absolute best. The breadth of the bowl allows the right amount of air to reach the wine and encourages swirling; the way the glasses narrow toward the rim concentrates the aromas instead of dissipating them. Even everyday wines strut their maximum stuff in a vessel shaped that way.

It's a sad truth that an engraved or tinted glass (even a traditional German Riesling glass called a Baden Römer) camouflages the wine and distracts from its beauty. Thick tumblers or anything made of plastic, wood, metal or clay are merely utensils. Sparkling wines deserve a long, narrow flute; the old-fashioned shallow Champagne coupe looks charming but extinguishes the fizz and blows off the bouquet before you can say Marie Antoinette.

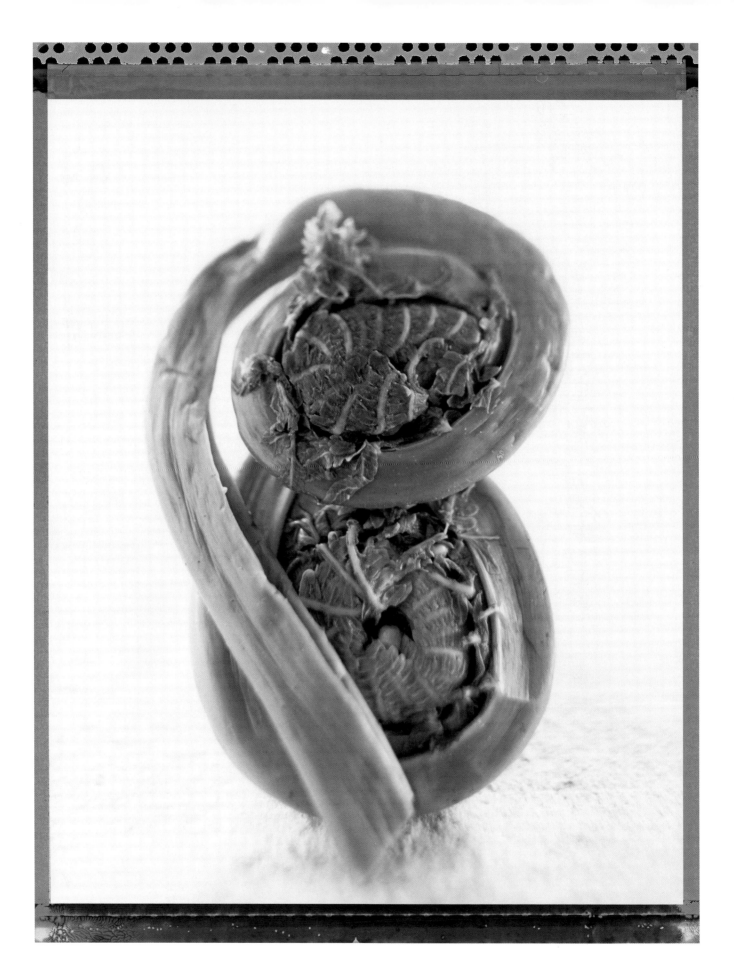

SPRING

spring food

EVERYONE HAS THEIR SPECIAL SIGNALS that spring has finally arrived—the early buds on the trees, daffodils raising their yellow heads, the sighting of the first robin.

My signs of spring are all about flavor and texture. When spring approaches, cooking changes. Gone is the desire for stews, hearty soups and rich puddings. The mood shifts to lighter, quick dishes. Starchy winter roots and slow-cooked foods give way to brighter tastes and a different approach to cooking. The season's first favas—tender, non-starchy beans that are finally making headway in North America—are gently sautéed. A walk in the woods may reveal earthy delicacies like fiddleheads and wild leeks, to be tossed into a soup or vegetable ragout. There's lots of fish, quickly braised or roasted, and salads livened up with seasonal specialties such as watercress and snow pea greens. And there are bright lemony flavors and the spring delights of fresh rhubarb, asparagus, sorrel, tiny new chives and the first fragrant fronds of chervil.

spring drinks

THERE IS A MOMENT EVERY YEAR when the sun first feels warm on my face and the notion of a glass of cold white wine leaps suddenly to mind. Perhaps it's the weather—the sense that an endless winter may be about to thaw, that the Campari days of summer are only weeks away. More likely it's the change in the way we eat: no more rib-sticking casseroles for a while, no more huddling around the fireplace with a hunk of Parmesan and a bottle of amarone. The sap green flavors of the year's early crops call for a racy Sauvignon Blanc: lighter days, lighter dishes, lighter wines.

But the climb from cold to heat can be steep, and there are days and nights when the new season stumbles, when windows must be closed and that amarone doesn't seem like such an outlandish idea. Crisp whites and big reds can share the same table. So can fresh rosés and opulent late harvest wines, ethereal cocktails and rich, dry oloroso sherries.

First Tastes of Spring

Polenta with Spring Vegetable Ragout
Tuna Confit
Fava Bean Sauté
Rhubarb Strawberry Crostata
SERVES 4

THIS DINNER COMBINES some new cooking techniques with the season's first fresh vegetables—asparagus, wild leeks and fava beans.

As soon as the snow disappears, fragile-looking wild leeks (also called ramps) peek out from under maple, beech and hemlock trees and deliver a bracing flavor that is garlicky and onion-like at the same time.

Favas (broad beans) are another rare spring treat. They are used extensively in Mediterranean and North African countries, where they are often dried for winter consumption. In Egypt they are used to make a pureed dip called ful, which is similar to hummus.

You can prepare the crostata and fava beans ahead of time. Reheat the favas and quick-cook the fish while you leave your guests to decide whether to drink white or red with the main course.

Manzanilla

THE GUESTS ARE AT THE DOOR and there will be smiles and kisses, a handing over of the tribute bottle, all the small rituals of welcome that lead at last to a single question: "What would you like to drink?" The polite guest refrains from an honest answer ("A glass of vintage Krug." "A gallon of gin if I'm going to have to sit and listen to endless news about your children.") and lobs the question back: "What have you got?" Now the evening begins.

Drinks before dinner—aperitifs—are amazingly useful things. They quench the thirst, soothe away stress, break the social ice, give us an initial topic of conversation and something to do with our hands. They also nudge the palate awake, leading off the long parade of good things to eat and drink around which the evening revolves. I like it when a host has put some thought into the matter, has found something interesting at the liquor store or decided on a particular cocktail that will glide smoothly into dinner.

The aperitif should suit the season and the temperature. It shouldn't be too sweet because sweetness shuts down the palate. Tartness or, better yet, a pleasing bitterness invigorates the taste buds.

As does salt, of course, though few drinks and only one wine I know of could actually be described as salty. That wine is manzanilla, the lightest and driest of all sherries. It comes from the northwestern area of the great triangular region where sherry is made, close to the coastal town of Sanlucar de Barrameda. They say the proximity to the ocean makes the difference, giving that salty hint to the wine, while the warm, moist wind off the Atlantic— the *poniente*—produces a thicker flor of yeasts on the surface of the sherry as it matures in the barrel. And it's true: if you move a butt of manzanilla inland to the town of Jerez, the flor thins and the wine slowly changes into a fino. With a sharp aroma and bone dry, delicately nutty intensity, manzanilla is a classic aperitif, brilliant with salted nuts and olives, and a clean, clear clarion call to table.

Polenta with Spring Vegetable Ragout

SERVES 4 AS AN APPETIZER

This foolproof oven method for making polenta means you'll never again have to stand stirring it over the stove. For a firmer polenta, reduce the water by up to 2 cups. (If you are using quick-cooking polenta, follow the package directions.)

Use all of the wild leeks, including the tulip-like leaves. If you can't find wild leeks, substitute green onions.

Polenta
2 tbsp olive oil
1/2 cup chopped onions
1 cup cornmeal
6 cups boiling water
2 tsp salt
1/4 cup butter
1 cup grated Parmesan cheese
Vegetable Ragout
2 tbsp olive oil
12 oz mixed wild mushrooms,
    trimmed and quartered

8 oz asparagus, trimmed and cut in
    2-inch pieces
1/2 cup green peas
1 bunch wild leeks (about 12), rinsed
1 cup chicken or beef stock
2 tsp balsamic vinegar
2 tsp chopped chervil or parsley
2 tsp chopped chives
2 tbsp butter
Salt and freshly ground pepper

Preheat oven to 350°F.
Heat olive oil in an ovenproof pot over medium-high heat. Add onions and sauté for 3 minutes, or until transparent.
Add cornmeal and stir to coat with oil. Pour in boiling water, whisking constantly to prevent lumps. Bring to a boil, stirring. Stir in salt.
Place pot in oven, uncovered, and cook for 45 to 60 minutes, stirring occasionally. Polenta should just hold its shape. Beat in butter and Parmesan.
Prepare ragout while polenta is cooking. Heat oil in a large skillet over medium-high heat. Add mushrooms and sauté for 2 minutes. Add asparagus and sauté for 1 minute longer. Add peas, leeks, stock and vinegar. Reduce heat and simmer for 3 to 4 minutes, or until asparagus is crisp-tender and sauce is slightly thickened. Remove from heat and stir in chervil, chives and butter. Season with salt and pepper.
Spoon polenta onto individual plates and top with vegetable ragout.

And to drink . . .

WHEN CHOOSING A WINE FOR A DISH, the first thing to consider is weight. Think of it as a boxing match: no matter how similar the talent and temperament and tenacity of the fighters, the bout is going to be less than meaningful if one pug is a bantam cock and the other is a gorilla. A rich, heavy dish works best with a heavy wine; a lighter wine suits lighter food.

Other traditional tenets have to do with the progression of wines. White precedes red, lighter precedes heavier, dry precedes sweet. There are umpteen triumphant exceptions, but by and large these rules make sense. The problems begin when a menu like this one crops up. The first course is richer, heavier and more intensely flavored than the second. One dictum says the wines should match the weight of the dish, so a heavier wine will precede a lighter, and that breaks a different law!

This is the moment to take a deep breath and relax. The lives of millions do not hang upon your decision. And options abound. The easiest solution is simply to break the rules and do exactly as you please. The vegetable ragout, with its intensifying dash of balsamic, its butter and olive oil, its heavenly, Parmesan-infused polenta, would be lovely with a soft, velvety New World Merlot. Bring it out.

Then again, whites can be heavyweights, too. Big, voluptuous, buttery Californian Chardonnays without too much oak absolutely adore the flavor of corn. Such a wine would clasp that polenta to its ample bosom and smile kindly upon the mushrooms. The balsamic is too small and well integrated a presence to offer any dangerous acidity.

So pass the buck. Serve both wines and shift the onus of decision onto your guests.

When referring to wild mushrooms in the recipes we mean a mixture of mushrooms such as shiitake, oyster, brown and white. Today these are cultivated, not wild.

Tuna Confit

SERVES 4

This amazing recipe is my take on a wonderful dish I had at L'Impero restaurant in New York. A confit usually refers to duck or goose that is cooked slowly in fat. In this case, tuna is cooked gently in olive oil. Don't be put off by the large amount of oil—the tuna does not absorb it.

Use a skillet or saucepan just big enough to hold the tuna snugly in a single layer. The olive oil should cover the fish completely.

Serve the tuna over the fava beans.

4 tuna steaks (about 6 oz each),
   1½ inches thick

Salt and freshly ground pepper
2 cups olive oil, approx.

Season tuna with salt and pepper.
Heat oil in a skillet over medium-low heat until a cube of bread bubbles very gently when dropped into oil. Temperature should be about 220°F.
Immerse tuna in oil and cook for 4 to 5 minutes, or until tuna is cooked on outside but still rare in center and feels soft to the touch. Immediately remove tuna to a strainer, drain, season to taste and serve.

Tuna For recipes that call for tuna to be eaten very rare, you'll want to buy the best-quality fish you can find. Choose species with the common names of yellowfin, bigeye and ahi—species that are not susceptible to parasites.

Tuna Confit; Fava Bean Sauté (p. 34)

And to drink . . .

THE FIRST COURSE WAS A WILD SUCCESS. The second must not be a disappointment. Tuna braised in olive oil is a good deal more delicate than might be supposed from reading the recipe. The fish is drained before serving, leaving the nutty, fruity flavor of the oil but little of its weight. The tuna itself is extraordinarily tender.

If you love red wine and feel that no dinner party is complete without it (which may sound obsessive but seems to be true of an amazing number of people), a wine made from Gamay or Pinot Noir grapes is in your immediate future. That old lore about not serving red wine with fish had a basis in science. The tannins in big red wines can have a bizarre reaction with the oils in oily fish, leaving an unpleasant metallic taste in the mouth. Gamay Noir, the easygoing sibling of Burgundy's great Pinot Noir, is usefully low in tannins. It is the grape of everyday Beaujolais and, much more interestingly, of cru Beaujolais wines (page 115). Lucy loves the fresh fruitiness of a Beaujolais with this dish, and I agree it's a fine combination. But there is always something more going on in a good Pinot Noir—something earthy, spicy and mushroomy under the fruit. A silky, middleweight Pinot Noir from a reliable producer in Oregon or New Zealand is my red this time.

That said, your ace in the hole is the same buttery Chardonnay you served with the first course. It has the weight to match this dish. Furthermore, just as it got on so well with the polenta, so it clasps hands with the fava beans. If oaked New World Chardonnays have a true affinity for simple food (and the range narrows when the wines are overripe, over-oaked and exaggeratedly potent), it is for the sweetly earthy flavors of corn and beans.

Fava Bean Sauté

SERVES 4

Favas are labor intensive to prepare, but they are worth the trouble. They are available fresh only in the spring and occasionally in the fall, but you can find frozen favas the rest of the year (the frozen favas are shelled but not skinned). Prepare them simply so as not to mask their earthy flavor. They can be eaten in a salad, simmered with asparagus or served with a sharp cheese like Asiago. Fold them into risotto just before serving or cook with couscous. If the beans are large and a bit tough, mash with butter or olive oil, garlic, paprika, cayenne, ground ginger and cumin and serve as a dip.

This is a marvelous side dish with fish, chicken or veal.

2 tbsp olive oil

4 slices prosciutto, diced

1 tsp chopped garlic

2 cups shelled and skinned fava beans

Salt and freshly ground pepper

Heat oil in a skillet over medium heat. Add prosciutto and garlic and sauté for 2 minutes, or until garlic is softened and prosciutto begins to crisp.

Add fava beans and sauté for 2 minutes longer, or until beans are heated through and tender. Season with salt and pepper.

How to Prepare Fava Beans Peel off the large pods to remove the beans nestled inside. Bring a pot of water to a boil, add the beans and blanch for 30 seconds. Drain and immediately plunge beans into ice water to cool. Slip the tough outer skin from each bean and discard. The beans are now ready for eating either raw or lightly cooked.

1 lb fava beans in the pod = 1 cup shelled beans

1 cup shelled beans = 1/2 cup skinned beans

Rhubarb Strawberry Crostata

SERVES 4 WITH LEFTOVERS

A crostata is a freeform tart made without a tart pan. I use dried cranberries to absorb some of the rhubarb juices while the tart is baking, but you could use raisins or omit the dried fruit altogether. This can be made a day ahead. It is a large tart for four people, but leftovers are great for breakfast. Serve with whipped cream, if desired.

Pastry
2 cups all-purpose flour
½ tsp salt
½ cup butter, diced
¼ cup shortening (page 8), diced
3 tbsp cold water, approx.
2 tbsp lemon juice

Filling
4 cups thickly sliced rhubarb
2 cups thickly sliced strawberries
⅓ cup dried cranberries
⅔ cup granulated sugar
3 tbsp all-purpose flour

Glaze
1 egg yolk
1 tbsp whipping cream
2 tsp granulated sugar

Combine flour and salt. Cut in butter and shortening until mixture is in tiny bits.

Combine 2 tbsp cold water and lemon juice and sprinkle over flour mixture. Gather pastry with your fingers until it holds together. Add an extra tablespoon of water if necessary. Form pastry into a ball, flatten into a disc, wrap in plastic and chill for 30 minutes.

Preheat oven to 425°F.

Roll out pastry on a floured board into a 14-inch circle (don't worry about making a perfect circle). Transfer to a parchment-lined baking sheet.

Prepare filling by tossing together rhubarb, strawberries, cranberries, sugar and flour. Spread fruit mixture over pastry, leaving a 2-inch border. Fold edge of pastry up over filling, leaving center open.

Beat together egg yolk and cream for glaze. Brush over pastry. Sprinkle with sugar.

Bake for 15 minutes. Reduce heat to 350°F and bake for 30 minutes, or until juices are bubbling and pastry is golden. Remove tart from oven and let sit until juices have thickened and cooled. Serve warm or at room temperature.

And to drink . . .

LATE HARVEST WINES are one of Canada's most notable oenological triumphs. The Rieslings and Vidals from Ontario's Niagara region are particularly well achieved, their fruity sweetness balanced by a delicious tang of acidity. Over the past ten years it has been interesting to see Canadian wine drinkers embrace the idea of dessert wines, prompted, no doubt, by the international success of our Icewines, the ultimate "late harvest" expressions. Our Select Late Harvest and slightly sweeter, richer Special Select Late Harvest wines are more versatile at the table than Icewine, fine matches for foie gras, creamy blue cheeses and innumerable fruit-based desserts and pastries.

The term late harvest is self-explanatory. Bunches of grapes are left on the vine beyond the time of harvest until they start to dry out, concentrating their sugars, acids and flavors. It's a gamble for the viticulturalists: birds, rain and mold can all take their toll on the crop. When the grapes are finally picked and pressed, the sticky juice is so sweet that there is plenty of residual sugar left in the wine even after fermentation, and the balancing acidity in a Riesling refreshes the palate with every sip.

A dessert wine should always be a touch sweeter than the dessert it accompanies. A Select Late Harvest Riesling from Ontario, or the equivalent from New Zealand, will harmonize with the slightly tart intensity of the fresh and dried fruits in this crostata.

Japanese Influences

Wasabi Shrimp with Cucumber Salad
Steak with Mushroom Miso Sauce
Soba Noodles and Spicy Greens
Chocolate Loonies with Blood Orange Curd

SERVES 4

FUSION COOKING, which combines local ingredients, distinctive seasonings and international techniques, suffered a bad reputation when its early popularity resulted in a glut of poorly executed dishes. But today these excesses have been trimmed away, and the ingredients and techniques involved have become part of modern cooking.

This special entertaining menu is influenced by Japanese ingredients adapted to North American tastes.

Cava

IT MAY SEEM ODD to begin a dinner full of Japanese references with a wine from Catalonia, but the choice is true to the ecumenical spirit of fusion. Cava is a light, delicate sparkling white wine made in the same way as Champagne, and I find it has a particular affinity with Japanese food. Eminently refreshing, it has less intensity, complexity and acidity than French Champagne and works beautifully with sushi and sashimi, allowing the subtle flavors of the rice and the fish to strut their stuff, picking no fights, even with pickled ginger. Cava just seems to dance around the palate, as weightless as its own bubbles.

Cava was invented in 1872 by Don Jose Raventos, a man of wealth and vision whose family had been making wine since the 1500s. An amateur chemist and Champagne fan, Don Jose excavated a cellar under the garden of his Barcelona town house and eventually sold his first seventy-two cases of fizz in 1879, choosing the old family name of Codorníu for the label. Catalans loved it, other winemakers followed suit, and by the end of the century the wine was internationally renowned. The traditional trio of grapes in the blend—robust, earthy Xarel-lo for structure, lighter Macabeo for fruitiness and the aromatic Parellada for elegance—is now frequently joined by Chardonnay, which adds the same brightness and charm it gives to Champagne.

As an aperitif, Cava is fresh, soft, cheerful and undemanding, with a gentle aroma of apples (Prosecco from Italy's Veneto region would be a similar alternative), but it has enough acidity to rouse a dormant appetite. Moreover, with this meal, the transition to chilled sake with the first course won't be too great a leap, and if some guests would rather forgo the sake and stick with the bubbly, all will be perfectly well in palate-land.

Wasabi Shrimp
with Cucumber Salad

SERVES 4 AS AN APPETIZER

Wasabi peas are peas that have been coated with wasabi and dried. They are sold in packages as a snack. When you grind them up they make a spicy, crisp coating for shrimp or chicken.

Cucumber Salad	Shrimp
1 seedless cucumber, thinly sliced	1 cup wasabi peas
1 tbsp salt	1 lb large shrimp, shelled
2 tbsp seasoned rice vinegar	Salt
1 tbsp granulated sugar	1 egg white
1 tbsp soy sauce	1/4 cup vegetable oil
1/2 tsp hot red pepper sauce	

Combine cucumber with salt in a colander and let sit for 30 minutes. Blot cucumber dry and place in a bowl.

Combine vinegar, sugar, soy sauce and hot pepper sauce. Pour half the dressing over cucumber and toss to coat. Let sit for 10 minutes. Drain and discard dressing. Toss cucumber with remaining dressing. (This double dressing technique will keep cucumber crisp for a longer time.)

Grind wasabi peas into a powder in a coffee grinder or food processor.

Sprinkle shrimp with salt.

Whisk egg white with a pinch of salt until foamy. Add shrimp and toss to coat. Roll shrimp in ground wasabi peas to coat.

Heat 2 tbsp oil in a large skillet over medium-high heat. Add half the shrimp and cook for 2 minutes. Turn and cook for 1 to 2 minutes longer, or until coating is crisp and shrimp is curled. Repeat with remaining oil and shrimp.

Serve shrimp hot or cold surrounded by cucumber salad.

And to drink . . .

LEARNING A LITTLE MORE ABOUT SAKE is one of life's abiding pleasures: that first-ever sip in a Japanese restaurant; the realization, years later, that it was better drunk cold than warm; the gradual discovery of the many different styles and levels of quality of this extraordinary brew. Really cheap sake, for example, can smell like a wet dog. A very good one can astonish your nose and palate with a swirl of ethereal suggestions—caraway, grape, tangerine, kumquat, banana—mere illusions created by the interaction of water, rice, yeast and a bacterium known as koji.

All sake begins as rice, each grain polished until thirty to sixty-five percent of its surface has been rubbed away. The rice is steamed, and some is used to cultivate koji, which will turn the starches in the rest of the rice into glucose. Meanwhile, yeasts are added to turn the glucose into alcohol. That's basically how sake is brewed. The more polished the rice, the better and finer the results. Daiginjo and Ginjo are generally considered the best and second-best styles of sake—some dry, some semi-dry, some clear as water, others unfiltered, thick and cloudy as milk.

In recent years, avant-garde restaurants in Toronto, New York and Vancouver have felt free to pair a tiny glass of chilled sake with an appetizer, especially if the dish contains soy or miso. It makes for a delightful change of pace in the progression of wines.

Steak with Mushroom Miso Sauce

SERVES 4

My nephews Daniel and Julian introduced me to their favorite steak dish at a Japanese restaurant. This is my interpretation. Use a combination of mushrooms such as chanterelles, morels and black trumpets or a simple mix of oyster and shiitake. Serve the steak surrounded by the soba noodles. The steak can also be barbecued.

Steak
2 tbsp soy sauce
1 tbsp mirin
1 tbsp vegetable oil
½ tsp granulated sugar
3 New York sirloin steaks (about 12 oz each), 1 inch thick, trimmed of fat
Salt and freshly ground pepper

Mushroom Miso Sauce
2 tbsp vegetable oil
1 tsp sesame oil
8 oz wild mushrooms, trimmed and sliced
1 cup chicken stock
¼ cup light miso
2 tbsp whipping cream
1 tbsp soy sauce
2 tbsp chopped chives

Combine soy sauce, mirin, oil and sugar. Brush on both sides of beef and marinate at room temperature for 30 minutes. Season beef with salt and pepper.
Heat vegetable oil and sesame oil in a skillet over medium-high heat. Add mushrooms and sauté for 3 minutes, or until softened.
Combine stock, miso, cream and soy sauce. Stir into mushrooms. Bring to a boil, reduce heat to low and cook for 1 to 2 minutes, or until slightly thickened.
Heat an oiled grill pan over high heat. Sear beef for 2 to 3 minutes per side, or until caramelized on outside but still rare in middle.
Cut steak into ½-inch slices. Drizzle with sauce and sprinkle with chives.

And to drink . . .

THE BEEF'S FINE. No problem there. Any number of reds (and even one or two really first-class German Rieslings) will pay court to the beef. The sauce, with its miso, soy and wild mushrooms, seems a more interesting proposition until you realize a heavenly match is staring you in the face: a good, rich, mature Californian Pinot Noir.

The maturity is important, partly because it can take a few years to shush the distracting chatter of ripe, primary fruit flavors in a Californian Pinot and also because an older wine is more likely to have acquired some of the earthy barnyard aromas that are such an attractive part of Pinot Noir's vast repertoire of special effects. Those aromas reach out to mushrooms whenever they wander by, and they speak the same language as the yeasty, fermented flavors of miso and soy.

One potential problem lies in the extreme saltiness of the miso and soy. Even with the calming influence of the cream, it may tend to make the tannins in a red wine taste bitter. Fortunately, Pinot Noir is less tannic than many reds, while its ripe fruit also has a soothing effect. Go for it.

Soba Noodles and Spicy Greens

SERVES 4

This dish has great taste, texture and visual appeal, and it can be served hot or at room temperature. If you buy wasabi powder, mix it with an equal amount of water to make the paste. This dish is a good vegetarian main course too.

Soba noodles are Japanese buckwheat noodles.

Spicy Wasabi Dressing
2 tbsp soy sauce
2 tbsp seasoned rice vinegar
2 tbsp sake
2 tbsp mirin
2 tbsp sesame oil
1 tbsp wasabi paste
Soba Noodles
8 oz dried soba noodles
4 green onions, slivered

2 tbsp vegetable oil
2 tbsp chopped gingerroot
1 tsp chopped garlic
½ tsp hot red pepper flakes
8 oz asparagus, trimmed and cut in
    2-inch lengths
4 cups sliced bok choy
4 cups baby spinach
Salt and freshly ground pepper
2 tbsp toasted black or white sesame
    seeds

Whisk together soy sauce, rice vinegar, sake, mirin, sesame oil and wasabi paste until smooth. Reserve.

Bring a large pot of water to a boil. Add noodles and cook for 2 to 3 minutes, or until tender but still with a slight bite in center. Drain and toss with green onions and half the dressing.

Heat vegetable oil in a large skillet over high heat. Add ginger, garlic and hot pepper flakes. Stir-fry for 30 seconds.

Add asparagus and stir-fry for 2 minutes, or until bright green. Add bok choy and stir-fry for 1 minute. Add spinach and stir-fry for 1 minute longer, or until wilted. Remove from heat and stir in remaining dressing.

Toss vegetables with noodles and season with salt and pepper. Sprinkle with sesame seeds.

Japanese Ingredients

Mirin is a Japanese rice wine made from fermented glutinous rice. It is very low in alcohol and quite sweet. It is used only in cooking and gives a shiny look to grilled dishes. If you don't have mirin, substitute granulated sugar (1 tbsp mirin equals 1 tsp sugar).

Miso is fermented soybean paste. It has a unique, slightly salty taste and is high in protein, amino acids, vitamins and minerals and very low in calories and fat. Miso is made by crushing boiled soybeans with barley or rice. Using a yeast-like mold, the mixture is then fermented, often for months or even years. Depending on the proportion of barley or rice to soybeans and salt, the miso can be light, sweet and mild or darker and more strongly flavored. Light (usually yellow) miso is delicate in texture and probably best suits our palates. The darker red or brown miso is best used in robust dishes.

Nori is thin sheets of seaweed (or, more properly, marine algae) used to wrap sushi. It often comes toasted but if not, fan the nori over a burner at low heat until crisp.

Rice Vinegar is made from fermented rice. It is milder than wine vinegar. Japanese seasoned rice vinegar has sugar added and is used for seasoning sushi rice and marinades. Use it in vinaigrettes for a less acidic taste.

Sesame Oil is an aromatic oil made from toasted sesame seeds. It is usually used to add flavor to a finished dish rather than in cooking. There are many types, from mild Middle Eastern oils to pungent Asian varieties, but I prefer the rich, smooth Japanese sesame oil. Adding just a few drops to vegetable oil will give fried dishes a good sesame flavor.

Soy Sauce is a sauce made from soybeans that have been fermented and steeped in brine. Thick, dark soy sauce is used to marinate meats and add color and flavor to rice or noodle dishes. Light soy sauce is used as a finishing sauce, as a condiment and to marinate poultry and fish. Medium-colored Japanese soy sauce can be used as a substitute for both light and dark.

Wasabi is also known as Japanese horseradish, but is not really horseradish. It is very hot and is usually served with sushi. The knobby green root grows in Japan but is hardly ever available fresh. Buy it in powdered form and mix with equal amounts of water or buy the less intensely flavored paste in a tube.

Chocolate Loonies with Blood Orange Curd

SERVES 4

This refreshing dessert contains one of my favorite combinations—chocolate and orange. Use regular seedless oranges if blood oranges are not available.

There will be orange curd left over. Serve it as a pudding or use as a filling for tart shells (page 224). You can also use this recipe to make lemon curd. Use lemon zest and juice instead of orange.

2 blood oranges	¼ cup butter
¼ cup orange liqueur	1 tbsp grated orange zest
6 oz bittersweet chocolate, coarsely chopped	2 tbsp blood orange juice
	1 tbsp lemon juice
3 tbsp whipping cream	2 eggs, beaten
Orange Curd	¼ cup whipping cream
½ cup granulated sugar	

Peel oranges, remove pith and separate oranges into segments. Pour liqueur over oranges and marinate for 2 hours at room temperature or refrigerate overnight.

Melt chocolate in a pot over low heat, stirring occasionally. Stir in cream and remove from heat.

Draw twelve 3-inch circles on a parchment-lined baking sheet. Spoon 1 to 2 tsp melted chocolate mixture over each circle and spread quickly with a spatula. Don't worry if discs are not perfect. Refrigerate until chocolate discs are cold and remove from parchment paper. Refrigerate until needed.

Prepare curd by combining sugar, butter, orange zest, orange juice, lemon juice and eggs in a heavy pot. Stir gently over low heat for 10 to 15 minutes, or until mixture coats back of a spoon. Do not let mixture boil or it will curdle.

Strain mixture into a bowl. Place plastic wrap directly on top of mixture to prevent a skin from forming. Refrigerate until cool.

Whip cream until it holds its shape. Fold whipped cream into orange curd.

Place one chocolate disc on a serving plate. Top with a generous spoonful of orange curd. Place another disc on top and top with another spoonful of curd. Top with a third disc.

Serve one loonie tower per person, accompanied by marinated oranges.

And to drink . . .

A DESSERT WINE MADE FROM Californian Orange Muscat grapes is going to be superb with this teetering tower of chocolate and orange curd. Muscat—in its infinite varieties and styles, perfumed and unmistakably "grapy"—is usually the first wine to reach for when chocolate appears.

But perhaps we should stay with the Asian theme to the end. A sweet plum wine from Japan introduces an intense new fruit flavor to play with the orange on the plate and has the moxie to stick up for itself when the chocolate lumbers over to hug it to death. But the wine has to be sweet. Gekkeikan Fushimi Kyoto is one particularly delightful version. The aroma is discreet but the taste of ripe plums lingers on the palate for ages. Many other Japanese plum wines (*ume-shu*) are deliberately drier, the better to carry the delectably sour flavor of the fruit, and would seem thin and out of place beside those loonies. If in doubt (and this is a good rule of thumb when faced with many a dessert conundrum), play it safe with a Muscat.

Spring Brunch

Vegetable Croustade • Brie and Cheddar Soufflé
Cherry Tomato and Onion Compote
Spirited Lettuce Salad with Creamy Tarragon Dressing
Maple-glazed Bacon • Lime and Ginger Muffins
Spring Fruit Salad • Coconut Macadamia Cookies

SERVES 12

WITH EASTER, MOTHER'S DAY and graduations on the spring calendar, brunch is an excellent way to entertain family and friends. Simple, wholesome food is the best choice. Choose recipes that can be made ahead of time and make sure you provide some vegetarian choices. For a special occasion a poached salmon or gravlax (page 298) looks spectacular, but you could also serve something as simple as bacon, sliced ham or, for my family, a tuna salad. I often supplement the menu with storebought bagels and croissants, butter, cream cheese and good jam as well.

Serve this as a buffet that will allow people to help themselves, even if you are seating them at the table. Though each dish serves ten, the complete menu should serve twelve or more.

Morning Glories

BRUNCH IS A CURIOUS MEAL. At worst, it can seem like a vast, unwieldy breakfast eating up the most precious hours of the day. At best, with the bright sun shining and the table laden with dishes, it can unfold into a lazy all-day party.

Although James the Champagne lover would serve Champagne or sparkling wine right through brunch, nonalcoholic drinks also have a role to play. Have jugs of fresh grapefruit and orange juice sitting out so guests can help themselves or mix with a little Champagne if they wish. There are also those sophisticated bottled fizzy drinks flavored with elderberry, elderflower or Asian herbs. And real iced tea or lemonade is always a treat.

To make your own iced tea, pour 4 cups boiling water over 8 good-quality orange pekoe or Darjeeling tea bags. Let sit for 10 minutes, then remove the tea bags. Stir in 3 tbsp granulated sugar and 4 slices lemon. Add 2 cups cold water, let cool completely and chill, covered, until needed. For the best iced tea, pour the chilled tea over ice cubes made with iced tea and garnish with fresh mint. You can also use your favorite fruit-flavored tea bags instead of regular tea, or even get creative and combine flavors. My favorite iced tea is made with strawberry tea bags and garnished with strawberries and lemon balm (an easily grown lemony herb).

Make a big jug of homemade lemonade, too. Pour 4 cups boiling water over 3 diced lemons. Sweeten with 3 tbsp granulated sugar and cool. Pour into a pitcher and refrigerate until needed. Pour into tall glasses over ice cubes and garnish with more lemon slices and fresh mint.

And to drink . . .

THERE IS NO NEED to chill Champagne or sparkling wine overnight. Refrigerate the wine for an hour, then move the bottles into a bucket or cooler containing a mixture of water and ice. As long as you can still see ice in the bucket, the bubbly will maintain a drinkable chill.

Exercise patience when pouring sparkling wine into a flute containing another liquid, especially a heavier fluid such as fruit juice or a liqueur. Pour just a little at first, wait until the head of foam subsides, then carefully fill the flute.

The Champagne Cocktail A timeless classic, the Champagne Cocktail seems to have emerged from the first golden age of mixology in the late nineteenth century but swiftly found favor wherever Champagne was enjoyed. In the 1920s, all the best London clubs and hotels had their own particular recipe, inspired (some say) by that of Harry Craddock, barman at the Savoy Hotel, whose book of cocktails was first published in 1930.

Drop a lump of sugar into a Champagne flute. Add two or three drops of Angostura bitters and let the sugar absorb them. Add a teaspoonful of brandy, top up with chilled Champagne and garnish with a slice of orange or a twist of orange zest. Before you drink, lift the glass and gaze into its purling golden depths. You may glimpse the real appeal of any classic cocktail—something more than a sociable restorative or a pretty mask for alcohol. It shimmers in the glass: the faint but unmistakable zest of a bygone decadence, a twist of gaiety and romance, a hangover from a more frivolous age.

The Buck's Fizz As a small boy growing up in England, I was enthralled by an old friend of my parents, a very elderly gentleman whom everybody called Buck. I remember him best at the long, leisurely picnics in the garden of his daughter's home in the country, sitting in a lawn chair with a rug over his knees. When passing clouds hid the sun, someone would keep an eye on the sky and then, at an opportune moment, ask Buck to bring the sun back. He would point upward with his walking stick and, to the endless delight and astonishment of the children, the sun would miraculously reappear. We assumed he was a wizard.

Buck's real name was Captain Herbert Buckmaster, and after the First World War he opened a gentlemen's club on Clifford Street in London called Buck's Club. At some time during the 1920s, the barman, Mr. McGarry, developed a particularly delicious cocktail made with fresh orange juice, Champagne and traces of two secret ingredients: the Buck's Fizz. Those mysterious components have never been divulged (a drop of gin? a suggestion of some sweet liqueur?), but even without them a Buck's Fizz is a delicious treat, mixed in proportions of two parts chilled, freshly squeezed orange juice to three parts chilled brut Champagne or sparkling wine. Carefully add the Champagne to the orange juice and drink at once. You'll think the sun has come out from behind a cloud.

The Black Velvet The idea of mixing equal amounts of Guinness stout and brut Champagne has been known to dismay both beer lovers and Champagne aficionados—until they try the drink. Legend insists that the Black Velvet was invented in 1861, after the death of Queen Victoria's husband, Prince Albert. While Britain and her Empire mourned, the staff at Brooks's Club in London showed their respects by adding black stout to Champagne to give it a respectfully funereal hue.

The drink caught on, and no wonder. Between the Champagne's sourness and the bitterness of the stout lies a broad area of harmony where the yeasty notes of the wine find similar qualities in the beer. The Velvet in the name refers to the smooth texture of the union. There doesn't seem to be a consensus about whether the Champagne or the Guinness should be poured into the jug first, but use caution: the combined fizz can turn a pitcher into Vesuvius.

The Royale Family In the early 1980s, a new kind of drink appeared in Europe—a blend of passionfruit juice and Cognac called Alizé. Delectably fresh tasting, it could be drunk on the rocks or with any number of mixes, from soda to other fruit juices. Mixed with dry sparkling wine in a ratio of about four parts bubbly to one part Alizé, it became an Alizé Royale—less sweet than the drink on its own and much more food friendly. Since then, a great many other, similarly exotic proprietary brands have appeared based on a variety of fruit juices and spirits. Some taste like candy, but most of them seem to have got the recipe right.

Vegetable Croustade

SERVES 10

This perfect brunch dish combines the bread and vegetables in one.
The yeast dough is spectacularly easy to make.

Yeast Dough
1 tsp active dry yeast
2 tbsp granulated sugar
⅓ cup warm water
1½ cups all-purpose flour
½ tsp salt
1 egg, beaten
3 tbsp butter, at room temperature
Filling
2 tbsp butter
3 cups chopped leeks

12 oz shiitake mushrooms, trimmed
  and sliced
2 tsp chopped garlic
¼ cup whipping cream
Salt and freshly ground pepper
8 oz goat cheese, crumbled
¼ cup fresh breadcrumbs
½ cup grated Parmesan cheese
2 tbsp butter, melted
Glaze
1 egg yolk
2 tbsp whipping cream

Sprinkle yeast and sugar over warm water and stir until sugar dissolves. Let stand for 10 to 15 minutes, or until foamy.

Combine flour and salt. Make a well in center and place egg, butter and yeast mixture in well. Stir together with a wooden spoon to form a soft, smooth dough. (Add a little flour if dough is sticky.)

Place dough in a lightly oiled bowl and cover with a tea towel. Put in a warm place for 20 to 30 minutes, or until slightly puffy.

Prepare filling by melting butter in a large skillet over medium heat. Add leeks and sauté for 1 minute. Add mushrooms and garlic and sauté for 5 to 6 minutes longer, or until mushrooms are soft. Add cream and cook for 30 seconds, or until cream just coats vegetables. Season with salt and pepper. Preheat oven to 400°F.

Punch down dough and roll out on a well-floured surface into a 14-inch circle. Place on a parchment-lined baking sheet.

Sprinkle goat cheese over dough, leaving a 2-inch border. Top with vegetable mixture.

Combine breadcrumbs, Parmesan and melted butter and sprinkle over vegetables. Fold pastry up over filling to form a border.

Combine egg yolk and whipping cream for glaze and brush over pastry. Bake for 20 to 25 minutes, or until pastry is golden and filling is hot.

Brie and Cheddar Soufflé

SERVES 10

This is my most requested brunch recipe. It is rich and extremely palate pleasing. Challah, brioche or even plain white bread will work well if the bread is thinly sliced. You can also add layers of cooked vegetables such as asparagus, spinach or mushrooms.

Serve the soufflé with the tomato compote on the side.

10 to 12 thin slices bread, crusts removed	1 cup finely chopped green onions
	¼ cup chopped parsley
1 lb Brie cheese, rind removed, cubed	2 tbsp Dijon mustard
4 cups shredded Cheddar cheese	2 tsp paprika
12 eggs	1 tsp hot red pepper flakes
3 cups milk or light cream	Salt and freshly ground pepper

Line bottom of a large buttered baking dish with a single layer of bread. Sprinkle half the Brie and Cheddar over bread. Cover cheese with a second layer of bread and sprinkle with remaining cheese.

Whisk together eggs, milk, green onions, parsley, mustard, paprika and hot pepper flakes. Season well with salt and pepper. Pour over bread layer. Refrigerate for at least 4 hours or overnight. Remove dish from refrigerator 1 hour before baking to bring it to room temperature.

Preheat oven to 350°F.

Bake for 45 to 60 minutes, or until puffy and golden. Let sit for 10 minutes before serving.

Cherry Tomato and Onion Compote Combine 1 lb halved cherry tomatoes with 1 cup chopped red or sweet onions and ¼ cup chopped fresh mint.

Combine 2 tbsp balsamic vinegar and ¼ cup olive oil. Toss with tomatoes and season with salt and pepper. Let sit for 1 hour before serving.

Makes about 4 cups.

Spirited Lettuce Salad with Creamy Tarragon Dressing

SERVES 10

A sharp salad like this one will contrast with the rich flavors of the croustade and the egg dish. Combine the greens ahead but do not dress until just before serving.

½ cup pine nuts
2 Belgian endives, thinly sliced
1 head radicchio, thinly sliced
1 head escarole, torn
1 bunch watercress, stems removed
1 cup thinly sliced red onions

Creamy Tarragon Dressing
1 small clove garlic, minced
2 tbsp mayonnaise
2 tbsp white wine vinegar
⅓ cup olive oil
2 tsp chopped fresh tarragon,
    or ½ tsp dried
Salt and freshly ground pepper

Place pine nuts in a dry skillet over medium-low heat. Toast, stirring occasionally, for 2 to 3 minutes, or until golden brown.

Combine endive, radicchio, escarole and watercress. Top with red onions and pine nuts.

Whisk together garlic, mayonnaise and vinegar. Slowly whisk in oil. Stir in tarragon and season with salt and pepper. If dressing is too thick, thin with a little warm water.

Pour dressing over salad and toss together.

Maple-glazed Bacon This deluxe bacon recipe can easily be prepared in quantity. I use double smoked bacon as it is less fatty and more flavorful than regular bacon.

Lay 1 lb bacon strips on a foil-lined baking sheet. Drizzle 2 tbsp maple syrup over bacon and sprinkle with coarsely ground pepper. Bake in a preheated 450°F oven for 7 to 10 minutes, or until crispy. Drain on paper towels. Serves 10.

Lime and Ginger Muffins

MAKES 12 LARGE MUFFINS

These are moist, trendy bran muffins with grown-up flavors. Make them a day ahead and warm in the oven before serving.

¼ cup finely chopped gingerroot
¾ cup granulated sugar
2 tbsp lime juice
1 tbsp grated lime zest
½ cup butter, at room temperature
2 eggs
1 cup buttermilk
1¾ cups natural bran

1 cup all-purpose flour
1 tsp salt
1 tsp baking soda
½ tsp baking powder
Glaze
¼ cup granulated sugar
¼ cup water
2 tbsp lime juice

Preheat oven to 375°F.

Combine ginger and ¼ cup sugar in a small pot. Add lime juice. Cook over medium heat for 3 minutes, or until sugar has dissolved and mixture is hot. Remove from heat and cool. Stir in lime zest.

Whisk butter with remaining ½ cup sugar until smooth. Whisk in eggs and buttermilk until blended.

Combine bran, flour, salt, baking soda and baking powder in a large bowl. Stir in buttermilk mixture. Stir in ginger-lime mixture. Do not overmix. (Don't worry if there are a few lumps.)

Spoon batter into 12 large well-greased or paper-lined muffin cups (each cup should be about three-quarters full). Bake for 20 to 25 minutes, or until a tooth-pick comes out clean.

Prepare glaze by combining sugar, water and lime juice in a small pot. Bring to a boil over high heat and boil for 1 minute.

Prick hot muffins several times with a skewer and brush with glaze. Cool in pan on a rack.

Spring Fruit Salad

SERVES 10

Finding seasonal fruits can be a challenge in spring, but here is an interesting salad using good fruit that is available all year. Serve it in a large glass bowl.

2 seedless oranges
1 cantaloupe
1/2 honeydew melon
1 pineapple
3 kiwi fruit
2 bananas
2 cups seedless red or green grapes

Dressing
1/2 cup plain yogurt
1/2 cup orange juice
2 tbsp lime juice
2 tbsp honey
1 tsp cardamom, optional

Peel oranges, removing all white pith. Cut out orange sections, saving any juice, and place in a serving bowl. Scoop out cantaloupe and honeydew with a melon baller, or dice. Peel and dice pineapple. Peel and thinly slice kiwi fruit. Peel and thinly slice bananas. Add prepared fruit with any juice and the grapes to the bowl.

Combine yogurt, orange juice, lime juice, honey and cardamom. Drizzle dressing over fruit. Toss and chill thoroughly before serving.

Coconut Macadamia Cookies

MAKES ABOUT 30 COOKIES

Macadamias are rich, fatty nuts that originated in Australia but now grow in Hawaii. They have a creamy taste and crunchy texture. Substitute cashews, if desired.

These can be made ahead and stored in a cookie tin for up to a week.

1 cup butter, at room temperature	1 1/4 cups quick-cooking rolled oats
3/4 cup granulated sugar	1 tsp baking powder
3/4 cup brown sugar	1/2 tsp salt
1 egg	3/4 cup shredded sweetened coconut
4 tsp grated orange zest	1 cup macadamia nuts, coarsely chopped
1 1/2 cups all-purpose flour	

Preheat oven to 350°F.

Cream butter and both sugars in a large bowl. Add egg and beat well. Add orange zest and beat well.

Combine flour, oats, baking powder and salt in a separate bowl. Beat into creamed mixture. Stir in coconut and macadamia nuts.

Roll dough into 1 1/2-inch balls. Place on parchment-lined baking sheets about 2 inches apart. Press down to flatten balls slightly.

Bake for 12 to 15 minutes, or until edges are golden. Cool on baking sheets for 2 minutes before removing to wire racks to cool completely.

Wine Tech

Tannins

I ONCE BIT INTO AN UNRIPE PERSIMMON. I knew it wasn't quite ready—still odorless and a little too firm—but I was hungry and it looked so tempting, a deep, rich yellow, glossy and promising much. So I bit, and was bitten right back. My whole mouth shriveled and clenched. It wasn't the burning sting of an acid but more like a withering astringency, an awareness of bitterness, a horrible dryness, as if I had stuffed my cheeks with cotton wool.

Unripe persimmons are laden with tannins, microscopic chemical compounds that have an obsessive attraction to proteins. Tannins bond with the proteins in animal hide and turn the hide into leather. They also bond with the fatty proteins in human saliva, making you feel as if your tongue and cheeks are suddenly lined with puckered suede.

And tannins lurk in other fruit, particularly in the skins, stems and seeds of grapes. Some thick-skinned varieties such as Cabernet Sauvignon, Syrah and Nebbiolo are especially well endowed. When the grapes are crushed, the acidic juice starts to leach out the tannins and pigments from the skins. The longer the juice stays in contact with the skins and seeds, the more tannins and color it gains. And when the juice starts to ferment, the newly formed alcohol speeds up the process. Put the young wine into a new oak barrel and the wood imparts different tannins of its own. A very young Cabernet Sauvignon can be so rich in tannins that tasting it is an unpleasantly astringent experience, especially with oily fish or soft cheese.

So why is the winemaker in his barrel cellar smiling as he tastes and then spits out the infant wine? Because tannins also have a positive role to play. They are preservatives, helping to keep the wine sound as it slowly matures. They help stabilize color compounds. They cling to yeast proteins left over from fermentation and drag them down to the bottom of the barrel, making the wine less cloudy. And in time their influence wanes. Ten years on, when you try that Cabernet again, the tannins have mellowed, their subtle presence bringing a certain sophisticated rigor to the wine, the way learning Latin as a boy (oh, the torment!) resonates quietly in the conversation of the man.

But what if you open your tannic red wine years too early? It was expensive (reds made for aging are always expensive) and all your wine books promised an epiphany, but when you pour a little to taste, you feel that telltale astringency on your gums and on the inside of your cheeks. It's as if all the fruit and spice and famous complexity of the Cabernet is hidden behind a leather curtain.

Fear not. This is no time to despair. Not with roast lamb or well-marbled roast beef on the menu.

There's a reason why industry dinners hosted by Bordeaux winemakers so often feature roast lamb. The wines they are hoping to sell are still young and tannic when sipped on their own, but they taste far better with lamb. All those delicious fatty proteins in the meat coat your mouth. The tannins make a beeline for the voluptuous lamb fats and put the squeeze on them. They meet, they cleave and then, locked in a molecular embrace, they are washed away, leaving the wine's fruitier attributes free to express themselves, and refreshing your mouth in the process.

Decanting is another emergency measure that can help mitigate aggressive tannins in a young wine. Oxygen ages wine almost as quickly as sunshine ages a vampire, so pour your vino into a decanter or splash it into a clean glass jug. Exposure to the air will soften the tannins and bring out the fruitiness in the wine.

One last tip: bring out the pepper mill and go easy on the salt. The effects are slight, but pepper mutes tannins while salt can make them taste bitter.

A Traditional Passover Seder

Gefilte Fish • Chicken Soup with Matzo Balls

Slow-cooked Veal Breast

Potato Kugel with Celery Root

Lemon Asparagus • Flourless Chocolate Cake

Orange and Almond Cake

SERVES 8

PASSOVER CELEBRATES THE EXODUS from Egypt of the Jewish slaves. They fled so quickly that they had no time to let their bread rise, so they baked it unleavened. Today this is symbolized by eating matzo (unleavened bread) for the eight days of Passover as well as eliminating yeast, flour and, depending on where you are from, legumes and any ingredient that may have come in contact with a grain.

The first and second nights of Passover are the Seder nights, celebrated with readings, songs and a multi-course Seder dinner. Today there is a fashion to serve Sephardic Seder dinners according to the traditions of the Mediterranean Jews, who are allowed to eat grains and rice. My Passover menu is based on the Ashkenazi traditions of the Jews of Eastern Europe. Most of the dishes can be prepared ahead of time and either baked or reheated when needed.

Kosher Wines

TWENTY YEARS AGO, North Americans knew what to expect when they opened a bottle of kosher wine. Behind those gaudy labels from Mogen David and Manischewitz were wines representing a long tradition—very heavy, very sweet, almost always red and made from New York–grown Concord grapes, with their unmistakable foxy flavor. Together with the sweet Carmel wines from Israel, they enjoyed a near monopoly on Passover tables.

Today that monopoly has been challenged and defeated. Dry kosher table wines from just about every wine-producing region in the world collectively outsell the old, sweet Concord bottlings. The new wines are made from vinifera varieties—anything from Chardonnay to Zinfandel—and they regularly win awards against the nonkosher competition.

Any wine can be kosher, provided it is made and handled from press to bottling line by Sabbath-observant Jewish men in a winery that has been cleaned and is supervised by a rabbi. Non-Jewish wineries can be leased for a number of days and used for this purpose (a long-standing practice in Europe), and there are some giant companies that routinely produce a kosher version of their bestsellers—Tio Pepe sherry, for instance. Kosher spirits and liqueurs are now far more available in North America than they used to be. A kosher Cognac or grappa after the Passover meal is a treat; Russian Jews favor kosher vodka.

The choice of kosher wines and spirits is greater than ever, but old habits die hard. Many people serve modern, dry kosher wines with the Passover meal, but the familiar bottle of sweet Concord wine still stands on the table, and during the Seder readings, when ritual calls for the drinking of four cups of wine, they pour the sweet Concord just as their parents and grandparents did. At Passover, family tradition has a way of superceding modern innovations.

Gefilte Fish

MAKES ABOUT 20 SMALL GEFILTE FISH

My mother, Pearl Geneen, makes the best gefilte fish because she treats them like French quenelles, cooking them for considerably less time than the two hours that many recipes recommend. The result is feather-light gefilte fish with enormous flavor. These are so good, I often serve them with horseradish as a nibble before a dinner party. The traditional mixture is whitefish, carp and pike, but my mother uses a blend of 1 lb halibut, 8 oz pickerel or tilapia and 8 oz haddock. You can also buy already blended traditional ground fish mixtures at many fishmongers.

2 lbs boneless, skinless fish	Salt and freshly ground pepper
1½ cups coarsely chopped onions	4 cups fish stock
⅓ cup coarsely chopped parsley	1 cup thinly sliced onions
¼ cup matzo meal	1 cup thinly sliced carrots
½ tsp saffron, optional	1 bay leaf
¼ cup cold water	6 peppercorns
2 egg whites	

Cut fish into large even-sized chunks.

Place chopped onions, parsley, matzo meal and saffron in a food processor. Pulse to combine. Add fish and pulse until ingredients are incorporated. Fish should be finely chopped but not pureed. With machine running, pour water and egg whites down feed tube. Turn off machine and stir in salt and pepper. Refrigerate mixture for 1 hour.

Combine fish stock, sliced onions, carrots, bay leaf and peppercorns in a wide shallow pot. Bring to a boil, reduce heat and simmer for 5 minutes.

Form fish mixture into oval balls, using ¼ cup for each (wet hands to form balls). Sauté a little bit of mixture to taste for seasoning. Season again if needed.

Place fish balls in stock, cover and simmer for 35 to 40 minutes, or until fish is firm to the touch. (You may have to do this in batches, depending on size of your pot.)

Remove fish balls to a dish and strain fish stock over top. Refrigerate for up to 3 days before serving.

And to drink . . .

IN THE LATE NINETEENTH CENTURY, Baron Edmond de Rothschild was visited by a group of Jewish farmers from Palestine who were trying to raise money for a well. He agreed to help, and he also sent a team of his Bordeaux wine growers back with the farmers to look into the possibility of viticulture. Their decision to plant vineyards of warm-climate French varieties—Carignan, Grenache and Mourvèdre, among others—was a good one and, in 1906, Rothschild turned the flourishing operation over to the growers, who formed themselves into a cooperative known today as Carmel.

Climatic heat has always been an issue for Israel's wines, and for decades their quality was compromised by flavors often described as "sunburned." By the 1970s, however, after considerable investment in equipment and imported expertise, Carmel was making some fine Sauvignon and Cabernet wines from its vineyards in northern Galilee. Even better fruit came to the wineries from the kibbutzim that had planted vineyards on the cooler Golan Heights. Eventually these kibbutzim formed their own company, Yarden Vineyards, and their wines have continued to improve ever since. Yarden's dry rosés made from Cabernet grapes are particularly lovely—fresh and fruity with an extraordinarily exotic floral bouquet.

Is that the wine for gefilte fish and chicken soup with matzo balls? It's a tough match, but there are a good many white and rosé options to consider—dry Chardonnays from Australia, Chile and California, South African Sauvignon Blanc, Austrian Welschriesling, even blush Zinfandel from California. I'd splurge and serve a Sauvignon Blanc with the gefilte fish and an off-dry Californian Chenin Blanc with the chicken soup.

Chicken Soup

SERVES 8

Plump, yellow-skinned kosher chickens make the richest chicken soup. It's probably because, according to the kosher laws, the chickens must be brined. However, you can also use capons, roasting chickens or pullets (older hens). Onion skins will give the soup a rich yellow color. For a full-flavored broth, ask your butcher for extra chicken bones, backs and necks. Adding chicken feet will make the stock gel and give it an especially intense flavor—just like old-fashioned chicken soup. Ground pepper sullies the soup, so use whole peppercorns.

If the chicken has any taste left, use it in chicken salads or a chicken pot pie. The soup will keep, refrigerated, for four days. Reheat the soup, ladle it into bowls and add one or two matzo balls to each bowl.

1 chicken (about 5 lbs), rinsed and cut in 8 pieces	3 carrots, cut in chunks
2 lbs chicken bones, backs or necks	3 stalks celery, cut in chunks
12 cups cold water, approx.	4 parsley sprigs
2 large onions, unpeeled, cut in chunks	3 cloves garlic, unpeeled
	6 peppercorns

Place chicken and bones in a large pot and add water until chicken is covered by about 2 inches. Bring to a boil. Skim off grayish froth that rises to surface. Add onions, carrots, celery, parsley, garlic and peppercorns. Reduce heat and simmer gently for 4 to 6 hours, or until soup is full of flavor. Strain, chill and remove fat before reheating.

Heat chicken soup thoroughly before serving. Taste and add salt if necessary.

Matzo Balls

MAKES ABOUT 16

Matzo balls are a kind of dumpling traditionally served at Passover with chicken soup. The test of a good Jewish housewife is her ability to create the perfect matzo ball. Some people say they should practically float in your mouth, while others like them heavy and dense. These matzo balls are light and airy. The secret ingredient is soda water, but ice water may be substituted.

If you cook these ahead, refrigerate them covered with a little cooking liquid to keep them moist, and reheat them in the soup.

1 cup matzo meal	4 eggs
¼ cup vegetable oil	½ cup soda water, cold
or melted chicken fat	Salt and freshly ground pepper

Combine matzo meal, oil, eggs, soda water, salt and pepper. Let sit for 30 minutes.

Bring a large pot of water to a boil over high heat. With wet hands, form matzo mixture into balls about 1 inch in diameter.

Drop balls into boiling water. Reduce heat to medium-low and simmer, covered, for 25 to 30 minutes, or until balls double in size and are cooked through.

Slow-cooked Veal Breast

SERVES 8 TO 10

Veal breast (veal brisket) is an underrated meat that should not be reserved just for Passover (use breadcrumbs instead of matzo meal if you are making this for other occasions). It is inexpensive, juicy, lean and easy to stuff. Make this ahead and reheat the meat in the sauce at 350°F for 30 minutes while the vegetable kugel is baking. Ask the butcher to cut a pocket for the stuffing.

Stuffing	Veal
1 tbsp vegetable oil	1 boneless veal breast (about 4 lbs)
1 cup chopped onions	2 tsp dried rosemary
½ cup matzo meal	Salt and freshly ground pepper
1 egg	1 tbsp vegetable oil
¼ cup finely chopped parsley	1 orange, peeled and thinly sliced
1 tbsp grated orange zest	6 cloves garlic, peeled
2 tsp dried tarragon	1 bay leaf
½ cup chicken stock or water	2 cups chicken stock or water
Salt and freshly ground pepper	
1 cup chopped pitted prunes or dried apricots	

Heat oil in a skillet over medium-high heat. Add onions and sauté for about 2 minutes, or until softened.

Combine onions with matzo meal, egg, parsley, orange zest, tarragon and stock. Season well with salt and pepper. Stir in prunes.

Fill veal pocket loosely with stuffing. Sew or skewer pocket closed. Sprinkle veal with rosemary, salt and pepper.

Preheat oven to 300°F.

Heat oil in a large casserole over medium-high heat. Brown veal on both sides, about 5 minutes per side.

Scatter orange slices, garlic and bay leaf over veal in casserole. Pour stock around veal. Cover and bake for 2 hours. Uncover and bake for 1 hour longer, or until veal is fork-tender. (Dish may be prepared ahead to this point.)

Remove veal from casserole and transfer to a carving board. Strain liquid, skim off any fat and return liquid to casserole. Bring to a boil on stovetop and cook for 1 minute to amalgamate flavors.

Slice veal and serve with sauce.

And to drink . . .

THOUGH NOT ORDERED BY RABBINICAL LAW, many households prefer to serve red wine rather than white or rosé at the Passover dinner. It was a red Bordeaux that first made me sit up and take notice of kosher wines back in the late 1980s. Sold under the somewhat long-winded name of Barons Edmond and Benjamin de Rothschild Haut-Médoc, it was actually a kosher bottling of Château Clarke, perhaps the most renowned cru bourgeois from the Haut-Médoc area of Listrac. A lovely wine, its success in this kosher incarnation seemed to open the North American gates for other kosher reds and whites from Minervois, Alsace and Italy.

These days, the choice is considerably more broad. Wafted by the winds of fashion, single-varietal kosher Merlots have now caught up with Cabernet Sauvignons in many parts of the continent. A dry Merlot made with the sun-ripened fruit of the south of France, California or Chile is a good match with Lucy's veal dish. The ripe aromas of the wine offer some balance to the stuffing of dried fruit and the hint of orange sweetness in the reduced sauce.

Potato Kugel with Celery Root

SERVES 8

A kugel is a sweet or savory dish set with eggs. To make the kugel moist, you need to use fat. Melted chicken fat would be the choice of many, but olive oil is an excellent alternative. Shred the carrots and zucchini with the grater blade of the food processor or by hand. If you wish, omit the celery root and add an extra pound of potatoes.

3 lbs Yukon Gold potatoes,
   peeled and halved
1 large celery root,
   peeled and quartered
1/3 cup olive oil
2 cups chopped onions

2 carrots, shredded
2 medium zucchini, shredded
4 eggs, beaten
Salt and freshly ground pepper
1/4 cup chopped coriander or parsley

Place potatoes and celery root in a large pot and cover with cold water. Bring to a boil. Reduce heat to medium and simmer for 15 to 20 minutes, or until vegetables are fork-tender. Drain well, return to pot and shake pot over turned-off burner to dry vegetables.

Heat 2 tbsp oil in a large skillet over medium-high heat while potatoes are cooking. Add onions and sauté for 7 to 10 minutes, or until softened and beginning to turn golden.

Preheat oven to 350°F.

Mash potatoes and celery root. Stir in cooked onions, carrots, zucchini, eggs and remaining 1/4 cup olive oil. Season with salt, pepper and coriander.

Transfer kugel mixture to an oiled baking dish. (Kugel can be prepared ahead to this point.) Bake for 35 to 40 minutes, or until kugel is browned on top and vegetables are heated through.

Lemon Asparagus

SERVES 8

I always serve a green vegetable with the Seder meal. You need the crisp crunch and the color for the palate and the plate.

2 lbs asparagus
2 tbsp lemon juice
Salt and freshly ground pepper

Peel asparagus if stalks are thick. Break off tough ends.
Bring a large skillet of salted water to a boil. Add asparagus and cook for 2 to 3 minutes, or until crisp-tender.
Drain asparagus and refresh with cold water. Drain well. Season with lemon juice, salt and pepper.

Asparagus Asparagus can be green or white. Green asparagus is generally grown in North America and Britain, while white asparagus is grown all over Europe. White asparagus is more tender than green asparagus and has a nutty, slightly bitter flavor. It is also more expensive.

Although green and white asparagus are the same plant, they are treated differently during their growing season. White asparagus is grown in beds with the earth piled on top of the plants. By being denied sunlight, the spears stay white. Green asparagus grows in the sun.

Flourless Chocolate Cake

SERVES 8 TO 10

Make this spectacular chocolate treat with margarine after a Passover meat meal because dairy cannot be served after meat in kosher homes. Make it with butter on other occasions.

The cake will seem undercooked until it is chilled. Serve it with whipped cream, if desired.

12 oz bittersweet chocolate, coarsely chopped	1 cup granulated sugar
½ cup butter or hard margarine	Topping
6 eggs, separated	2 oz bittersweet chocolate, coarsely chopped

Preheat oven to 350°F. Grease base and sides of an 8-inch springform pan and line with parchment paper.

Melt chocolate and butter in a heavy pot over medium-low heat, stirring constantly, until smooth.

Place egg yolks in a large bowl. With an electric mixer, slowly beat egg yolks with ½ cup sugar until mixture has tripled in volume and beater leaves a trail in mixture. Fold in chocolate mixture.

Beat egg whites in a separate bowl until foamy. Slowly add remaining ½ cup sugar and beat until egg whites are thick, glossy and hold stiff peaks.

Stir one-quarter of beaten egg whites into chocolate mixture to lighten it. Gently fold in remaining egg whites.

Spoon mixture into prepared pan and bake for 40 to 50 minutes, or until cake is slightly wiggly in center and has a crust on top (crust may crack).

Cool on a wire rack for 30 minutes. Chill overnight. Remove sides of pan and paper and place cake on a platter.

Melt chocolate for topping in a small heavy pot over low heat. Drizzle over cake before serving.

Orange and Almond Cake

SERVES 8

This dessert combines oranges and nuts with egg whites for leavening. It produces a moist, interesting cake that is perfect for the end of the Seder. Serve it garnished with orange slices, if desired.

2 large seedless oranges, unpeeled	1¼ cups granulated sugar
4 eggs, separated	2 tbsp icing sugar
1½ cups ground almonds	

Place whole oranges in a pot and cover with water. Bring to a boil, reduce heat and simmer, covered, for 1½ hours, or until very soft. Drain, cool and chop.

Preheat oven to 375°F. Grease an 8-inch springform pan and dust with Passover cake flour. Line bottom with parchment paper.

Add oranges, egg yolks, almonds and 1 cup granulated sugar to a food processor and pulse until well mixed. Scrape mixture into a bowl.

Whisk egg whites with an electric beater until frothy. Keep beating while adding remaining ¼ cup granulated sugar. When egg whites are thick and glossy and hold stiff peaks, stir one-quarter of egg whites into orange mixture, then fold in remaining whites. Spoon batter into prepared pan.

Bake for 45 minutes. Check cake and cover loosely with foil if cake is getting too dark. Bake for 15 minutes longer, or until a cake tester comes out clean. Cool cake in pan on a rack. Remove sides of pan, place cake on a serving platter and dust with sifted icing sugar.

A Dinner of Lemons

Sorrel Soup
Roasted Halibut Tagine
Israeli Couscous
Lemon Ginger Yogurt Cake
SERVES 4

LEMONS ADD SPARKLE TO FOOD. Vegetables like sorrel add a lemony zing to salads and soups, lemon juice lightens salad dressings and flavors sauces, while the grated zest lifts desserts to new heights. In Moroccan dishes lemons are salted and brined to conjure up yet another level of flavor.

This is a menu with a citrus edge that is perfect for lifting you out of the winter doldrums.

The Dry Martini

I WISH I COULD REMEMBER the first time I saw a Dry Martini. It must have made a deep impression, for the idea of it lingered in my young imagination, inexplicably glamorous and unattainably adult, as cold and clear and shimmering as the sun on Arctic ice. I knew there was mystery in its making, watching the grown-ups frown with concentration as they bent over the glass, alchemists with a secret formula. Years later, when at last I felt its smooth, cold weight on my tongue, I knew I had come of age.

I still believe a Dry Martini is the perfect cocktail, as long as it's perfectly made. And that's where the trouble starts, for every confirmed Martini drinker has a beloved recipe, to be championed to the point of belligerence. Hemingway (who seems to have left personal instructions for mixing every conceivable cocktail in every bar he ever visited) relished a ratio of fifteen parts gin to one part dry vermouth. Mixing it that dry seems to me to be missing the point. Ten to one allows the cocktail maximum self-expression—the subtle, complex, bittersweet botanicals of the vermouth interlocking with the similar properties of the gin, graced by the heat within the chill and the salt-sour shadow of the olive.

Or perhaps you prefer a sliver of lemon zest. For me, the choice of olive or twist depends on whether the brand of gin has a dominant citrus note (opt for an olive) or leads off with juniper (balance it with a twist).

That decided, retrieve your bottle of French Noilly Prat vermouth from the fridge and your Plymouth gin from the freezer (keeping it there eliminates the need for contact with frozen water). Pour 2 oz gin into a cold Martini glass with 1 tsp vermouth. Stir it once or twice, if you have the patience, and garnish. It sounds so simple, but the difficulty of balancing such subtleties time after time is what puts the art in Martini. Like people or dreams, no two are ever quite the same, and that in itself is a wonder and a joy.

Sorrel Soup

SERVES 4

French sorrel tastes like a bite of tart green apple with a lemony edge. But it is difficult to find. You must look for it in season at farmers' markets or grow it yourself (it is an easy-to-grow perennial that will give you years of pleasure). Garden sorrel will also work in this soup, and I have added apple to give it more of a French sorrel flavor.

Add the lemon juice at the end. The amount will vary depending on the tartness of the sorrel.

This soup is excellent served hot or cold.

2 tbsp butter	2 bunches sorrel (about 2 cups packed)
1 cup chopped onions	¼ cup whipping cream
1 cup diced peeled potatoes	Salt and freshly ground pepper
½ cup diced peeled tart green apples	Lemon juice
4 cups chicken stock	

Heat butter in a pot over medium heat. Add onions, potatoes and apples and sauté for 3 minutes, or until slightly softened.

Add stock and bring to a boil. Reduce heat and simmer for 10 minutes, or until potatoes are tender.

Stir in sorrel and simmer for about 2 minutes, or until sorrel has wilted.

Puree soup. Return soup to pot and add cream.

Bring to a boil, reduce heat and simmer over low heat for 5 minutes. Season with salt and pepper and add lemon juice to taste.

And to drink . . .

YIKES! A SOUP THAT TASTES OF SORREL (alias sourgrass or cuckoo's sorrow)—a herb as sharp and subtle as any in the garden. Already dismayed by having to match a soup, the old-time wine matcher is tempted to admit defeat and move rapidly on to the next course.

Then again, everyone has just sat down, expectant smiles on their faces, and glasses are standing empty. The challenge must be met. And Lucy's soup turns out to be less tart than you might expect if you have ever chewed on a sorrel leaf. If anything, the principal acidity comes from that fresh green apple in the recipe. So we need a dry white wine with a tangy acidity of its own but with enough body to stand up to the cream and potato in the soup. A dry Alsatian Riesling fits that description, or an Austrian Grüner Veltliner. Or you could step in a different direction and pour everyone a small glass of cold, extra-dry white vermouth.

Scruples of mastic, spikenard and saffron, costmary and wormwood from Pontica or Thebes: steep them without heating in eighteen pints of wine . . . The recipe comes from ancient Rome, but the notion is as old as wine itself. The ancients had a mighty pharmacopoeia of herbs and spices, flowers, leaves, barks, gums and roots. It was their custom to use wine, often sweetened with honey, as a medium for their remedies, and the herbs in their turn improved the flavor of the wine. After Rome fell, the old knowledge was kept alive in the cellars of the great monastic houses, evolving into a host of forms from patent medicines to unique liqueurs. The herb wormwood was a particularly versatile ingredient, pleasantly bitter and prized as a vermifuge and general stomach-settler. Later, its silky gray leaves yielded the toxic oil that put the sin in absinthe, France's popular narcotic aperitif, until the drink was outlawed in 1915. But its tiny yellow-green flowers, free of the poison, were used in more gentle decoctions, such as the wine-based tonics prepared for individual customers by the apothecaries of northwestern Italy. In 1786, one of these herbalists, Antonio Carpano of Turin, decided to produce his own bittersweet, aromatic preparation commercially. He needed a name for it and hit upon vermouth, from *Wermut*, German for wormwood.

Today's dry white vermouths are excellent aperitifs, those bitter botanicals calibrating the palate for what lies ahead. I also love serving them with a soup that has a sharp herbal flavor; they can handle sorrel with their eyes shut. Ice breaks the bouquet, so chill the bottle thoroughly in the refrigerator and serve a couple of ounces straight up.

Roasted Halibut Tagine

SERVES 4

James might claim that in the interest of taxonomical exactitude, this dish should not actually be called a tagine, since it isn't cooked in the traditional Moroccan cooking vessel. However, it does contain Moroccan flavors. The fish is covered with spices and roasted, so it is low in fat as well as tasty.

Preserved lemons can be found in Moroccan restaurants and in some gourmet shops, or you can prepare your own. You could also omit them. The dish will have a different flavor but will still be good.

¼ cup coarsely chopped fresh coriander	Pinch ground cinnamon
	Salt and freshly ground pepper
¼ cup coarsely chopped parsley	4 halibut fillets (about 6 oz each)
1 tbsp coarsely chopped garlic	3 fresh or canned tomatoes, pureed
¼ cup lemon juice	¼ cup sliced preserved lemon rind (page 78)
3 tbsp olive oil	
2 tsp ground cumin	½ cup green olives
2 tsp paprika	Fresh coriander sprigs
¼ tsp cayenne	

Combine coriander, parsley and garlic in a food processor and process until chunky.

Add lemon juice, oil, cumin, paprika, cayenne and cinnamon and process until combined. Season with salt and pepper.

Reserve 2 tbsp spice mixture for sauce. Spread remaining mixture over fish fillets and marinate for 30 minutes.

Preheat oven to 425°F.

Combine tomatoes, preserved lemon rind and reserved spice mixture.

Spread tomato mixture in a baking dish just large enough to hold fish in a single layer. Top with marinated fish.

Bake fish for 12 to 15 minutes, or until white juices appear at edges. Serve fish with sauce and garnish with olives and coriander sprigs.

And to drink . . .

MY MEMORIES OF TAGINES IN MOROCCO are all from south of the Atlas mountains, of eating in small inns where there was little else on the menu and where the dish was always a rough assembly of hunks of lamb, preserved lemons, olives and a quart of olive oil. Heavy stuff, and the local wine that cut through it best—a very cold, not very interesting rosé—contributed little but refreshment.

This recipe is different. It's fish, it's low in fat and light in weight, and it has quite a high level of acidity from the tomatoes, preserved lemons and lemon juice. The wine you select must have enough acidity of its own not to be intimidated. And then there are all those spices leaping up from the page to terrify whoever pulls the corks. How can a wine cope with such an array?

In fact, quite easily. When combined and sweetened with garlic and the juices from the fish as it cooks, the acids and spices mellow delightfully, though they would still bully a delicate, merely fruity wine. Something with flavor and character will be required.

My first choice would be a Viognier either from the south of France (where this great grape is performing well and far more affordably than in its classic Rhône role as Condrieu) or from California's recently rejuvenated Lodi region. A good Viognier with plenty of peachy, subtly spiced personality can stand up curiously well to quite strongly spiced cooking. A dry German Muscat, seeming so fey and perfumed in the glass, can also show surprising immunity to peppery heat and spices. Australian Sémillon or Marsanne might be other contenders.

Israeli Couscous

SERVES 4

Israeli couscous is larger than the more familiar Moroccan couscous. The pea-sized pasta can be found in many grocery stores in the rice section. It is sometimes labeled super couscous, pearl couscous or toasted couscous. Unlike Moroccan couscous, Israeli couscous can be prepared the same way as pasta; boil it in plenty of salted water or stock.

2 cups dried Israeli couscous	2 tbsp chopped fresh coriander
1 tbsp butter	Salt and freshly ground pepper

Bring a large pot of salted water to a boil over high heat.
Sprinkle in couscous and boil for 5 minutes, or until tender. Drain well.
Stir in butter and coriander. Season with salt and pepper.

Preserved Lemons Lemon rind preserved in salt and lemon juice is used as an ingredient and garnish in many Moroccan recipes. Preserved lemons have an amazing flavor that cannot be duplicated by fresh lemons. They are wonderful in salads and in chicken and fish dishes.

To make preserved lemons, wash lemons well. Spread ¼ inch coarse salt over the base of a jar. Cut each lemon into 4 wedges but do not cut all the way through. Sprinkle or rub 2 tsp coarse salt over lemon flesh.

Pack lemons in jar, cover and marinate at room temperature for one week, shaking jar daily to distribute juice and salt. After a week, fill jar with more fresh lemon juice. Cover with ½ inch olive oil to seal. Let jar sit at room temperature for at least 4 weeks.

To use, scoop flesh from rind. Rinse rind. Slice or chop rind to use in recipes.

Lemon Ginger Yogurt Cake

SERVES 4 WITH LEFTOVERS

This is a one-bowl cake that works brilliantly. Just beat everything together and bake. Serve with fresh mangoes or kiwi. It makes a lovely breakfast cake, too.

½ cup butter, at room temperature

2 eggs

1½ cups all-purpose flour

¾ cup granulated sugar

1 tsp baking soda

1 tsp ground cardamom

½ tsp salt

2 tbsp grated lemon zest

1 tbsp minced ginger in syrup

½ cup plain yogurt

1 tsp vanilla

Glaze

¼ cup granulated sugar

2 tbsp lemon juice

2 tbsp minced ginger in syrup

Preheat oven to 350°F. Grease an 8-inch square cake pan and line with parchment paper.

Add butter, eggs, flour, sugar, baking soda, cardamom, salt, lemon zest, ginger, yogurt and vanilla to a large bowl.

Beat with electric beaters for 3 minutes, or until mixture is well combined.

Pour batter into prepared pan. Bake for 30 to 40 minutes, or until a cake tester comes out clean.

Cool cake in pan for 10 minutes. Prick surface liberally with a skewer.

Prepare glaze by combining sugar, lemon juice and ginger in a small pot. Bring to a boil and cook for 2 minutes, or until slightly thickened.

Pour warm glaze over cake. Cool cake in pan for 30 minutes. Lift out onto a wire rack and cool completely.

And to drink . . .

FRUIT WINES ARE WORTH SEEKING OUT. They inhabit a little world unto themselves, made from the fermented juice of all manner of berries, apples, pears and stone fruits. Some are as sweet as syrup; others are bone dry and perform perfectly well with savory food. They can't match the complexity of a great wine made from grapes, but they bring other subtleties of freshness, flavor and perfume to the table.

The main disadvantage of fruit wines is that they are usually unfamiliar. When matching them to food, therefore, you have to taste them first, assess their body, their sweetness, relative acidity and intensity of flavor. Lucy's delicate cake, with its lemon-cardamom nuances, deserves something sophisticated and refined that is still slightly sweeter than the cake itself. I have tasted medium-sweet apricot wines from Ontario and England that fit the bill precisely, their aromatic scent adding a delicious dimension to the dessert. Similar wines made from apples or pears would work equally well.

If none are to be found, go to Plan B—one of the lighter dessert wines made from grapes, but something with real finesse. It might be a late harvest Riesling from Ontario, a late harvest Sauvignon from Chile, or a Monbazillac, a Coteaux du Layon or a sweet Jurançon from France.

The Wine-tasting Shower

Caramelized Onion Tarts
Roasted Salmon with Hoisin Glaze
Snow Pea Greens and Mushroom Salad
Apple and Fennel Slaw • Rainbow Rice
Heart-shaped Meringue Cakes with Apricot Cream

SERVES 8

THE WINE SHOWER is one of the most popular new ways to entertain the prospective bride and groom. Our wine-tasting shower is a kind of wine primer—a fun and enlightening way to honor a couple, or just a great way to enjoy an evening with good friends.

As it will already be late, the food after the tasting should be quite light and simple, with everything prepared ahead of time so the host can enjoy the party, too. With the meal, guests can drink the wines they have enjoyed most during the tasting.

This menu expands easily or can be halved to make an elegant dinner for four.

The Set Up

CHOOSING THE WINES FOR A TASTING presents infinite options—Old World versus New, wines made from the same grape but from different countries, different vintages of a single wine, etc. Our tasting takes things right back to basics—three whites and three reds, each made from a world-famous grape variety.

Figure out how many bottles you will need, allowing for ten to twelve tastings per bottle. Prudent hosts may wish to buy a spare bottle of each wine in case one is corked. The reds should be at room temperature; chill the whites for an hour before serving.

Provide water and plain white bread to clear the palate, and more water to rinse glasses between each wine. Empty rinsed glasses into a wine bucket. Give guests paper and pencils to write down their own impressions of the wines before you begin to discuss them.

Professional wine tasters can be proper little martinets, insisting on laboratory conditions for their work—clear, bright northern light, tasting glasses washed without detergent, an aroma-free environment, silence. A colleague wearing perfume or aftershave is instantly evicted. They are right, of course, but such an ambiance can put a sodden damper on your shower. That said, the whole exercise will prove much more enjoyable if taken a little bit seriously.

How to Taste Wines

GET HOLD OF some appropriate glasses; rent them, if necessary. Look for plain stemware with a bowl that becomes narrower toward the rim. That shape concentrates the aromas of the wine. Standard tasting glasses are fine, but something a little bigger is even better.

Start by pouring an inch of wine into the glass.

Look Lift the glass and tilt it away from you, holding it against a white background. Observe the clarity and the color, especially at the rim. Put the glass down and swirl it by holding the bottom of the stem, pressing down lightly and moving the glass in a small circle. Watch the wetness left on the inside of the glass sink back into the wine. The slower these "legs" run, the more alcoholic the wine is likely to be.

Sniff Swirling also helps release aromas, as esters in the wine evaporate. Lift the glass to your nose and take several little sniffs. Concentrate on how your olfactory system interprets what you're smelling. Most of us would recognize and agree on certain smells—woodsmoke, pine needles—but aromas in wine are subtler and more subjective. We tend to interpret them by analogy—raspberry jam, roses, tobacco leaf, kerosene—though it's often because identical aromatic molecules exist both in the wine and in something more familiar. First impressions are more accurate than revised opinions.

Taste Take a decent sip of the wine and let it rinse your mouth. Don't swallow. Note the mouth-feel or weight of the wine. Is it light, heavy or somewhere in between? Note your basic physical responses. Does it taste sweet? Is the acidity making the sides of your tongue tingle? Are tannins puckering your cheeks?

Now consider the flavors as they dance around your mouth. Do they match what you smelled in the wine? Are they changing?

Finally, swallow the wine and concentrate on the aftertaste. How long does it last (a sign of a good wine)? What is the final farewell?

All in all, was the wine pleasingly balanced and, most important, did you like it?

This tasting introduces the world's six major varietals—three white and three red. Taste them in the order given—light- to full-bodied whites and then light- to full-bodied reds.

White Wines

Riesling Every wine writer I've ever met adores Riesling. All agree it is a superb food wine, that it is unequaled in its versatility (making innumerable styles of wine from bone-dry aperitifs to the most opulent late harvest and Icewines), that it can express the terroir of the place where it's grown and yet still keep its integrity. It is wonderful, and inexplicably unfashionable.

Where flavor is concerned, young dry or off-dry Riesling is all about fruit or flowers: the sharpness of lime and minerally slate in wines from the Mosel; apple or lemon or white flowers in Ontario's excellent offerings; riper lime and passionfruit in Australia; citrus and orange in some I have loved from New Zealand. But that primary fruit changes with the passing years. Good German and some Canadian Rieslings develop fascinating mature aromas of kerosene and honey. And always the grape's calling card reveals its identity: a tongue-tingling acidity to balance the intensity of flavor.

Sauvignon Blanc Or just Sauvignon these days, since Sauvignons Gris, Noir, Jaune and Violet are so rarely seen. The Sauvignon our parents knew came from the Loire—sharp, minerally Sancerre and Pouilly-Fumé—or from Bordeaux, where it was smoothed with Sémillon to produce such divinities as dry white Château Haut-Brion and sweet, immortal Sauternes.

Then, suddenly, New Zealand burst onto the scene with an array of pungent, fruit-driven wines that ran the gamut from green pepper and gooseberry through melon to passionfruit and beyond, the difference depending on climate and how ripe the grapes were when they were picked. Bobby-dazzlers, they established a different Sauvignon standard, and it has been interesting to watch some French producers drift toward it. South African Sauvignons are improving all the time, while Californian versions are riper, softer and often muted by a touch of oak.

Chardonnay "Don't hate me because I'm beautiful!" pleads the blonde cheerleader in the teen flick. It could also be Chardonnay's lament, perennially voted the grape most likely to be liked. Indeed, the variety is so popular it has now become unpopular in certain quarters (such are the ironies of fashion), with wine writers reminding anyone who will listen that there are other white grapes out there. Unfair, I suppose. It isn't Chardonnay's fault.

As the noble white grape of Burgundy, Chardonnay has an impeccable pedigree. Our grandparents acknowledged white Burgundies as the best white wines in the world (with great German Riesling the only contender) and were taught the nuances of the region: how wines from Chablis, in Burgundy's cold northern reaches, were steely, acidic but capable of fabulous elegance; how the villages around Mâcon, in the south, produced smoother, rounder wines, while a Meursault from the heartland of the Côte d'Or would probably be richer and more buttery than either. Then Chardonnay started to travel, and more dramatic differences came into play. In the warm summers of California or Australia, the delicate Burgundian aromas of crisp green apple, pear, citrus or melon became voluptuous, more like ripe peaches or even pineapples.

Who would have guessed the refined French beauty would look so great with a tan and her hair down? The New World winemakers started to have fun. In Burgundy, their counterparts had instinctively given more aromatic and flavorful wines a little longer aging in oak barrels. These new Chardonnays had far more obvious fruitiness, so why not give them far more oak, especially since customers seemed to love oak's spicy vanilla bouquet? It all got horribly out of hand. In the late 1980s, I remember some highly renowned, very heavy and potent Chardonnays that tasted like essence of shoe. It was tough to match them to food. It was hard, sometimes, even to finish the glass.

Now balance has been restored. In California, Chardonnays from Sonoma County's Russian River region or cool, foggy Carneros can be quite magnificent—juicy, tangy, middleweight, perfectly balanced. In Australia, Margaret River and Yarra Valley offer much the same quality. As for the great white Burgundies, they are what they have always been: cool, subtle, sophisticated and expensive—the stuff of fantasies.

Red Wines

Pinot Noir Everyone, once in their lives, should set aside an evening and drink a really fabulous bottle of Burgundy. As the aromas and flavors evolve in the glass—so complex and persistent, so much more aromatic than the silky, graceful, light body of the wine might seem to be able to bear—realization dawns. So this is what all the fuss is about. Life will never be the same. The true Pinot Noir lover is doomed to spend his drinking life in restless search of perfection.

Pinot Noir is notoriously difficult to get right. Indifferent Burgundies can be terribly disappointing. The best Pinots from Oregon sometimes come close. Californian Pinots, from top producers in the Santa Barbara, Carneros and Russian River regions, tend to be riper and more fruit-forward, with spicy oak adding complexity—delicious but different, though some do achieve the gamey farmyard aromas that Burgundy fans crave. Vibrant stars also shine from Ontario and from New Zealand's Martinborough, Central Otago and Marlborough regions.

Merlot Bordeaux's other great grape, the dominant partner in the blended wines of St. Émilion and Pomerol, Merlot is currently California's darling. Smooth and velvety, it is rarely as heavy as Cabernet Sauvignon or as austere. You might find plums and blueberries in the bouquet, even hints of chocolate when the wine is more mature.

Where food matching is concerned, Merlot rides its bike down the middle of the road. It has a weight and intensity that suits contemporary North American cooking, especially the style that used to be known as Cal-Ital, and it copes well with a little spice. It even flatters Cajun-style blackened chicken livers. Only a cynic would suggest that Merlot's popularity owes a lot to the fact that, like Chardonnay, it's such a pretty word to say.

Cabernet Sauvignon Long-lived, complex, noble—the clarets of the Médoc and Graves are the benchmark of all red wines for many oenophiles, a sensory swirl of black currant, cedar, pencil shavings, cigar boxes and all manner of other fanciful allusions. In Bordeaux, the experience of centuries has led to Cabernet Sauvignon being blended, as often as not, with Cabernet Franc, Merlot and one or two minor varieties to soften and round out the corners. Imitated everywhere, this Bordeaux blend, or "meritage," is only one of many successful liaisons—Cab with Shiraz in Australia, with Sangiovese in Italy, with Tempranillo in Spain. Yes, Cabernet Sauvignon travels well, always wearing its cloak of black currants. In California, it is the red of the cult wines, many of them so ripe, tannic and potent that they merely bully food at the table. In Canada and New Zealand, a long warm autumn is needed to fully ripen the fruit and avoid green, vegetative nuances. You can always tell a good Chilean Cabernet. It's as if the winemaker took a wallpaper brush and painted a vibrant purple stripe across your palate.

Caramelized Onion Tarts

MAKES ABOUT 24 TARTS

This is my daughter Katie's favorite recipe in the book. The easy, no-fail, rich shortbread-like pastry is best used in individual tarts, although you can use it for single-crust pies, too. However, if you don't want to make your own pastry, buy puff pastry. It works very well as long as you roll it out thinly and prick it before chilling. Serve these after the tasting, while you are setting up the buffet.

Use Vidalia, Spanish or other sweet onions, which caramelize beautifully.

Cream Cheese Pastry
2 cups all-purpose flour
Pinch salt
3/4 cup butter, diced
6 oz cream cheese, diced
Filling
2 tbsp butter
1 tbsp olive oil
6 cups thinly sliced sweet onions

Salt and freshly ground pepper
1 cup red wine
1/2 cup chicken stock
1 tsp granulated sugar
3/4 cup whipping cream
1 tsp dried thyme
1/4 cup chopped parsley
1 cup grated Pecorino or Asiago cheese

Place flour, salt, butter and cream cheese in a food processor and pulse until mixture just begins to form a ball. Turn out mixture and press into a flat disc. Wrap and chill for at least 30 minutes.

Roll pastry out thinly on a floured surface. Cut 3-inch circles to fit 2-inch muffin or tart tins. Fit pastry into tins, prick and refrigerate for 30 minutes (pastry can also be formed into 1-inch balls and patted into tins).

Heat butter and olive oil in a large skillet over medium heat. Add onions and salt them immediately to help remove water. Sauté for 5 minutes, or until softened.

Add wine, stock and sugar. Bring to a boil, reduce heat to medium-low and cook for 30 to 35 minutes, or until onions are very soft and liquid has almost evaporated. Season well with salt and pepper.

Add cream and thyme and cook for 5 minutes, or until onions are a creamy mass. Remove from heat and stir in parsley and cheese.

Preheat oven to 375°F.

Fill tart shells with onion mixture. Bake for 20 minutes, or until pastry is crisp and filling is heated through. Serve warm or at room temperature.

Roasted Salmon with Hoisin Glaze

SERVES 8

This is one of the most popular recipes I have ever developed. It looks beautiful and is so easy and versatile. Serve it cold or at room temperature on a buffet table or hot at a dinner party. Roasting the salmon gives a firmer texture than poaching. Roast at 450°F for 10 minutes per vertical inch when the salmon is measured at its thickest point.

2 center-cut salmon fillets (about 2 lbs each)	Ginger Mint Mayonnaise
	1 cup packed fresh mint leaves
¼ cup hoisin sauce	½ cup coarsely chopped green onions
¼ cup white wine	¼ cup drained pickled ginger, coarsely chopped
2 tbsp balsamic vinegar	
2 tbsp vegetable oil	1 tsp grated lime zest
1 tbsp hot Asian chili sauce	3 tbsp lime juice
Salt and freshly ground pepper	½ cup mayonnaise
	¼ cup plain yogurt
	Salt and freshly ground pepper

Place salmon skin side down on an oiled foil-lined baking sheet.

Combine hoisin, wine, vinegar, oil, chili sauce, salt and pepper. Spread over top and sides of salmon. Marinate for 1 hour at room temperature or refrigerate for up to 4 hours.

Preheat oven to 450°F.

Roast salmon for 15 to 25 minutes, or until white juices just begin to appear on sides. Remove from oven. Fish will continue to cook as it cools.

Prepare mayonnaise while salmon is cooking. Combine mint leaves, green onions, pickled ginger, lime zest and lime juice in a food processor and process until slightly chunky.

Combine mint mixture with mayonnaise and yogurt. Season with salt and pepper and place in a serving bowl.

Serve salmon with mayonnaise alongside.

Snow Pea Greens
and Mushroom Salad

SERVES 8

If snow pea greens are not available, use two bunches of watercress leaves.

½ cup vegetable oil	1 tsp hot Asian chili sauce
1 tbsp sesame oil	1 tsp finely chopped gingerroot
3 tbsp rice vinegar	8 large shiitake mushrooms, trimmed
3 tbsp soy sauce	8 oz snow pea greens
1 tsp brown sugar	¾ cup chopped green onions

Preheat oven to 450°F.

Whisk together vegetable oil, sesame oil, vinegar, soy sauce, brown sugar, chili sauce and ginger.

Brush mushrooms with vinaigrette and place cut side up on a baking sheet.

Bake mushrooms for 5 minutes. Turn and bake for 5 minutes longer, or until tender. Cool and slice.

Place snow pea greens on a platter. Top with sliced mushrooms and sprinkle with green onions. Drizzle with remaining vinaigrette.

Asian Chili Sauce Asian chili sauce is hot and zingy and can be used to flavor all types of food. There are two kinds. Sambal oelek is a chunky mixture of chopped chilies with a touch of vinegar. It is best used in dishes that you want to be hot but not sullied by other flavors. Sriracha chili sauce usually comes in a squeeze bottle; it is much smoother in texture and contains added garlic, sugar, vinegar and salt.

Apple and Fennel Slaw

SERVES 8

This slaw has a good crunch and contrasts nicely with the salmon, though it is also good with grilled chicken or pork. It will be easier to prepare if you have a mandolin (page 9) or julienne grater. Otherwise thinly slice by hand. (If you use a four-sided box grater the texture will be too soft.) Use Cortland apples if you can find them. They keep their color better than other apples.

Dressing	Slaw
¼ cup cider vinegar	2 Cortland or Spy apples, unpeeled
1 tsp grainy mustard	1 large bulb fennel, trimmed
½ tsp ground fennel seeds	½ cup very thinly sliced red onions
½ cup olive oil	2 tsp chopped fresh thyme
Salt and freshly ground pepper	Salt and freshly ground pepper

Whisk together vinegar, mustard, fennel seeds, oil, salt and pepper.
Grate apples and fennel with julienne blade of a mandolin or grater.
Combine apples, fennel, red onions and thyme.
Add dressing to salad and toss. Season with salt and pepper.

Rainbow Rice

SERVES 8

Bake this rice in the oven for a perfect texture. If you want to make it ahead, spread the cooked rice on a baking sheet to cool. Reheat covered on the baking sheet for 10 minutes at 350°F.

3 cups uncooked basmati
  or Thai jasmine rice
2 tbsp butter
1 cup chopped onions
¾ cup diced red peppers
¾ cup diced green peppers
1 tsp chopped jalapeño peppers

1 tsp chopped garlic
Salt and freshly ground pepper
3 cups chicken stock or water
3 bay leaves
2-inch stick cinnamon
1 cup green peas
3 tbsp chopped parsley

Preheat oven to 350°F.

Soak rice in cold water for 30 minutes. Rinse and drain well.

Heat butter in a deep ovenproof skillet or wide pot over medium heat. Add onions, red and green peppers, jalapeño and garlic and sauté for 2 minutes, or until slightly softened.

Add rice and stir to coat with butter mixture. Season well with salt and pepper. Stir in stock, bay leaves and cinnamon stick and bring to a boil.

Cover and bake for 20 minutes, or until rice is tender. Remove from oven and stir in peas. Cover and let sit for 5 minutes. Remove bay leaves and cinnamon. Stir in parsley and reseason if necessary.

Heart-shaped Meringue Cakes with Apricot Cream

SERVES 8

A simple dessert that can be made ahead up to the point of adding the topping (add topping about three hours before eating). The topping is made with dried fruit because fresh fruit is not at its best in spring, but you can also make this with fresh raspberries or strawberries.

This recipe makes his-and-her cakes.

8 egg whites
2 cups granulated sugar
2 tbsp white vinegar
1 tsp salt
Topping
2 cups dried apricots

2 cups water
¼ cup apricot brandy or orange liqueur
2 cups whipping cream
1 cup shaved bittersweet chocolate
1 cup shaved white chocolate

Preheat oven to 275°F. Line 2 baking sheets with parchment paper. Trace 2 large heart shapes, about 10 inches across, on paper.

Beat egg whites with an electric mixer until foamy. Beat in sugar 2 tbsp at a time, beating well after each addition.

Add vinegar and salt and beat until mixture is thick and glossy and forms stiff peaks.

Spread meringue mixture inside heart shapes, building up sides slightly.

Bake for 1½ hours, or until meringues are creamy colored and crisp on outside. Turn off oven and let meringues sit in oven for 30 minutes. Cool on a rack and remove parchment paper.

Place apricots, water and brandy in a pot and bring to a boil. Simmer over medium heat for 5 to 10 minutes, or until apricots are soft. Cool.

Puree apricot mixture, adding extra water if puree is very stiff. It should be just thick enough to coat a spoon.

Whip cream until stiff peaks form.

Spread whipped cream over meringue hearts. With a spoon, streak apricot puree through cream. Sprinkle with chocolate shavings.

Fast and Fresh
Pasta and Salad

Peppery Lettuce Salad with Hazelnut Parmesan Crisps
Pasta with Asparagus, Oyster Mushrooms and
Goat Cheese
Instant Coconut Cream Tart

SERVES 4

A SPRING DINNER WITH SPARKLE. Use the fresh produce that is appearing in stores to revive your palate. Make the Parmesan crisps and the pie in advance, and the final preparation will take no time at all.

And to drink . . .

Goat cheese and Sancerre is a classic match, but why not try something new—a Pinot Grigio from northern Italy? Once they were all light, racy and rather shy in terms of flavor, but the current trend among many producers is to coax more out of the grapes, making these wines considerably more interesting and giving them much more to talk about with food.

Peppery Lettuce Salad
with Hazelnut Parmesan Crisps

SERVES 4

Use any peppery lettuce—slightly bitter dandelion greens, arugula, frisée or mixed baby lettuces (mesclun). For a vegetarian menu, omit the prosciutto. Use Grana Padano or Parmigiano Reggiano cheese in the crisps.

Hazelnut Parmesan Crisps
¾ cup coarsely grated Parmesan
    cheese
2 tbsp finely chopped toasted hazelnuts
Vinaigrette
2 tbsp lemon juice
2 tbsp olive oil

1 tsp maple syrup
Salt and freshly ground pepper
Salad
1 bunch peppery lettuce, stemmed
    (about 6 cups)
4 slices prosciutto

Preheat oven to 350°F. Line a baking sheet with parchment paper.
Combine Parmesan and hazelnuts. Drop 8 spoonfuls of Parmesan mixture onto baking sheet 3 inches apart.
Bake crisps for 8 to 10 minutes, or until golden. Cool on baking sheet.
Whisk together lemon juice, oil and maple syrup. Season with salt and pepper.
Toss lettuce with vinaigrette and pile on individual plates.
Coil each slice of prosciutto into a rose shape and set a rose in center of each mound of greens. Garnish each serving with two Parmesan crisps.

Pasta with Asparagus, Oyster Mushrooms and Goat Cheese

SERVES 4

Replace asparagus with blanched fiddleheads if desired. Oyster mushrooms are easy to obtain, but use morels or blue-tooth mushrooms if you can find them.

1 lb dried penne or other short pasta	1 tbsp grated lemon zest
1 tbsp olive oil	2 tsp finely chopped garlic
1 tbsp butter	8 oz soft goat cheese, crumbled
1 lb asparagus, trimmed and cut in 2-inch lengths	½ cup whipping cream
	¼ cup slivered fresh basil
6 oz oyster mushrooms, trimmed and torn in strips	2 tbsp slivered fresh mint
	Salt and freshly ground pepper

Cook pasta in a large pot of boiling salted water for about 10 minutes, or until *al dente*. Drain, reserving ½ cup cooking water.

Heat olive oil and butter in a large skillet over medium heat while pasta is cooking. Add asparagus stems and sauté for 2 minutes, or until asparagus begins to soften.

Add mushrooms and asparagus tips and continue to cook for 2 minutes, or until mushrooms are wilted.

Add lemon zest and garlic and cook for 30 seconds. Add two-thirds of the goat cheese, cream and reserved pasta-cooking water and stir well.

Add cooked pasta and half the basil and mint. Season with salt and pepper and toss well.

Divide pasta among 4 bowls. Top each portion with remaining goat cheese, basil and mint.

Instant Coconut Cream Tart

SERVES 4 WITH LEFTOVERS

This will remind you of your favorite coconut cream pie, but you will be astonished at how quick it is to make. For an even easier version, buy a prepared Graham cracker crumb base. As an added touch, spread the tart with whipped cream before sprinkling on the toasted coconut.

Crust
8 oz gingersnap cookies
1/2 cup butter, melted

Filling
1/2 cup butter
1/2 cup coconut milk
8 oz white chocolate, coarsely chopped
1 cup flaked unsweetened coconut

Place cookies in a food processor and process until cookies resemble fine crumbs (you should have about 2 cups). Add melted butter and process until crumbly.

Press cookie mixture into base and sides of an 8- or 9-inch tart pan or pie plate. Heat butter and coconut milk over medium heat until it comes to a boil. Remove from heat and stir in white chocolate until smooth. Stir in 1/2 cup coconut. Pour filling into shell. Refrigerate for 2 hours, or until set.

Preheat oven to 350°F.

Spread remaining coconut over a baking sheet and toast in oven for 5 minutes, or until golden. Sprinkle toasted coconut over chilled tart.

Coconut Milk   Coconut milk is produced by extracting the juice from the coconut flesh (the liquid inside the coconut is actually coconut water, not milk). The first pressing of the coconut flesh produces thick coconut cream, and the second pressing produces the lighter milk. Canned coconut milk usually separates, with the thick cream on the top and the milk on the bottom. Unless the recipe calls for coconut cream, combine the two consistencies before using. "Light" coconut milk does not contain the cream from the first pressing.

A Drop More

Gin

THE BRITISH EMPIRE—the empire on which the sun never sets. It's a resonant phrase, conjuring up (at least in my mind) an image of a perpetual happy hour, the sun poised for all eternity just below the yardarm, a never-ending preprandial chotapeg enjoyed on the veranda of the officers' mess. The drink might be a Pink Gin or sometimes a Gin and It or a Gin and French, but more often it's a gin and tonic, the refreshing aperitif of peppery colonels and their ladies.

Wherever the English ventured, gin was an essential part of their kit, but only in Canada did it find its way onto the map. In 1829, Sir Felix Booth, proprietor of Booth's gin, sponsored Captain John Ross's attempts to find the Northwest Passage. While his ship, *Victory*, ended up trapped in the Arctic ice for four years, Ross spent the time exploring—hence the Gulf of Boothia and the Boothia Peninsula, the most northerly point of continental America. Ross also identified the magnetic North Pole, and I like to think he toasted his success with a precious tot of Booth's, undoubtedly served well chilled.

Gin is so closely associated with the English that it comes as a surprise to discover it was invented in the Netherlands, taking its name from *genever* or *jineverbes*, Dutch words for juniper. The idea of putting juniper berries and other botanicals into a pot still along with a mash of malted grain is usually credited to one Dr. Sylvius, a professor in the medical faculty of the University of Leyden during the 1650s. The good doctor may have borrowed the notion from the local firm of Lucas Bols, which was already distilling a kind of gin as early as 1575. Bols still makes a geneva, but anyone used to gin in the English style will find it strangely pungent and highly flavored, with an aroma of grain and a taste that owes as much to caraway as juniper. It's delicious as a well-chilled shot with a twist of tangerine zest.

By the time the Dutch prince William of Orange and his English wife, Queen Mary, came to the throne of England in 1689, gin was fairly well known in London and the southern coastal towns. William gave it a tremendous boost by banning imported French brandy and simultaneously making it legal for anyone to distill their own gin. For the next 150 years, bootleg gin—dirt cheap and dangerously impure—was the all-pervasive vice of the urban poor. Inevitably, crude proto-cocktails evolved. Hatfield was the name for gin and ginger beer, popular in warm weather, while Purl was a mixture of gin and heated beer, beloved of Thames watermen. Gin and soda with a garnish of lemon was simply known as "the British soldier's delight."

But it was the men of the Royal Navy, not the army, who raised gin back to respectability. Down by the harbor in the Devonshire port of Plymouth stands an old monastery, built by the Black Friars in 1425. When Henry VIII dissolved the monasteries, the building was put to many uses, including that of a town meeting place. In 1620, the Pilgrim Fathers spent their last night there before setting off for America. (By an astonishing but totally irrelevant coincidence, the sect had recently come from Leyden, where they had settled eleven years earlier to avoid persecution. Moreover, most of the passengers on the *Mayflower* were Londoners. Thus the three cities most involved in the invention and perfection of gin are also inextricably linked to the colonization of America.) In 1793, the former monastery was transformed into a distillery for the manufacture of Plymouth gin, and so it remains, the oldest working distillery in England. Naval officers of Nelson's era discovered it quickly, and it was soon commonplace on board a flagship to offer Plymouth gin as well as Madeira or sherry as an aperitif before a formal dinner. Sailors first mixed it with lime juice to make a scurvy-busting prototype of the Gimlet, and navy doctors also created the Pink Gin by adding a drop or two of Angostura bitters to a shot of Plymouth.

The war with Napoleon was no more than a memory when the newly invented patent still gave London-based distillers a chance to make a cleaner, more delicate kind of spirit. Bone dry and subtly flavored with a complexity of exotic botanicals, London gin has become the dominant style worldwide. Different brands have their own nuances of taste, some weighting the balance toward citrus rather than juniper, others achieving layers of spicy floral aroma. Plymouth gin remains my favorite—fuller, earthier and more fruity than the London style, the juniper not showing off but playing nicely with the other botanicals. Order a Plymouth Martini and the hippest downtown lounge starts to look like the deck of a frigate. Order three and you're sailing.

Fast and Fresh
Spring Chicken

Fiddlehead Soup with Orange Dust
Maple and Chili-infused Chicken with Watercress Salad
Spicy Orzo
Kiwi and Lime Parfait

SERVES 4

THIS LIGHT AND LIVELY DINNER is highlighted by a delicate pale green soup dusted with dried orange zest. Many trendy chefs are using dusts as a garnish. They can be made from ground citrus fruits, mushrooms, tomatoes—anything that is, or can be, dried.

Spring is tree-tapping time, and the first maple syrup is fresh and light. It adds flavor to the chicken and a subtle sweetness to contrast with the peppery watercress.

And to drink . . .

The chicken's sweet-sour marinade strides forward like Goliath from the ranks of the Philistines. Your David is a Riesling—ideally an off-dry version from Ontario's Beamsville bench (the slight residual sugar and lively acidity meeting the maple and vinegar head on) or a kabinett from Germany's Pfalz region.

Fiddlehead Soup with Orange Dust

SERVES 4

Earthy-tasting fiddleheads are the young edible tips of the ostrich fern. Hand-picked near woodland streams, they are a gourmet's delight, partly because their season is so short.

This is a bright spring soup that can be made with frozen fiddleheads all year. Use asparagus instead of fiddleheads for another excellent soup.

12 oz fiddleheads	1 tsp grated orange zest
2 tbsp butter or olive oil	Salt and freshly ground pepper
1 cup chopped onions	¼ cup whipping cream
1 tsp chopped garlic	¼ cup chopped chives
4 cups chicken stock	2 tbsp orange dust, optional

Wash fiddleheads in at least four changes of water to help get rid of brown papery substance covering them. Swish them around in the water to release dirt. Cut off tough brown base of fiddleheads.

Melt butter in a large pot over medium heat. Add onions, garlic and fiddleheads and sauté for 3 minutes.

Add stock and bring to a boil. Reduce heat and simmer, covered, for 20 to 25 minutes, or until fiddleheads are soft.

Puree soup. If desired, strain soup to remove any fibers. Return soup to pot.

Add orange zest to soup and simmer for 5 minutes. Season well with salt and pepper. Ladle soup into bowls. Drizzle each serving with cream and sprinkle with chives and orange dust before serving.

Orange Dust Remove the zest from 2 large oranges. Use a zester if possible for uniformly thin strips. Place zest in a small pot and cover with water. Bring to a boil, drain and return zest to pot. Cover with water and repeat twice more (this helps the zest dry evenly). Dry zest on paper towels. Place zest on a sheet of parchment paper and microwave on High for 7 to 8 minutes, or until zest is dry and crisp but not brown. Grind to a powder in a coffee or spice grinder.

Makes about 2 tbsp.

Maple and Chili-infused Chicken with Watercress Salad

SERVES 4

Peppery watercress goes well with this sweet-tart chicken. Chipotle or ancho chili powder is the best for this dish, but if it is unavailable, use regular chili powder.

Use chicken thighs on the bone instead of breasts if desired.

Serve the chicken over the salad and surround with orzo.

Chicken
1/2 cup maple syrup
1/4 cup cider vinegar
2 tbsp vegetable oil
1 tbsp chili powder
1 tbsp grated lemon zest
Salt and freshly ground pepper
4 single chicken breasts, on bone, with skin (about 12 oz each)

Watercress Salad
2 tbsp olive oil
1 tbsp balsamic vinegar
1 tsp maple syrup
Salt and freshly ground pepper
1 bunch watercress, trimmed
1/2 cup thinly sliced red onions

Combine maple syrup, vinegar, oil, chili powder, lemon zest, salt and pepper.
Place chicken breasts skin side up in a foil-lined baking dish just large enough to hold chicken in a single layer. Pour marinade over chicken. Marinate for 30 minutes.
Preheat oven to 400°F.
Bake chicken in marinade for 30 minutes, or until juices are clear.
Prepare salad while chicken is baking. Combine oil, vinegar, maple syrup, salt and pepper.
Toss watercress and onions with dressing.
Serve salad on individual plates and top with chicken.

Spicy Orzo

SERVES 4

A starch with a little fire in it goes perfectly with the sweet chicken dish, but you can omit the hot pepper flakes.

2 cups orzo	1 tsp hot red pepper flakes
2 tbsp butter	Salt and freshly ground pepper

Bring a large pot of salted water to a boil. Add orzo and boil for 9 minutes, or until tender.
Drain well and stir in butter, hot pepper flakes, salt and pepper.

Kiwi and Lime Parfait

SERVES 4

This parfait can also be made with mango, papaya or a mixture of tropical fruits.

2 limes	1½ cups drained yogurt
⅓ cup granulated sugar	4 kiwi fruit, peeled and sliced

Grate zest from limes and squeeze juice (you should have about ¼ cup).
Whisk together lime juice, zest, sugar and yogurt.
Layer lime cream and kiwi fruit in sorbet glasses.

Drained Yogurt To drain yogurt, set a cheesecloth-lined sieve over a bowl. Place 3 cups yogurt in sieve, cover and refrigerate overnight (I prefer not to use fat-free yogurt). Discard any liquid and use drained yogurt in recipes or as a substitute for sour cream.

Makes about 1½ cups.

A Drop More

Sherry and Madeira

STRANGE ARE THE MYSTERIES OF SHERRY, the world's most undervalued wine. The vineyards around Jerez, in Andalusia, have a surreal appearance—treeless plains of dazzling white, chalky soil. It seems impossible much could grow there, but the ground absorbs winter rain, eking it out to the Palomino vines during the scorching summer while moist ocean breezes cool the foliage. Palomino yields a dry, fairly uninteresting white wine. This is left to finish its fermentation until around November, during which time a veil of living yeasts called the flor forms on its surface, subtly changing the young wine's character while protecting it from the air.

In January, the new wines are sampled and their destiny decided. Grape spirit is added to the darker, slightly heavier wines, raising the alcohol to 17.5 percent, killing the flor and letting oxygen get at the wine. These will evolve into oloroso sherries. The paler, more elegant wines are marked as fino and fortified to only 15 percent, ideal for prolonging the growth of the flor.

Now the wines are moved into oak barrels called butts, which are filled to only five-sixths capacity. The flor continues to protect and modify the finos, kept alive by the solera system. Imagine this as a stack of partially filled butts with the oldest at the bottom, the youngest on top. Sherry ready for bottling is drawn out of the bottom butt, leaving it about two-thirds full. The butt is topped up from the one above, which is replenished from the younger one above that, and so on. The new sherry is added to the top butt. Mixing with older vintages speeds up the maturation of the younger sherries, educates them beyond their years and ensures consistency of style. When the flor on a fino does fail, exposing it to the air, the sherry evolves into an amontillado—darker, nuttier, but still light on the palate.

True amontillados, like finos and olorosos, are magnificent in their complexity, but there is another, rarely encountered sherry style that I find even more delicious: palo cortado. This is a fino that seems all set to evolve into an amontillado, but then suddenly starts to look more like an oloroso—like a boy soprano whom the choirmaster expects to sing tenor when his voice breaks but who ends up a deep baritone. Dry, elegant, smooth and tangy as an amontillado, yet rich and rounded as an oloroso, palo cortado is glorious wine.

So why does sherry fail to receive the admiration it deserves? I'm afraid the blame lies with all those commercial sweet cream sherries that tradition insists are the favorite tipple of genteel aunts, Anglican vicars and university professors. Made by blending commonplace finos or olorosos with treacly, super-sweet wines pressed from dried Pedro Ximénez or Moscatel grapes, many of them end up tiresomely dull and one-dimensional, damaging the reputation of their more dazzling cousins. The silver lining, of course, is that great sherry is still delightfully affordable.

Madeira If sherry's popular image has been tarnished by cheap versions, Madeira's has almost been destroyed. Lying 465 miles off the coast of Morocco, the uninhabited island was discovered and claimed for Portugal in 1419 by Captain Zarco the Cross-Eyed. So dense was the vegetation that exploration proved impossible, so the wise captain decided to burn a way through the forest. He lost control of the fire, which smoldered for seven years, destroying all trace of plant life on the island but leaving rich potash soil that turned out to be well suited to vines. The first colonists, a group of Portuguese convicts, planted whatever they could get their hands on—Monemvasia from Crete (the grape used to make sweet Malmsey), Sercial from Germany, Verdelho from Italy and Bual from Portugal. The vines flourished and eventually attracted the attention of English wine merchants. By the seventeenth century, they had set up a lucrative trade with the American colonies.

An Atlantic crossing is harsh treatment for a barrel of wine. Fortified with alcohol to preserve them, baked by the tropical sun, the Madeira wines became oxidized and cooked, but surprise! It made them taste better. Soon the producers learned to imitate the sea crossing by leaving their wine barrels in the attic for years, to heat up and cool down with the seasons. Thus Madeira was born, relished by eighteenth-century connoisseurs who discovered that the finest vintages could be left to mature in the barrel for up to one hundred years and would last indefinitely in the bottle.

They still can. I have tasted nineteenth-century Madeiras that are amazingly lively and vibrant, their aroma filling the room as the cork is pulled, their aftertaste lingering on the palate for what seems like hours. Some great Madeira is still made in the traditional way. Cheap Madeira, its maturation hastened by artificial heating, is sadly far more common, little more than a parody of one of the world's most extraordinary wines.

SUMMER GARDENING PARTY

•

COTTAGE RETREAT

•

SOPHISTICATED GRILLING

•

FISH ON THE GRILL

SUMMER

FAMILY REUNION

•

FAST AND FRESH
FINGER-LICKING GOOD

•

FAST AND FRESH
MARKET SPECIAL

summer food

LEARNED MY FIRST LESSON about summer cooking many years ago when I was first engaged. To show my fiancé that I could really cook, I bought a goose from the supermarket near our cottage on Lake Simcoe. I slavishly followed the Julia Child directions on roasting goose and after many exhausting hot hours in the kitchen proudly brought out the golden bird to be carved. It was so tough that you could have used it for a football.

Later, after we were married, we spent a long hot summer in Ottawa. We were invited to dinner with friends in their hot little flat in their hot little building. The wife was French and she served a huge platter of vegetables, ham and hard-boiled eggs with a powerful dip that made my senses sing. It was aioli, garlic mayonnaise. The heat went unnoticed as we ate this simple but terrific food.

Both of these incidents taught me about summer cooking. Summer is for light, simple meals—lots of grilling, spices that bring out natural flavors, salads of local greens and vegetables, the perfect tomato dripping with juice, corn so fresh you hardly need to cook it, tiny blueberries and ripe strawberries that go straight into your mouth, not the pot.

Summer is for time out of the kitchen, not in it.

summer drinks

SOME DRINKS SEEM TO BELONG EXCLUSIVELY to hot summer days and nights. Pimm's, for example, requires ripe summer fruit and warm sunshine to show its best. A Campari and soda, indispensable in August, slips out of the picture after Labor Day. Cool white and pink wines come into their own but reds aren't abandoned—not as long as there's meat on the barbecue.

During the summer, the weather becomes a serious factor in matching wines to food, as the need for wine to refresh the palate is more important than ever. And when the party moves outdoors (as it always seems to at our house, given the least encouragement), the choice of wines changes slightly again. The subtle aromatic nuances of some rare old vintage disappear in the breeze or are swamped by the scents of the garden and the neighbor's char pit. Wines of vigor and forthright character, lighter body and tingling acidity suddenly seem most attractive.

Summer Gardening Party

Green Pea Soup with Mint Gelato

Pork Tenderloin on a Bed of Leeks and Fennel

Sweet Potato Ginger Pancakes

Peach and Blueberry Cobbler

SERVES 4

WHEN SUMMER APPROACHES, my husband and I hold a gardening party with a couple of our green-thumbed friends. We invite them over for the afternoon to garden and plant, and then we have a simple dinner with some good wine to celebrate the season. The following weekend we go to their house and repeat the exercise. By gardening together we get lots accomplished and benefit from the input of people who know a lot more than we do.

For a post-gardening meal, I concentrate on make-ahead dishes that can be popped in the oven. Here is one of our most popular menus. Garnish with newly sprouted herbs from the garden and throw a few organic pansies on the plates for color.

Pimm's

THE DROWSY HEAT of a summer afternoon—green lawns sloping to the lake—the brow-mopping cut and thrust of a game of croquet. Is that Lucy and her friends busy among the rose beds? It's the perfect moment for the bittersweet refreshment of a Pimm's.

Pimm's was invented in 1840 by James Pimm, an ambitious Londoner who started out selling oysters from a barrow and ended up with a chain of fashionable seafood restaurants. As a gimmick, and to refresh his suave clientele, he began to search for an original house cocktail, playing around with gin, aromatics and various flavorings. Eventually he stumbled onto something rather sophisticated—pleasantly bitter and fruity, but not too sweet. Pimm served it up as a "cup," mixed with fresh fruit and tart lemonade, and created a craze that kept him in clover for the rest of his life—or at least until 1880, when he sold the secret recipe to an entrepreneur named Horatio Davies. A self-confessed Pimm's enthusiast, Davies carried his passion to the farthest corners of the British Empire. Wherever the upper classes lifted a cricket bat, racquet or oar, they did so in the expectation of a tankard of Pimm's as reward for their manly exertions.

Ardent republicans may wish to disassociate Pimm's from this milieu of members' enclosures, marquees by the Thames and Oxford punting parties. Some mix Pimm's with Champagne, tonic water or dry ginger ale. Others, flirting with anarchy, add extra gin or serve it in the continental way, on the rocks as a delicious aperitif.

But the structure of English society is based on there being a right and a wrong way of doing everything, and that includes making a perfect Pimm's.

Slice half a cored but unpeeled apple, half an orange, half a lemon and a handful of strawberries. Tip the fruit into a jug and add about 2 cups Pimm's No. 1 Cup. Refrigerate for no more than 20 minutes. Just before serving, add about 4 cups very cold fizzy lemon pop (like Sprite or 7-UP). Pour into half-pint glasses, each containing two cubes of ice, letting some of the fruit share the journey. Garnish with a twist of cucumber peel and/or a couple of mint leaves and/or some tiny blue borage flowers. Drink it in a sun-filled garden for the full effect (though it's also remarkably good indoors, with Chinese and Thai food).

Green Pea Soup with Mint Gelato

SERVES 4

The trend to garnish cold soups with gelato is rampant in fine restaurants. Here is an easy version. Use a mild lettuce such as Boston or romaine.

The gelato can also be served on top of fresh fruit or between courses as a palate cleanser. It can be made a week in advance as long as it is well wrapped before freezing. Alternatively, omit gelato.

Mint Gelato	Green Pea Soup
¼ cup granulated sugar	2 cups green peas
¼ cup water	½ cup diced peeled potatoes
2 tsp grated lemon zest	1 cup chopped green onions
1 tbsp lemon juice	2 cups shredded lettuce
1¼ cups slivered fresh mint	4 cups chicken stock
½ cup mascarpone	¼ cup whipping cream
1 egg white	Salt and freshly ground pepper

Bring sugar, water, lemon zest, juice and 1 cup mint to a boil in a pot over high heat. Reduce heat to medium and simmer for 5 minutes. Cool syrup and strain.

Beat mint syrup into mascarpone. Stir in remaining ¼ cup mint until well combined. Freeze for at least 2 hours.

Place frozen mixture in a food processor with egg white. Puree and refreeze.

Combine peas, potatoes, green onions, lettuce and stock in a pot over medium heat. Bring to a boil. Reduce heat and simmer for 10 minutes, or until potatoes are tender.

Puree soup in a blender until mixture is very smooth. Add cream and season well with salt and pepper. Chill.

Ladle soup into bowls and top each serving with a small scoop of gelato.

And to drink . . .

NOT ENTIRELY COINCIDENTALLY, the garnish of mint on your preprandial Pimm's forms a delicate green bridge to Lucy's delicious soup. Despite its mentholated soul, mint turns out to be a surprisingly innocent herb where wine matching is concerned, though the same cannot be said for gelato, with its sweet-tart intensity and palate-numbing chill. So consider this soup holistically. Imagine the sweetish, fresh flavor of the peas and the hint of mint, the smooth texture thickened with potato and cream and enriched by the slowly melting mascarpone in the gelato. The first wine that springs to mind is a crisp, dry Austrian Grüner Veltliner with a voluptuous body.

Grüner Veltliner is a grape whose hour is almost upon us. It is Austria's premier white variety, and top examples from the Kamptal and Traisental regions are showing up increasingly often in our restaurants and wine stores. The typical nose reminds me of a green apple but with mineral and often peppery notes, though some Grüners also seem floral. While it lacks the zingy acidity of Riesling, it has enough of an edge to refresh the palate and a lingering flavor that will hold its own against this soup. Look for a fuller-bodied version by checking the label for the "alcohol by volume" measurement. Anything over 13 percent will do the trick; a Grüner of only 12 percent will seem too thin with this dish.

That's one suggestion, playing to the "green" taste of the peas, lettuce, green onions and mint in the recipe while cutting through the richness. Another might be a buttery, full-bodied Californian or Chilean Chardonnay without much oak. Chardonnay has a way of ingratiating itself with cream, chicken stock and potato, and it can find nuances in the flavor of peas that remind you of their family ties with beans and other legumes. This is definitely a moment to hunt for extra glasses and open both wines.

Pork Tenderloin on a Bed of Leeks and Fennel

SERVES 4

In this dish, tarragon highlights the slightly licorice flavor of the fennel. The recipe also works with veal tenderloin.

The vegetable mixture can be made ahead of time and the pork popped into the oven at the last minute. The pork could also be grilled.

1 tbsp Dijon mustard	1 bulb fennel, trimmed and thinly sliced
1 tbsp chopped fresh tarragon	3 leeks, trimmed and thinly sliced
1 tsp cracked peppercorns	¼ cup chicken stock
2 tbsp olive oil	¼ cup white wine
1½ lbs pork tenderloin	2 tbsp whipping cream
Salt and freshly ground pepper	1 tbsp lemon juice
1 tbsp butter	

Preheat oven to 400°F.

Combine mustard, 2 tsp tarragon, peppercorns and 1 tbsp oil. Reserve.

Heat remaining 1 tbsp oil in a large skillet over medium heat. Season pork with salt and pepper. Add pork to skillet and brown on all sides, about 4 minutes in total.

Transfer pork to a baking dish and spread mustard mixture over top and sides. Bake for 17 to 20 minutes, or until just a hint of pink remains in pork.

Prepare vegetables while pork is cooking. Heat butter in a large skillet over medium heat. Add fennel, leeks and remaining 1 tsp tarragon and sauté for 3 minutes, or until crisp-tender.

Add stock, wine and cream. Cover and cook for 5 to 7 minutes, or until vegetables are tender.

Uncover, increase heat and cook for 2 to 3 minutes, or until liquid is reduced and slightly thickened. Stir in lemon juice. Season well with salt and pepper.

Cut pork into slices ½ inch thick. Place overlapping slices on leek and fennel mixture.

And to drink . . .

THE CONVENIENCE OF THIS LOVELY SUMMER MENU is that the wines that worked with the soup can stay on the table for the arrival of the pork. The Grüner Veltliner may seem a little uneasy in such meaty company, but in Austria, a mature Grüner with a good body would not seem outlandish with pork. Unlike Rieslings, these wines do not develop petrol aromas as they age; the white pepper spiciness that often hovers in the aroma may become a little less fleeting, which would flatter both the pork and the pancakes. The full-bodied Chardonnay, always amiable, simply nestles down with the leeks in their creamy sauce, especially if the same wine has been used in the sauce's preparation. It also works well with Dijon mustard, won't bicker with the fennel and welcomes a roasted tenderloin of pork oozing with pale, sweet, rich juices.

But what if some of your gardening buddies are red wine aficionados and have only been sitting so patiently while you elaborated upon the virtues of Grüner Veltliner because they were waiting for a wine they could get their teeth into? I'm afraid they may be disappointed. Serving a heavy-duty red on a warm summer night only makes sense if the barbecue is fired up. With the pork, something soft and fruity, served slightly chilled, is in order—perhaps a cru Beaujolais from the north of the region. The best Beaujolais comes from ten communes, and you'll see their monikers on the labels—St.-Amour, Julienas, Chénas, Moulin-à-Vent, Fleurie, Chiroubles, Morgon, Regnié, Brouilly and Côte de Brouilly.

Sweet Potato Ginger Pancakes

SERVES 4

These pancakes can be made ahead and reheated in a 400°F oven for 5 minutes before serving. Grate the sweet potatoes and onion by hand or in a food processor.

3 cups packed grated peeled
    sweet potatoes
½ cup grated onions
2 tbsp grated gingerroot
1 egg

¼ cup all-purpose flour
½ tsp baking powder
Salt and freshly ground pepper
2 tbsp vegetable oil, approx.

Squeeze all excess moisture from grated sweet potatoes and onions and combine.

Stir in ginger, egg, flour, baking powder, salt and pepper.

Heat 2 tbsp oil in a large heavy skillet over medium-high heat. Drop sweet potato mixture into hot skillet ¼ cup at a time and flatten with a spoon. Cook on both sides for about 3 minutes per side, or until pancakes are golden brown and crisp. Continue to cook pancakes in batches until all batter is used (about 12 pancakes), adding more oil as needed.

Drain pancakes on paper towels.

Peach and Blueberry Cobbler

SERVES 4 WITH LEFTOVERS

The cornmeal gives this topping an unusual crunch. Leftovers are wonderful for breakfast the next day. The cobbler can also be made with other fruit combinations such as apricots and raspberries.

4 cups sliced peeled peaches (5 or 6)	**Topping**
1 cup blueberries	½ cup all-purpose flour
2 tbsp lemon juice	½ cup cornmeal
2 tbsp brown sugar or to taste	¼ cup brown sugar
1 tbsp cornstarch	¼ tsp grated nutmeg
1 tbsp butter	¼ cup butter, diced
	½ cup whipping cream

Preheat oven to 350°F.

Combine peaches, blueberries, lemon juice, brown sugar and cornstarch. Place in a buttered 8-inch square baking dish and dot with butter.

Combine flour, cornmeal, brown sugar and nutmeg for topping. Cut in butter until mixture is crumbly. Stir in cream until mixture is just moistened.

Drop batter by heaping spoonfuls onto fruit mixture. Topping will spread slightly during baking.

Bake for 30 minutes, or until topping is golden and fruit is bubbling. Serve warm.

And to drink . . .

LUCY LOVES TO USE the soft fruits of summer in her desserts (and who can blame her), which gives me plenty of opportunities to bring out lightly chilled Select Late Harvest Rieslings or Vidals from Ontario. Vidal, especially, is a peachy-keen companion. If you enjoy Icewine with afters (some people find it too unctuous, too sweet and intense, a substitute rather than an accompaniment to dessert), this is a bona fide moment to uncork the precious elixir.

Another ideal partner is a mature Vouvray of the medium-sweet (*moelleux*) or sweeter, heavier, botrytized *liquoreux* variety. These wines come from France's Loire region and are pressed from late-harvested Chenin Blanc grapes—unquestionably the variety's finest hour. Rich and sweet, they also have a powerful backbone of acidity and are traditionally discouraged from undergoing a malolactic transformation—the process that occurs in a new wine (sometimes naturally, sometimes with the vintner's assistance) by which tart malic acids change into smoother, creamier lactic acids. Vouvray makers like to get their wines into bottle as soon as possible, forcing the vintage to mature much more slowly than it would in a tank or barrel. As a result, young Vouvrays can be surprisingly tart, but that same acidity gives them a very long life. A sweet Vouvray from a top producer hits its prime after decades and can last in a well-kept cellar for more than a century. Such wines, naturally enough, are rare and expensive; a young, run-of-the-mill Vouvray is a far less interesting proposition.

Cottage Retreat

Grilled Margarita Pizza

Grilled Sirloin of Beef

Grilled Mushrooms and Potatoes

Tomato Salad

Sour Cherry Crunch

SERVES 4

WHEN WE GO TO THE COTTAGE, food is the most important element of our planning. If we are having guests, I make sure I am very well organized so I can enjoy the time and relax, as well as being a hospitable host. A few hours' preparation at home takes the tension out of the whole weekend.

We like comfort food at the cottage—nothing too complicated. Much of the meal is usually barbecued. Salads are ideal (no pots and pans); dessert is made ahead and brought from home. In this menu, I have used one large steak instead of several smaller ones. It is easier to deal with if you are cooking for a crowd because it leaves room on the barbecue for vegetables.

The Margarita

SOME THINK OF FIRECRACKERS AND PIÑATAS, the sound of a mariachi band on the street of a dusty border town. For others it's tight jeans and cowboy boots, sunset over the desert and lonesome songs by The Eagles on a jukebox in a cantina. Either way, the Margarita is tequila's finest hour, the cocktail of the Tex-Mex revolution and the best possible source of dietary salt.

Any cocktail that bears a person's name has a story behind its creation, and the Margarita's is more romantic than most. In *An Encyclopedia of Drink and Drinking*, Frederick Martin gives a tantalizing (and somewhat cold-hearted) glimpse of what must have been a moment of poignant tragedy. The Margarita, he writes, is "said to have been named by a bartender in Virginia City in memory of his 'gal' who died in his arms after getting in the way of a bullet during a shooting."

No date. No background. No motive. Did the accident happen during the days when the West was wild and woolly? Somehow I never pictured those cowboy barkeeps toying with cocktail shakers and Cointreau. Or perhaps Margarita bought hers at a much later date, the innocent victim of a holdup in the rough-and-ready Nevada of the thirties.

Though the first known tequila shipment crossed the Mexican border in 1873, the spirit only became fashionable in the U.S. in the 1960s, thanks to a vogue among Californian university students. They may have confused mezcal (tequila's crude country cousin) with mescal, the hallucinatory peyote, although there is no connection. Perhaps they just enjoyed the macho American tequila ritual—a lick of salt from the thumbnail or from the skin between thumb and forefinger, a shot of spirit, a sucking squeeze of fresh lime. That ritual is mimicked by the Margarita. Salt rims the glass, so you taste it first; then comes the tequila and citrus. Insinuated into the mix is the Cointreau or Triple Sec, boosting the fruit and adding depth and richness of flavor.

To make one, wipe the rim of a cocktail glass with a wedge of lime and dip it in salt. Combine 1½ oz tequila, ½ oz Cointreau and 1 oz freshly squeezed lime juice in a cocktail shaker with cracked ice. Shake hard and strain it into a glass.

Grilled Margarita Pizza

MAKES 4 9-INCH PIZZAS

The drink may have been named after a bartender's moll, but when it comes to pizzas, Margarita just refers to a classic Italian pizza traditionally topped with tomato sauce and buffalo mozzarella (*mozzarella di bufala*). If you don't want to make your own dough, buy prepared dough or use prebaked pizza bases. Sprinkle the finished pizzas with some fine olive oil.

1 cup warm water	2 cups tomato sauce, storebought or
2 tsp active dry yeast	homemade
1 tsp granulated sugar	2 cups shredded Fontina or mozzarella
2½ cups all-purpose flour, approx.	cheese
1 tsp salt	¼ cup slivered fresh basil

Stir together warm water, yeast and sugar. Let stand for 5 minutes, or until frothy.

Combine flour and salt in a food processor. With machine running, pour yeast mixture into flour and process until well combined. Continue to process for 2 minutes, or until dough is soft and slightly sticky.

Knead dough on a well-floured board, adding flour if necessary, for about 2 minutes, or until smooth and elastic. Place dough in an oiled bowl in a warm place, cover and let sit until doubled in bulk, about 1 hour. Punch dough down and divide into four balls.

Roll out dough on a floured surface to make four 9-inch crusts. (You can also spread dough with your fingers.)

Lay 2 pizza crusts on grill over medium heat. Grill for about 3 minutes, or until edges begin to puff and bottom is slightly crisp.

Turn off one burner. Turn crusts and place over indirect heat. Spread each crust with ½ cup tomato sauce, ½ cup cheese and 1 tbsp basil. (If you use prebaked pizza crusts, simply place over turned-off side of grill and add toppings immediately.) Close grill lid and cook for 3 to 4 minutes, or until cheese has melted. Serve immediately. Repeat with remaining ingredients.

And to drink . . .

MORE THAN THE AUTOMOBILE, almost as much as the television, the barbecue is a cornerstone of the North American male domestic experience. Unless they happen to be freemasons, barbecuing is the only time most men will don an apron, even if it means wearing the thing over a parka, for true barbecue devotees cook al fresco deep into autumn and beyond.

The weather may not be a factor to the determined grillmeister, but it can't be ignored when choosing wines to accompany food off the coals. A mighty Cabernet or Shiraz that would be the natural choice for a superb piece of barbecued beef in springtime or fall is too ponderous in the heat of summer. Nuances of aroma also tend to get lost in the great outdoors, banished by breezes, gusts of smoke from the grill and the sharp scents of suntan oil and mosquito repellent.

Before the meat makes its appearance, however, there is the matter of the pizza—a simple pizza, to be sure, but a pizza still, bearing the wine matcher's burden, a deliciously tangy tomato sauce. Finding a wine for tomatoes is always a challenge, because they are so high in natural sugars and acidity. Tomato sauce is even tougher since its whole purpose is to intensify the sweet and tart qualities of the fruit. Even mitigated by crunchy dough and melted cheese, that sauce must be addressed. You could clout it over the head with a red Zinfandel or Baco Noir, but you wouldn't wear a tweed overcoat on a day like this, so why ask your palate to do the equivalent? A decent Valpolicella or Barbera or a Cabernet Franc from the Loire has the forward fruitiness and necessary acidity to get the job done in a debonair and suitably summery manner. Chilling it for a little while in a bucket of ice water will stop the wine from wilting in the heat. Better yet, perhaps, reintroduce your guests to the forgotten joys of dry rosé wine—a fragrant Syrah rosé from France's Pays d'Oc, for example, or a Cabernet rosé from Australia's Margaret River region or one of northern Spain's dry, pungently fruity rosados. If you've never seen a wine waltz with a tomato, this is your chance.

Grilled Sirloin of Beef

SERVES 4

For the best grilled steak, the thickness of the meat is most important. A steak that is 2 inches thick will form a crust on the outside and be juicy and red in the middle. (A 2-inch–thick boneless sirloin may weigh 3½ to 4 pounds, but the meat is so succulent that you can use the leftovers in a steak salad or sandwiches the next day.)

1 boneless sirloin steak (about 3 lbs),
   2 inches thick, trimmed
2 tbsp olive oil
2 tbsp dry seasoning rub (page 128)

Garnish
1 bunch arugula, trimmed
1 cup finely chopped red onions
¼ cup finely chopped parsley
1 tbsp fleur de sel or kosher salt
1 tbsp cracked peppercorns

Brush steak with oil on both sides and sprinkle rub all over.

Grill beef over high heat for 10 minutes. Turn and continue to grill for 5 to 10 minutes longer for medium-rare, or until steak reaches desired degree of doneness.

Place steak on a carving board and let rest for 5 minutes (meat will continue to cook as it sits). Carve steak against grain into thin slices.

Fan beef slices on a serving platter over bed of arugula and sprinkle with onions, parsley, fleur de sel and peppercorns.

And to drink . . .

GORGEOUS GRILLED SIRLOIN OF BEEF, running with juices, its surface crusted, smoky and caramelized from the heat, deserves our full attention. A big red wine is required, loaded with charisma and personality but still relatively light on its feet. Oak is no problem—oakiness harmonizes beautifully with the charred flavors of the grill—and ripe fruitiness would be an asset. Above all, with this menu, that big red should have a powerful acidity to cut through the richness of the food and refresh the palate, to match the sweet acid of the tomatoes in the salad and generally to hold the wine together on a hot July day. A fine Chianti Classico Riserva fits the bill perfectly.

Chianti, of course, is a sprawling region in central Tuscany, close to Florence; Chianti Classico is its heartland. "Riserva" means that this is a Chianti Classico made from the estate's best grapes and aged longer in wood. The wood in question used to be huge old *botti* of Slavonian oak that lost any chance of making an impact on the wine decades ago. These days it might mean new French barriques, adding their spicy note to the Sangiovese grape's own deep cherry flavors. The best riservas from a wonderful vintage like 1997 or 1999 can show amazing nuances of licorice, tobacco and violets weaving among those cherries. Some have a substantial body, but good Chianti (and there is still a broad range of quality, even in a famous year) always balances its weight and intensity with an uplifting acidity—one reason why it is such a great partner for food.

Grilled Mushrooms and Potatoes

SERVES 4

The best accompaniment for barbecued steak. Parboiling the potatoes means they will cook more quickly on the grill and retain a soft, floury texture.

4 Yukon Gold potatoes, unpeeled, cut in ½-inch slices
4 Portobello mushrooms, trimmed
⅓ cup olive oil

3 tbsp balsamic vinegar
2 tsp chopped fresh basil
1 tsp chopped garlic
Salt and freshly ground pepper

Place potatoes in a pot and cover with cold water. Bring to a boil over high heat and boil for 4 minutes. Drain and combine with mushrooms.

Whisk together oil, vinegar, basil and garlic. Add to vegetables and toss to coat. Marinate for 1 hour.

Remove vegetables from marinade and season with salt and pepper.

Grill potatoes over high heat for 7 to 8 minutes per side. Grill mushrooms for 5 minutes per side.

Slice mushrooms and potatoes and serve with steak.

Food Tech

The Best Steak on the Grill

I BELIEVE THE VERY BEST STEAK for barbecuing is top-quality ribeye. I like to buy a ribeye that is about 2 inches thick and divide it between two people. With a larger steak, the meat develops an outside crust but remains rare inside.

For those who prefer their steak on the bone, rib steaks or Porterhouse (a combination of T-bone and tenderloin) are winners. For the best flavor, look for well-marbled Prime or Triple A grade beef. Dry-aged beef (beef aged for at least 21 days on the carcass) has even more flavor. These steaks need nothing but a liberal sprinkling of salt and pepper, and a little garlic if you like it. Use kosher salt, which has coarser crystals and a more complex taste than table salt. Pepper loses its flavor after grinding, so it is always best to grind as you need it.

After much experimentation on the grill, I've decided it's best not to fool with the steaks too much. Flip them only once. For a professional look, give the steaks a quarter turn after a few minutes of grilling to create the cross-hatched grill marks.

To feed a crowd, my preferred steak is boneless sirloin. However, as it doesn't have quite as much flavor and texture as the top-quality cuts, a barbecue sauce (pages 158 and 348) or a dry seasoning rub is a good addition (I also use a rub when I am barbecuing flank steak).

Here is my seasoning rub recipe. It can easily be doubled or tripled.

Combine 1 tbsp paprika, 1 tsp chili powder, 1 tsp dry mustard, 1 tsp dried thyme and 1 tsp kosher salt. Stir to combine and store in an airtight container. Sprinkle liberally on steaks or chops, adding freshly ground pepper.

Grilled Sirloin of Beef (p. 124)

Tomato Salad

SERVES 4

The best-quality tomatoes need little embellishment. Heirloom tomatoes are grown from old seeds and have the long-forgotten real tomato flavor. They are appearing more and more in upscale grocery stores and farmers' markets. They can be dark red, striped, green or orange, and they deliver a flavor punch and mouth-watering juiciness. If they are unavailable, just use the very best tomatoes you can find in this salad.

To make this even more special, use a high-quality extra-virgin olive oil and either Maldon salt, sea salt or fleur de sel. There is enough acid in the tomatoes that you won't need to add any vinegar. When you have excellent ingredients, simplicity is the key.

4 to 6 heirloom tomatoes
Handful fresh basil leaves

Salt and freshly ground pepper
2 to 4 tbsp extra-virgin olive oil

Core tomatoes and slice lengthwise so slices hold together. Arrange tomato slices on a platter or stack with basil leaves on individual serving plates. Sprinkle tomatoes with salt and pepper and drizzle with oil.

Sour Cherry Crunch

SERVES 4

Frozen sour cherries are widely available in summer. They have already been pitted and are very easy to use. If you use fresh sour cherries, pit them by squeezing the fruit between your fingers.

Gooseberries in season are also good in this. Top and tail them and increase the granulated sugar to ½ cup if they are very sour.

Demerara sugar adds extra crunch to this dessert.

1½ lbs sour cherries, pitted	¾ cup Demerara sugar
⅓ cup granulated sugar	Pinch ground ginger
1 cup all-purpose flour	Pinch ground cinnamon
	⅓ cup butter, diced

Preheat oven to 350°F.

Toss cherries with granulated sugar and place in a buttered 8-inch baking dish.

Combine flour, Demerara sugar, ginger and cinnamon. Cut butter into flour until mixture resembles coarse breadcrumbs. Sprinkle topping over fruit.

Bake for 35 to 40 minutes, or until top is golden brown and fruit is bubbling. Serve hot or cold with ice cream.

Demerara Sugar Demerara sugar is an unrefined brown sugar. It has a coarser grain than other brown sugars and is wonderful in coffee and for baking when you want crunch. It also never seems to harden like other brown sugars.

Beware of imitation brown sugars. Some are in fact refined white sugar with color added back in. Unrefined brown sugar is made from sugarcane, and the natural color and flavor have not been removed.

And to drink . . .

THERE'S AN OLD QUESTION DEVISED TO CONFOUND wine snobs: "Can you find a wine to go with my grandma's cherry pie?" You could ask the same thing about Lucy's Sour Cherry Crunch, and a single answer would serve. Fortified cherry wine has delighted connoisseurs and grandmothers in northern and eastern Europe for centuries. The Danes make a particular speciality of it, but the Poles and Croatians keep pace. Their methods differ slightly but all involve cherries, alcohol, sugar and a base wine, usually made from grapes or raisins. The result is a heavy, intensely cherry-flavored treat, sweeter and infinitely simpler than port but almost as delicious.

These cherry wines have many uses. A measure added to a flute of sparkling wine produces a fascinating hybrid of a Kir Royale. When served with dessert, the added alcohol literally fortifies the wines against the most direct or the most insidious attack. Even ice cream and dark chocolate cannot disconcert their defences. It must be said, a little goes a long way. For that reason, you might want to pour the cherry wine over ice when offering it alongside the crunch. And if pairing cherry with cherry seems a tad too co-ordinated—like wearing a shirt and tie of an identical pink—rest assured there is enough going on in the ginger and cinnamon crunch to keep the twins apart.

Sophisticated Grilling

Chilled Cucumber Soup with Shrimp

Grilled Bombay Lamb with Mint Salsa

Zucchini Pilau

Indian Chopped Salad • Indian-style Ratatouille

Raspberry Tart with Mint and Lemon Cream

SERVES 6

THE KIDS ARE GONE FOR THE SUMMER, and burgers, ribs and hotdogs have been banished from the grill. Now is the time to entertain friends with a little flair and sophistication, and here is a summer menu that fits the bill.

Indian spicing is multi-layered. The many different spices and combination of textures in this menu give intense flavor, zest and style to familiar foods.

The dessert is not Indian but definitely a crowd pleaser.

Sangria

SANGRIA, FOR ALL ITS SPANISH ASSOCIATIONS, is essentially a punch, and therefore all the punch bowl caveats apply. The host must be alert to rapidly melting ice, to fruit growing soggy and discolored, to fizz falling flat. There are few drinks sadder than a jug of sangria that has been left out in the sun. Warm, sticky and diluted, it might as well be abandoned to the wasps.

In my youth, English holidaymakers discovered cheap vacations to the coast of Spain, returning with fond memories of refreshing, slyly potent sangria and often a hideous glazed jug in which to make their own. Adding brandy and lemonade was a way to use up bottles of rock-bottom Rioja that friends brought to parties.

We learned our lesson. Undrinkable wine makes undrinkable Sangria, so whichever of the innumerable recipes for the drink one may favor, it's important to begin with a wine that gives pleasure on its own.

To steep or not to steep: that is the question. I used to be a steeper, slicing a peach, half an orange and a handful of strawberries into the brandy and Cointreau and letting them stay in the refrigerator overnight, sharing their flavors with the spirit. Yes, they ended up mushy, but it was worth it for the taste.

These days, I'm not so sure. Perhaps it is a matter for the individual conscience. The bottle of good Rioja should certainly spend an hour in the fridge, alongside a jug containing 2 oz Spanish brandy, 2 oz Cointreau or peach schnapps and the freshly squeezed juice of an orange. If the fruit has been withheld from this mixture, add it just before serving, along with the chilled red wine. Stir. Pour it into large glasses containing a cube or two of ice. A splash of soda can follow, if desired.

Chilled Cucumber Soup with Shrimp

SERVES 6

This refreshing summer soup is a little like an Indian raita, and it looks especially wonderful served in glass bowls. Moisten the rims of the bowls with water and dip them in chopped fresh mint. Zucchini can be substituted for the cucumber.

Chilling dulls seasonings, so taste and season with salt and pepper after refrigerating.

1 seedless cucumber, sliced
1 cup chopped green onions
1 tsp chopped garlic
4 cups chicken stock
¼ cup whipping cream
   or plain yogurt

2 tbsp chopped fresh mint
1 tbsp lime juice
Salt and freshly ground pepper
1 cup cooked baby shrimp
2 tbsp chopped chives

Combine cucumber, green onions, garlic and stock in a pot. Bring to a boil over medium heat. Reduce heat and simmer gently for 20 minutes, or until vegetables are cooked.
Puree soup until smooth.
Stir in cream, mint and lime juice. Refrigerate overnight.
Season with salt and pepper just before serving. Garnish with shrimp and chives.

And to drink . . .

WHILE THE MARRIAGE OF SOUP AND WINE is a surmountable dilemma, a cold soup with cream presents an extra obstacle to the union. Cream coats the mouth, and though a crisp dry white wine will soon counteract this effect, it could also disrupt the delightful balance of ingredients in the soup. A dry, relatively neutral white from Italy—a Soave, for instance—could come along for the ride, but my instinct (and I never thought I'd hear myself say this) is to sit this course out where wine is concerned and marshall all forces for the kaleidoscopic flavors that lie ahead.

Which wines work with Indian food? Given the infinite range of cuisines in the vast subcontinent, one might as well ask which wines work with European food. Over the years, I have spent many pungent evenings with sommeliers and Indian restaurateurs, working our way through dozens of different dishes with dozens of wines on the table, looking for pitfalls and epiphanies. Most of the time we have found that the general logic of wine and food matching still holds. Intensely flavored dishes dismantle or kill light, delicate wines and mask the precious subtleties of rare old vintages. Sauces dramatically sharpened with vinegar, tamarind or lime, not to mention chutneys and pickles, are as dangerous to wine as any food with a searing acidity. The richness and weight of dishes made with ghee, yogurt or coconut milk call for wines with a decent body of their own. Above all, and I suppose this is in direct contradiction to the above, generalizations are even more risky than usual. Each dish must be judged on its own merits.

Grilled Bombay Lamb with Mint Salsa

SERVES 6

Ask for a butterflied lamb leg—a leg that has been boned and opened up. Indian curry pastes, which are now available in many supermarkets, come in different heats, and they do not have the raw taste of curry powder. If they are unavailable, use 2 tsp curry powder mixed with 2 tbsp vegetable oil.

Garnish the lamb with lime wedges and fresh mint sprigs and serve with the rice and mint salsa.

1 butterflied leg of lamb (about 3 lbs)
2 tbsp mild Indian curry paste

2 tbsp finely chopped gingerroot
1 tbsp finely chopped garlic
½ cup plain yogurt

Trim fat from lamb.
Combine curry paste, ginger, garlic and yogurt. Spoon marinade over lamb and refrigerate for 6 hours or overnight.
Place lamb fat side down on a grill over high heat and sear for 3 minutes. Turn lamb and sear for 3 minutes on second side. Close lid, reduce heat to medium and grill for 10 minutes. Turn again and grill, covered, for 10 minutes longer, or until lamb is medium-rare.
Remove lamb from grill and let rest for 10 minutes. Slice against grain and transfer to a platter.

Mint Salsa This salsa is great with lamb and fish. It can also be tossed with pasta for a salad.
    Combine 2 cups mint leaves, 1 tsp chopped garlic, ¼ cup olive oil and ¼ cup plain yogurt in a food processor. Process until a thick puree. Add 2 tbsp lemon juice and season with salt and pepper.
    Makes about 1 cup.

And to drink . . .

THIS GLORIOUS GRILLED LAMB with its intensely flavored marinade deserves to walk down the sensory aisle with a red wine of stature. Nothing too tannic, I would suggest, since the heavy-duty spices in the curry paste seem to me to accentuate tannins, but something with masses of character and loads of ripe fruit. A good, serious Californian red Zinfandel would be my opening bid, a wine full of opulent, soft blackberry flavors with its own hint of spiciness. Such Zins are famously able to handle the sweet-sour challenges of grilled meats in piquant barbecue sauces or rubs, largely by opening their big purple arms and giving everything on the plate a soothing hug of fruit.

There are alternatives. If the table decides that the Zinfandel you have found is a little too big and jammy, jump to Plan B—a Rhône-style blend from California or Australia. Producers there have been having all kinds of fun with old vineyards of Grenache, Syrah and Mourvèdre, creating warm, earthy blends that show more obvious and riper fruit than the French originals. At their best with powerfully herbal dishes, these wines can also survive the hot embrace of South Asian spices, looking over the marinade's shoulder to commune directly with the lamb.

Both a Zinfandel and a New World Rhône-style red should be fine with the spiced ratatouille, but the chopped salad, tangy as raw chutney, has such vibrant acidity that it might prove a problem. A sip of water or a forkful of rice between tastes of salad and wine is the easiest solution.

(from top) Indian-style Ratatouille (p. 139);
Mint Salsa (p. 136); Indian Chopped Salad (p. 138)

Zucchini Pilau

SERVES 6

An easy rice dish. You can use carrots, peas, green beans or other vegetables instead of the zucchini.

2 cups uncooked basmati or
   long-grain rice
2 tbsp butter
1 onion, sliced
2 medium green zucchini, diced
1 medium yellow zucchini, diced

1 tsp cumin seeds
2-inch cinnamon stick, broken in pieces
4 cloves
3 cardamom pods, crushed, optional
2 cups water
Salt to taste
2 tbsp chopped fresh mint

Soak rice in cold water for 30 minutes. Rinse and drain well.
Heat butter in a pot over medium heat. Add onion and sauté for 3 minutes. Add green and yellow zucchini and sauté for 2 minutes.
Stir in cumin, cinnamon, cloves and cardamom and sauté for 1 minute.
Add rice and water. Bring to a boil over high heat and boil for 2 minutes. Cover and leave on lowest heat for 10 minutes.
Season with salt. Sprinkle with mint before serving.

Indian Chopped Salad

SERVES 6

When I was in India, this refreshing, tangy salad was served with nearly every main course. If you cut all the vegetables into a large dice, their crunchy texture will contrast with the softer textures of the meat and curried vegetables.

2 cups diced sweet onions
4 tomatoes, seeded and diced
½ seedless cucumber, diced
1 tsp chopped jalapeño pepper

Salt and freshly ground pepper
¼ cup lime juice
½ tsp granulated sugar
¼ cup chopped fresh coriander

Combine onions, tomatoes, cucumber and jalapeño. Season with salt and pepper.
Combine lime juice and sugar. Toss with vegetables and coriander.

Indian-style Ratatouille

SERVES 6

In this dish, the vegetables are first roasted and then combined with spices and sautéed together, as for a ratatouille. If you cannot grind your own spices, buy them already ground.

This dish can be made up to a day before serving.

1 large eggplant	Salt and freshly ground pepper
1 large sweet onion, peeled	1 tbsp cumin seeds
4 plum tomatoes, halved and seeded	1 tbsp coriander seeds
1 jalapeño or serrano pepper, halved and seeded	1 tbsp chopped gingerroot
	1 tbsp chopped garlic
¼ cup vegetable oil	1 tsp garam masala
	¼ cup chopped fresh coriander

Preheat oven to 450°F.

Peel 1-inch strips from eggplant, leaving about 1 inch between strips. Cut eggplant and onion into rounds about ½ inch thick.

Brush eggplant, onion, tomatoes and jalapeño with 2 tbsp oil and season with salt and pepper. Place on an oiled baking sheet.

Roast vegetables for 15 minutes. Turn and roast for 10 to 15 minutes longer, or until browned and tender. Cool, peel jalapeño and cut all vegetables into chunks.

Place cumin and coriander seeds in a small dry skillet over medium heat and cook, stirring constantly, for 2 minutes. Grind in a coffee or spice grinder.

Heat remaining 2 tbsp oil in a skillet over medium heat. Add ginger and garlic and sauté for 1 minute. Add toasted seeds and sauté for 1 minute.

Stir in vegetables, cover and simmer gently for 5 minutes, or until thick. Stir in garam masala and salt. Sprinkle with fresh coriander.

> **Coriander** Known as cilantro in Mexican cooking, coriander has a sweet, citrusy, flowery taste, and it is an essential ingredient in many Asian dishes. In Thai cooking even the roots are used. It is an annual and easy to grow.
>
> Coriander wilts quickly, but if you place its roots in a little water in a jar and cover the leaves with a plastic bag, it should keep for two weeks in the refrigerator.
>
> Coriander seeds are often ground and used as a fragrant seasoning.

Raspberry Tart
with Mint and Lemon Cream
SERVES 6

A beautiful tart with just a hint of mint and lemon in the custard. Glaze it up to an hour before serving but don't refrigerate after glazing, or the glaze may run.

1 recipe Sweet Tart Pastry (page 224)	¼ cup granulated sugar
1½ cups milk	¼ cup all-purpose flour
¼ cup chopped fresh mint	3 tbsp butter
1 tbsp grated lemon zest	1½ cups fresh raspberries
3 egg yolks	½ cup raspberry jam, sieved
	¼ cup raspberry wine or framboise

Roll out pastry and fit into an 8- or 9-inch tart pan. Prick pastry with a fork and refrigerate for 15 minutes.

Preheat oven to 350°F.

Place parchment paper or foil in pastry shell and fill with rice or dried beans. Bake for 15 minutes. Remove weights and bake for 5 to 10 minutes longer, or until pastry is pale gold. Cool.

Prepare filling by combining milk, mint and lemon zest in a heavy pot over medium heat. Bring to a boil, reduce heat and simmer for 3 minutes. Cool. Strain milk mixture, discarding mint and lemon.

Whisk together egg yolks, sugar and flour. Pour in milk mixture, whisking constantly. Return to pot and bring to a boil over medium heat. Stirring constantly, cook for 2 to 3 minutes, or until thickened.

Stir in butter. Transfer to a bowl. Place plastic wrap directly on custard to prevent a crust from forming. Cool.

Spoon custard into pastry shell and top with berries.

Combine jam and wine in a pot over medium heat. Bring to a boil and simmer for 2 minutes, or until slightly thickened. Brush glaze gently over fruit and let cool.

And to drink . . .

THERE ARE SEVERAL OPTIONS FOR THIS DESSERT. Most of my classic European wine-and-food-matching tomes suggest a Sauternes, but I sometimes wonder if such received wisdom isn't an echo from a past when the range and number of dessert wines were more limited than they are today. It is true, however, that a Sauternes, a Monbazillac or a sweet wine from the Loire are all pretty fabulous with this scrumptious tart and, served well chilled, they aren't too heavy for a summer night. Something higher up the scale of saccharine opulence might be. A small glass of very sweet, fortified framboise is a little too fulsome and probably also too obvious, even though you may have used it in the glaze for the tart and have three-quarters of a bottle left.

Sparkling Moscato d'Asti has the refreshing levity to cut through a hot summer night and the sweetness to shine when dessert is in the offing. But I would go with the safe bet and buy a couple of half bottles of Monbazillac. Like Sauternes, it is made from Sémillon, Sauvignon and Muscadelle grapes, but in Bergerac, not Bordeaux, which has a charmingly diminishing effect on the relative price of the wine. Botrytis often adds its honeyed overtone to the golden liquid.

Better make that three or four half bottles.

Fish on the Grill

Bruschetta with White Beans, Arugula and Prosciutto
Spiced Yellow Tomato Soup
Grilled Whole Snapper with Provençal Vinaigrette
Lentil Salad
Peach and Raspberry Compote

SERVES 4

GRILLING A WHOLE FISH can seem like a challenge. Fear of turning the fish, fear of over- or under-cooking it and the fuss of dealing with bones sends many barbecuers running to the safety of everyday fish fillets. But there really isn't any reason to worry—grilling whole fish is easy and the results are especially tasty.

Campari

SWEET AS MEMORY, bitter as middle age, as scarlet as Satan's tights, a Campari and soda is the most refreshing drink in the world. It's the perfect aperitif if you're having lunch in Italy in July and arrive at the restaurant early. It can be a lifesaver on sweltering Mediterranean nights when your shirt clings to your back and nothing else seems able to quench your thirst. But such is the compelling balance of the elixir that another becomes an immediate priority.

Campari is a concoction unlike any other. It was invented in 1862 by a former barman called Gaspare Campari and it made his fortune as the speciality of the chic café he owned in the center of Milan. Almost at once, apparently, people started mixing it in equal proportions with the local sweet red vermouth, a cocktail that was eventually dubbed the Americano, perhaps because visiting American tourists enjoyed its relative sweetness, with or without a splash of soda.

Delicious though it is, the Americano has sometimes been criticized for a lack of rigor. Count Camillo Negroni, a Florentine aristocrat who did his drinking during the 1920s, always demanded the addition of gin to the cocktail, and this supercharged version has been known as a Negroni ever since. It's a tricky drink to perfect and some people find it too strong and too bitter, especially if they don't know the secret ingredient—a few drops of juice squeezed from a slice of orange. Add them to a generous ounce of gin, a meager ounce of Campari and three-quarters of an ounce of sweet red vermouth and serve it straight up or on the rocks with a slice of orange as garnish. An optional dash of soda can lengthen matters but the orange slice is essential, as it is with a regular Campari and soda. Orange clasps hands with the flavor of bitter oranges in the Campari, slightly soothing the bitterness of the quinine. Using lemon as a garnish has almost the opposite effect and throws the whole drink off kilter. Flamboyant mixologists have been known to take orange's affinity with the Negroni one step further, holding a lighted match over the cocktail with one hand and pinching a piece of orange peel with the other, about an inch from the flame. The sudden squirt of the fruit's essential oils ignites in a tiny but melodramatic sputter of fire.

Bruschetta with White Beans, Arugula and Prosciutto

MAKES 12 HORS D'OEUVRES

Substitute slivered red peppers for the prosciutto, if desired. Buy a jar of pimentos or grilled red peppers, or roast your own.

You may have topping left over; it should keep, refrigerated, for one week.

1 19-oz can white kidney beans, rinsed and drained	Salt and freshly ground pepper
1 clove garlic, coarsely chopped	12 slices Italian baguette (about ½ inch thick)
½ tsp paprika	1 bunch arugula leaves, trimmed and shredded
3 tbsp olive oil	8 slices prosciutto, slivered

Puree beans, garlic, paprika and oil. Season with salt and pepper. If mixture is too thick to spread, thin with a little mayonnaise.

Grill baguette slices on both sides until golden. Spread with bean puree. Sprinkle with arugula and prosciutto.

Spiced Yellow Tomato Soup

SERVES 4

Yellow tomatoes are less acidic than red ones. You can also use red tomatoes in this soup, but taste for acidity and add a pinch of sugar if needed.
    Serve this soup hot or cold.

2 tbsp butter	1-inch strip orange rind
½ cup chopped onions	2 lbs ripe tomatoes, diced
½ cup chopped carrots	3 cups chicken stock
1 tsp ground coriander	Salt and freshly ground pepper
1 tsp ground allspice	¼ cup whipping cream, optional
Pinch ground cloves	2 tbsp chopped fresh mint

Heat butter in a pot over medium heat. Add onions and carrots and sauté for 2 minutes. Add coriander, allspice, cloves, orange rind and tomatoes. Stir together.

Add stock and bring to a boil. Season with salt and pepper. Reduce heat and simmer for 20 minutes. Remove orange rind.

Push soup through a food mill for the smoothest texture, or puree in a food processor or blender. Return to pot.

Add cream and mint. Simmer for a few minutes to amalgamate flavors. Taste and adjust seasonings if necessary.

And to drink . . .

WHEN TOMATOES ARE THE PRINCIPAL INGREDIENT in a dish—even sweet, ripe, locally grown yellow tomatoes—the high-acid warning light starts to flash. If a wine doesn't have enough acidity of its own to cope with the tomatoes, it could well end up tasting flabby and dull.

New Zealand Sauvignon has what it takes—a clean, green scythe of fruit that offers one of the most unmistakable olfactory footprints on the planet. This intensity of aroma is partly explained by a molecule in the grape called methoxypyrazine, which the human nose interprets as the smell of green grass. There is three times as much of it in the average New Zealand Sauvignon as in the same variety from, say, Australia. Whether it manifests itself as grassiness, gooseberries, passionfruit or something in between depends partly on ripeness at harvest time, but also on location. In Marlborough in the cooler South Island, Sauvignon tends to be sharper, greener, more like a mouthful of gooseberries. Versions from warmer Hawke's Bay often seem fuller and more reminiscent of melon. Some winemakers temper the acidity of their Sauvignon by leaving a trace of residual sugar after fermentation or by blending in a little soothing Sémillon. Not that there is any doubt about the grape and the provenance once that bouquet streams up out of the glass. A fine wine for tomatoes.

Grilled Whole Snapper
with Provençal Vinaigrette

SERVES 4

When grilling whole fish, you can remove the head if you wish, but the fish will retain more moisture if you leave the head on.

Herbes de Provence is a prepackaged mix of dried Provençal herbs. If you can't find it, use a combination of dried rosemary, thyme, oregano and savory.

Have the fishmonger clean the fish so that it is grill-ready. Substitute striped bass for the snapper if desired.

2 whole red snappers (about 2 lbs each)	2 tbsp finely chopped roasted red peppers
½ cup olive oil	1 tsp finely chopped garlic
1 tbsp finely chopped garlic	1 tsp grated lemon zest
⅓ cup fresh thyme stalks	3 tbsp balsamic vinegar
Provençal Vinaigrette	½ cup olive oil
2 tsp herbes de Provence	Salt and freshly ground pepper

Rinse fish. Whisk together oil and garlic. Brush over skin and cavity of fish. Stuff thyme stalks into cavity. Marinate at room temperature for 30 minutes. Whisk together herbes de Provence, red peppers, garlic, lemon zest, vinegar and oil. Season with salt and pepper. Reserve vinaigrette.

Grill fish over medium-high heat for 6 to 10 minutes per side, depending on thickness of fish, until flesh is white and moist and just comes away from bone. Use a large spatula to turn fish (tongs may break it).

Transfer fish to a platter and cut fillets off bone. Place fillets on serving plates and drizzle with vinaigrette.

> **Grilling Fish** To prevent fish from sticking to the grill, spray or brush the fish with oil before grilling. The skin will caramelize slightly and release from the grill on its own. You can also rub the grill with oiled foil just before grilling or, if your fish is small enough, use a grill basket.
>
> Cook whole fish until the eye turns white and the flesh next to the bone is slightly pink.

And to drink . . .

I LOVE A WHOLE FISH COOKED ON THE GRILL—the skin crisp and slightly smoky, the flesh soft and moist, its juices seized by the heat. The lentil salad is also a major part of the experience, with the delicately earthy taste of the lentils sparked by lemon and onions.

Snapper is a medium-weight fish in terms of texture, so start thinking about wines with more body than light summer whites. New World Sauvignon is definitely a contender, especially since the dish provides its own acid balances in the Provençal dressing for the fish and the lemon and tomatoes in the lentil salad. No need, then, to put away that half-finished New Zealand Sauvignon that you opened for the tomato soup. Sémillon also springs to mind—the sort of Sémillon produced in Australia's Hunter Valley, the one place in the world where Bordeaux's "other" white grape really shines on its own. Big-bodied and with aromas that are often difficult to describe (lime? honeysuckle? milk?), these wines are sometimes barrel-fermented, and the well-integrated oak picks up the flavors of the grill on the snapper's skin in a most delectable way.

As a third wine to set out on the table I was going to suggest a smooth, oaky white Rioja, but Lucy tells me she loves drinking a cold rosé from the south of France with this dish—a wine from Provence or the Pays d'Oc. It sounds like a very good idea, and one should never argue with the cook.

Filleting Cooked Fish With a sharp knife, remove the dorsal fin on the back of the fish. Cut off the head and tail.

If you wish, remove the top layer of skin with a knife. It should peel off easily. Slide a fish knife or pastry server under the fillet. Gently lift the fillet off the bone and transfer to a platter.

Using a knife and fork, lift the exposed bone and pull it away from the fish to expose the second fillet. Transfer the second fillet to the platter. If the fillets are large, cut them in half.

Lentil Salad

SERVES 4

I love the contrast of grilled fish with these flavorful lentils. Use lentils du Puy—the small green lentils from France. They retain their texture when cooked and never go mushy. If you can't find them, use regular green lentils.

1 tbsp olive oil
1/2 cup chopped onions
2 tsp chopped garlic
1 tsp hot red pepper flakes
1 cup dried lentils du Puy
1 bay leaf
2 slices lemon (about 1/2 inch thick)
Salt and freshly ground pepper

Dressing
1 tsp grated lemon zest
2 tbsp lemon juice
1 tbsp finely chopped fresh oregano
1/3 cup olive oil
Garnish
1 cup chopped red onions
1/2 cup black olives, pitted and sliced
2 tomatoes, seeded and chopped
2 cups slivered fresh spinach

Heat oil in a pot over medium heat. Add onions and garlic and sauté for about 2 minutes, or until fragrant. Stir in hot pepper flakes.

Add lentils and sauté for about 1 minute, or just until lentils are coated with seasoning mixture.

Add enough water to cover lentils. Add bay leaf and lemon slices, squeezing lemon gently. Bring to a boil, reduce heat to medium-low, cover and simmer for 35 to 45 minutes, or until lentils are tender.

Drain off any excess water and remove lemon slices and bay leaf. Season lentils well with salt and pepper.

Whisk together lemon zest, lemon juice, oregano and oil. Toss warm lentils with dressing.

Sprinkle lentils with red onions, olives, tomatoes and spinach. Taste and re-season if necessary.

Food Tech

Smoking on the Grill

TRUE BARBECUING GIVES FOOD A SMOKY TASTE. If you use a charcoal barbecue, it is easy to throw soaked wood chips on the coals to create the smokiness. But with a gas barbecue it is a little more difficult. You need to buy or create a smoker basket.

To make your own smoker basket, place about 2 cups soaked wood chips (I like to use mesquite or applewood) in a double wrap of foil. Puncture the foil with lots of holes and place it under the barbecue grill. You can also use a foil container or buy a smoker pan. Follow the manufacturer's directions to determine how long you need to soak the wood before using. Preheat the grill over high heat. When the barbecue is full of smoke, grill the meat or fish.

A favorite dish in my family is hot smoked salmon. Even our fish haters like it. The combination of smoking and grilling makes the salmon very flavorful and juicy. I cook the salmon on a cedar plank to enhance the smoky flavor.

Soak a cedar plank for 2 hours before using to help prevent flare-ups, and have a water sprayer on hand while cooking to douse any flames. The plank can often be washed and reused.

Smoked Grilled Salmon Combine 1 tbsp maple syrup, 1 tbsp dry mustard, 2 tsp kosher salt and 1 tsp cracked peppercorns. Spread over a 2-lb salmon fillet. Marinate for 30 minutes.

Place a smoker basket with wood chips on coals. Heat grill over high heat until you see some smoke.

Place a soaked cedar plank on grill and leave for 3 to 4 minutes, or until you smell smoke. Immediately turn plank and place fish on top.

Cover grill and cook salmon for 10 to 15 minutes, or until fish is just cooked. Cut salmon into serving portions on plank and slide off onto serving plates.

Serves 4 to 6.

Peach and Raspberry Compote

SERVES 4

A fresh, fast dessert that looks great and tastes even better. It can be made in individual glass bowls or one larger bowl. I usually press the raspberry puree through a sieve to remove the seeds, but it is not essential.

2 cups fresh raspberries, or 1
   12-oz package unsweetened
   frozen raspberries, defrosted
2 tbsp granulated sugar
2 tbsp orange juice

6 peaches, peeled and sliced
3 tbsp icing sugar
3 tbsp peach schnapps, optional
¼ cup chopped almonds or pecans
Sprigs of fresh mint

Combine raspberries, granulated sugar and orange juice and puree in a food processor.

Place one-third of peach slices in a glass bowl or individual wine glasses. Sprinkle with 1 tbsp icing sugar, 1 tbsp peach schnapps, half the almonds and half the raspberry puree.

Repeat layers, finishing with peaches, icing sugar and schnapps. Top with mint.

Mint Fresh mint adds a cool, clean taste with sparkle. It is a most versatile herb, and with the popularity of Asian cooking, it appears everywhere. There are more than twenty-five species of mint and more than six hundred varieties. Most of us are familiar with the frizzy leaves of spearmint and the refreshing taste of English mint, but try yellow-flecked ginger mint, pineapple, apple, chocolate and many others.

   Mint grows very easily (too easily for some) so try planting a few varieties in your garden and experiment.

And to drink . . .

A LATE HARVEST WINE FROM THE NEW WORLD or a Sauternes, Barsac or any of their more affordable kin will all perform superbly with this dessert. An Ontario late harvest Vidal brings an extra note to the harmonious chord, since Vidal often shows a distinct peachiness at the late harvest level.

A more fanciful finale might be a Kir Royale made with demi-sec Champagne rather than the traditional Crémant de Bourgogne, and raspberry liqueur instead of Burgundy's rich black currant liqueur, Crème de Cassis. Not a Kir Royale at all, in fact, now that I come to think about it. You and your guests will have to come up with a more appropriate name for the cocktail.

One tip: pour the Champagne first, then add a tablespoon of raspberry liqueur. Doing it the other way round can cause an eruption of foam. And pour the drinks mere seconds before you serve them. As with any Champagne cocktail, the extra ingredients curtail the wine's natural effervescence. The mousse is short-lived, and its loss is keenly felt.

Wine Tech

Oak

WE ALL KNOW THE AROMA AND TASTE OF OAK—the toasty vanilla nuances that time spent in a French oak barrique can lend to Chardonnay, or the more forward cinnamon and coconut notes a Californian Pinot Noir picks up as it matures in an American oak barrel.

Oak seasons wine. It giveth and it taketh away, smoothing rough edges, filling out body, dimming primary fruit flavors, prolonging a wine's life even as it ages.

It all begins with an oak tree—one of three species of white oak, two of which grow in Europe, the other in North America. The tree might be 150 years old when it falls to the ax, cut in the autumn when the sap is down. The wood is left out for years in the open air to be mellowed and seasoned by rain and sun, until the cooper begins to saw or, better yet, split it into staves. With extraordinary skill, he then shapes, heats, bends and hoops all the staves together to make a watertight container, held together not by nails or glue but by its own tensile structure. Flame "toasts" the interior, essentially caramelizing the lignins in the oak (the greater the degree of toasting, the more the wine shows those smoky, toasted aromas) and at last the barrel is ready. One 225-liter new oak barrique will sell to some favored winery for about six hundred dollars.

My own education in wood took place years ago in the barrel cellar of a castle in the Italian Alps. The progressive young owner had decided that French oak barriques were the way of the future, but before he made the alarmingly large investment his ambition required, he took a year to conduct a number of experiments.

First he showed me the huge oak and chestnut casks that the family had used to age wines for generations. They were merely vessels, contributing nothing of their own to the wine, but because wood is porous they allowed minuscule amounts of oxygen to reach the precious liquid. That is the real point of barrel aging, he explained. The innumerable molecular activities between wine and air soften tannins, encourage clarification and bring everything into balance until the time comes to bottle.

Then he led me into another dungeon where recently fermented Chardonnay had been drawn into new barriques made from oak cut from different French forests. Tasting, I agreed that each had its own personality. This one more tangy or smoky or toasty, another with less pronounced vanilla, that one with a scent of leather. In a corner were barriques in which the wine had been fermented as well as aged. I expected the oak effect to be more intense, but in fact it was milder, more finely integrated. The yeasty lees that remained in the barrel had got in on the molecular act, muting the oak's own phenolic influence. For me, it still tasted too crudely of wood, but my host explained he would be blending these wines with Chardonnay that had spent its whole, brief life in steel tanks, playing with the proportions until he got it just right. Next year, the new oak barriques would have lost a lot of their punch. After three or four years, they would be as neutral as his grandfather's massive casks.

There are other, cheaper ways to get an oaky effect into wine. Throw a bucketful of oak chips into the fermentation tank (it happens all the time), and you'll capture the flavor. But you lose out on oak's more significant contribution—the maturing effects of real time in a barrel. Oak-chipped wines do not age gracefully.

Great wines are made in the vineyard, but winemakers also play a part. When the grapes are surrendered at the winery door, oak is one of the alchemical tools at the vintner's disposal. A judicious use of it is like a pinch of salt in a recipe, enhancing the main ingredients. Too much oak is like too much salt—dramatic but quickly exhausting. Generally speaking, the more intense and tannic the wine, the more oak it will take. Balance is everything. Consider a wine like Ontario's Baco Noir, a robust, inky, acidic hybrid with a flavor like blackberries. The few winemakers who persist in working with the variety age it in plenty of new American oak, adding a vital dimension of smoky spice. They are dressing a biker in a tuxedo, but when barbecued ribs or some down-home game stew is on the menu, Baco can handle the action. Oaky and smoky rhyme during barbecue season.

Family Reunion

Great Grilled Chicken with Smoky Barbecue Sauce
Family-style Bean Salad
Mediterranean Roasted Potato and Fennel Salad
Uncaesar Salad
Butter Tarts • Chocolate Cupcakes

SERVES 8

MY HUSBAND'S FAMILY used to have family reunions every summer at the Maxville Highland Games in eastern Ontario. Although the family has been in Canada since the early 1800s, they are still Scottish in their souls. Reunion food, however, was not Scottish. It was a humdrum potluck of jellied salads, cold turkey and three-bean salads. Although we always looked forward to the games, we never looked forward to the food.

A family reunion is a time to feel good about being together, and food is part of those feelings. Here is a savory menu that can be delegated to various family members. Everything is served cold except for the chicken, and it can be served cold, too, if desired. The desserts don't need plates and they will please both kids and adults. The menu is also excellent for a picnic. It can easily be doubled or tripled.

The Bloody Caesar

IMAGINE THAT RASPUTIN, charismatic but sinister spiritual adviser to the last tsarina, had met and married Mary Tudor, queen of England and enthusiastic burner of heretics. Imagine that their union had been blessed with a son. I suspect he would have turned out to be a rather intense young man with a tendency to do unspeakable things in the name of religion.

Genetics work differently in the world of cocktails. A Rasputin is vodka and clam juice poured over ice and garnished with an olive stuffed with an anchovy (there was always something fishy about the mad monk). A Bloody Mary, of course, mixes vodka and tomato juice, seasoned barely at all or hot as hellfire, depending upon the whim of the bartender. Bring them together and you have a Bloody Caesar, an all-Canadian cocktail as wholesome as Sunday brunch.

The Bloody Caesar was invented in 1969 by Calgary barman Walter Schell to mark the opening of Marco's Italian restaurant. Looking for a twist on the Bloody Mary, he rimmed a glass with celery salt, dropped in some ice, a pinch of cayenne pepper, two dashes of Worcestershire sauce and a little salt and pepper. Then he poured in four ounces of Mott's Clamato juice and an ounce of vodka. A celery stalk and a lime wedge for garnishes and the cocktail was finished. That is the original recipe, preserved for posterity by the helpful people at Mott's, who have calculated that Canadians drink about 220 million Bloody Caesars a year, the last time I checked. The figure does not include Caesar's sibs—the Cleopatra (using gin instead of vodka), and the Red Eye, Quebec's own distinct variation made with equal parts Clamato and beer.

The reason for all this information is that a tray of Bloody Caesars is a useful thing to have around when hordes of hungry relatives appear in the garden on a bright summer's day, especially with several fresh and well-dressed salads in their immediate future. Younger members may wish to imitate their folks by sipping on Virgin Caesars, made just the same way but without the vodka.

Great Grilled Chicken with Smoky Barbecue Sauce

SERVES 8

You can use boneless chicken thighs in this recipe. The chicken can also be served on buns with mayonnaise flavored with a bit of lemon.

Chipotle peppers are smoked jalapeños. They are sold in cans preserved in a hot tomato sauce called adobo. Use both the peppers and the sauce in this recipe. If you can't find chipotles, use 2 tbsp chili powder and 1 tbsp tomato paste in the sauce, and 1 tsp chili powder in the marinade.

Chicken
1 lime, cut in pieces
2 cups fresh mint, basil or coriander, including bits of stem
1 tbsp coarsely chopped garlic
2 tbsp soy sauce
1 tsp adobo sauce
1/4 cup vegetable oil
Salt and freshly ground pepper
12 boneless single chicken breasts, skin on

Smoky Barbecue Sauce
1 1/2 cups mayonnaise
1 tbsp adobo sauce
1 tbsp lime juice
1 tbsp honey
2 tsp chopped chipotle peppers
1 cup chopped red onions
2 tbsp chopped fresh coriander
Garnish
1/2 head Boston lettuce
1/2 seedless cucumber, thinly sliced
1 sweet onion, thinly sliced
2 tbsp slivered fresh mint

Place lime, mint, garlic, soy sauce, adobo sauce and oil in a food processor and pulse until slightly chunky. Season well with salt and pepper.

Toss chicken with marinade. Refrigerate for up to 12 hours.

Prepare sauce by combining mayonnaise, adobo sauce, lime juice, honey, chipotles, red onions and coriander.

Remove chicken from marinade. Place skin side up on a grill over high heat. Close lid and cook for 5 minutes. Reduce heat to medium. Turn chicken and cook for 5 to 6 minutes longer, or until juices run clear. Slice thickly.

Line a platter with lettuce leaves and sprinkle with cucumber and sweet onion. Top with chicken slices and sprinkle with slivered mint. Serve barbecue sauce on the side.

And to drink . . .

FOUR WINES WILL GRACE THE TABLE THIS TIME, partly to show suitable largesse to the extended family, partly because it's couth to offer a choice and partly because New World Chardonnay, while not fabulous with green beans and tomatoes, is a famous partner for Caesar (or, in this case, Caesarish) salad. It's the richness of the dressing and especially the Parmesan cheese that seems to form the bond. Look for a well-balanced, medium-bodied wine with a decorous amount of oak and juicy fruit—something from California's central coast, Washington State or Australia's Margaret River, or a reserve Chardonnay from British Columbia or Ontario.

As an added bonus, the same wine works well with the roasted fennel and potatoes and flatters the barbecued chicken, its mild oak harmonizing with the flavors of the grill-crisped skin. But I fear for any Chardonnay that ventures too close to Lucy's smoky barbecue sauce. Like a good girl in a dangerous neighborhood, it must run the gauntlet of sweet-tart-spicy intensity, and I don't think it will emerge with honor intact. Guests who lavish the sauce over their meat might be directed toward a glass of red wine, specifically a red from Portugal's Dao region. Robust and fruity but with excellent underlying acidity and an intriguing hint of bitterness, this wine won't seem too heavy on a summer's day.

Lucy's other salad leads me back to white. The grassy chlorophyll flavor of green and yellow beans finds an echo in Sauvignon, either from the New World or a Sancerre or Pouilly-Fumé from France's Loire region. And Sauvignon has the acidity to survive an encounter with a vinaigrette.

One last bottle to open might be a dry, fruity rosé from the south of France or from Spain. This is not to prove any particularly famous alchemy of grape and ingredient. It's more that a fresh, crisp rosé with an aroma of wild strawberries or red currants or violets is a lovely thing to have around on a hot afternoon. Guests who find Chardonnay or Portuguese Dao too heavy and Sauvignon too sour will be delighted by your decision.

Family-style Bean Salad

SERVES 8

A family favorite that is easy to make and has a flavor that is a bit unusual and very refreshing. The vinaigrette will discolor the beans after several hours. Dress salad one hour before you need it.

12 oz green beans, trimmed
12 oz yellow beans, trimmed
3 tbsp soy sauce
3 tbsp rice or wine vinegar
½ cup vegetable oil

1 tsp sesame oil
Salt and freshly ground pepper
1 cup slivered green onions
2 tbsp toasted black or white
 sesame seeds

Bring a large pot of salted water to a boil. Add green and yellow beans and cook for 3 minutes, or until tender but still crisp. Drain and cool under cold running water. Drain again.

Whisk together soy sauce, vinegar, vegetable oil and sesame oil. Season with salt and pepper.

Toss beans and green onions with dressing. Garnish with sesame seeds.

Bloody Caesar (p. 157)

Mediterranean Roasted Potato and Fennel Salad

SERVES 8

This attractive and unusual potato salad is good served with cold salmon, grilled chicken and ribs.

2 lbs red potatoes, cut in 1-inch pieces
1 large bulb fennel, trimmed and cut
   in 8 wedges
¼ cup olive oil
Salt and freshly ground pepper
Vinaigrette
3 tbsp red wine vinegar
2 tbsp grainy Dijon mustard

2 anchovy fillets, chopped
½ cup chopped roasted red peppers
½ cup olive oil
Salt and freshly ground pepper
Garnish
½ cup chopped red onions
¼ cup chopped parsley

Preheat oven to 450°F.

Toss potatoes and fennel with oil, salt and pepper. Spread on baking sheets in a single layer. Roast, stirring occasionally, for 25 to 30 minutes, or until browned and tender.

Prepare vinaigrette while vegetables are roasting. Whisk together vinegar and mustard. Stir in anchovies and red peppers. Slowly beat in olive oil. Mixture should thicken. Season with salt and pepper.

Cut fennel into 1-inch pieces and combine hot vegetables immediately with dressing.

Stir in onions and parsley. Taste and adjust seasonings if necessary. Serve at room temperature.

Uncaesar Salad

SERVES 8

Not quite a Caesar but with a similar taste, this salad is great for a buffet table or served as a first course. The meaty macadamia nuts take the place of croutons.

Dressing
¼ cup mayonnaise
¼ cup grated Parmesan cheese
2 anchovy fillets
1 tsp chopped garlic
3 tbsp lemon juice
1 tsp Worcestershire sauce
½ cup olive oil

Salt and freshly ground pepper
Salad
1 large head romaine lettuce, torn in pieces
¾ cup diced pancetta, sautéed until crisp
1 cup macadamia nuts
½ cup shaved Parmesan cheese

Place mayonnaise, Parmesan, anchovies, garlic, lemon juice and Worcestershire sauce in a food processor or blender and puree. With machine running, slowly add olive oil. Season with salt and pepper. Add a little water if dressing is too thick.

Combine lettuce with pancetta and macadamia nuts. Add dressing and toss. Garnish with shaved Parmesan.

Washing Greens Wash greens in lots of water, spin dry with a salad spinner, wrap in paper towels and store in a plastic bag in the refrigerator for up to a week. You can also buy prewashed mixes of baby lettuces (look for the organic ones). There are generally three to eight varieties in each mix. Asian salad mixes usually combine tatsoi, mizuna, baby spinach and other greens. Mesclun mixes usually contain arugula, mache, oak leaf, frisée, radicchio and baby romaine. Often a few herbs such as chervil and Italian parsley are included.

Salad Greens

LETTUCE USED TO MEAN BORING ICEBERG (now making a comeback), but today we have a choice of many different greens to make our salad bowls interesting and exciting. Here are some of the greens that I like to use in salads.

Arugula This variety of lettuce adds a peppery, nutty taste to salads. It is excellent served with a main course as well as mixed with other greens. Actually a field lettuce, it is also known as rocket or rucola.

Belgian Endive Elongated and elegant, Belgian endive has a slight bitterness that is a good counterpoint to assertive ingredients. It is also delicious braised in a little stock with butter and sugar.

Bibb Lettuce Small, mild and sweet, this lettuce has a bit more texture than Boston lettuce, although they are in the same family. Soft leaf lettuces like Bibb and Buttercrunch are known as butterheads because of their melt-in-the-mouth texture. They are best dressed with light vinaigrettes.

Escarole This pale green, slightly bitter, frilly-edged green is a member of the chicory family. Mix it with frisée and other chicories in salads containing assertive ingredients such as blue cheese, nuts and bacon. It is also good stir-fried.

Frisée A finely curled, frizzy-leafed endive that ranges in color from yellow-white to darker green. Buy young, small heads and use as part of a salad mix or in an assertive salad with ingredients like chicken livers or poached eggs.

Mache Also known as lamb's quarters, corn salad or field salad, this lettuce is now grown in California as well as in France. Remove the little roots before serving. The spoon-shaped leaves have a nutty, buttery flavor and are good served alone or combined with other mild lettuces.

Mizuna This delicate green with jagged green leaves and white stalks is appearing in markets more frequently. Use it as part of a salad mix or to garnish Asian dishes.

Oak Leaf This loose-leafed lettuce with crunchy stems comes in red and green varieties. It can be served in a mixed salad or on its own.

Radicchio Part of the chicory family, its intense burgundy color and peppery flavor add life to salads. It comes as a round cabbage-like head or as an elongated head called treviso radicchio.

Tatsoi Also known as spoon cabbage, tatsoi is an Asian green with a spoon-shaped leaf and a mild peppery flavor.

Watercress A member of the nasturtium family, this spicy green is good in salads and sandwiches.

Butter Tarts

MAKES 12 TO 14 TARTS

Julia Child once divided foods into two groups—sinkers or not. Sinkers were foods that you ate over the sink because they were so drippy and delicious. These butter tarts are sinkers. They are runny and rich and you can't stop eating them. If you don't want to make the pastry, buy premade tart shells.

½ cup butter, at room temperature
1 cup brown sugar
½ tsp salt
1 tbsp white vinegar

1 tsp vanilla
2 eggs
1 cup corn syrup
1 recipe Perfect Flaky Pastry
½ cup raisins

Cream together butter, brown sugar and salt with a whisk or a wooden spoon. Stir in vinegar, vanilla, eggs and corn syrup. Don't overmix. Chill for 30 minutes. Preheat oven to 350°F.
Roll out pastry and cut into 4-inch rounds. Fit rounds into tart pans or muffin cups.
Place 1 tsp raisins in each tart shell.
Stir filling mixture. Spoon filling over raisins. Shells should be about three-quarters full.
Bake tarts for 25 to 30 minutes, or until filling is set. Cool in pan on a rack. Tarts take about 2 hours to firm up (refrigerate to speed up process).
Loosen tarts with a small, sharp knife and ease out of pan.

Perfect Flaky Pastry

MAKES ENOUGH PASTRY FOR 2 SINGLE-CRUST PIES OR 12 TARTS

This easy, no-fail, all-purpose pastry can be made by hand or in the food processor. Although shortening contains trans fat, the proportion in this recipe is very small. You can replace it with margarine, lard or extra butter, but the combination of butter and shortening gives the pastry a perfect flavor and texture. Use this pastry for quiches and fruit or meat pies.

3 cups all-purpose flour

1 tsp salt

¾ cup butter, diced

¼ cup shortening (page 8), diced

½ cup cold water

1 tbsp white vinegar or lemon juice

Sift together flour and salt. Cut in butter and shortening until mixture resembles coarse breadcrumbs.

Combine water and vinegar. Sprinkle liquid over flour mixture. Using your fingers, work in liquid and gather dough into a ball. Divide dough into two equal pieces.

Roll out dough as needed or wrap in plastic wrap and chill until needed.

Chocolate Cupcakes

MAKES ABOUT 18 CUPCAKES

These are rich and moist and easy to serve. The method is based on a recipe from wonderful chef and teacher Marcel Desaulniers. For a sinful addition, add 1 cup chopped white chocolate to the mixture before baking. Ice the cupcakes if desired and decorate with white or dark chocolate shavings.

1 cup whipping cream	5 eggs
1 lb bittersweet chocolate, coarsely chopped	¾ cup granulated sugar
	1 cup all-purpose flour
	½ tsp baking powder

Bring cream to a boil in a pot over medium heat. Stir in chocolate and remove from heat. Stir cream and chocolate together until smooth. Let cool.

Preheat oven to 325°F.

Whisk together eggs and sugar with an electric mixer until batter triples in volume and beaters leave a trail in batter. Stir in chocolate mixture and beat on low speed until incorporated.

Combine flour and baking powder and stir into chocolate mixture.

Line muffin pan with baking cups. Fill cups with batter almost to rim.

Bake for 30 to 35 minutes, or until a toothpick inserted comes out clean. Cool before icing.

Dark Chocolate Icing Bring ¾ cup whipping cream to a boil in a pot over medium heat. Immediately remove from heat and stir in 12 oz chopped bittersweet chocolate. Stir together until chocolate has melted. Beat in ¼ cup butter.

And to drink . . .

CUPCAKES AND BUTTER TARTS are delicious in their own right or with a cup of tea. It might even be argued that these sweet treats need no alcoholic accompaniment at all. By way of rebuttal, slide out a small glass of slightly chilled aged tawny port and insinuate it close to the butter tart. Human curiosity will do the rest.

Tawny port begins its life like all other ports (except white port), as a blend of grapes grown on the sun-parched stone terraces of Portugal's Douro region. During fermentation, the sweet, dark purple juice is drawn into barrels that are already partially filled with neutral spirits, ending fermentation and trapping all those sugars and rich extracts in the wine. The following spring, the barrels (called pipes) travel to the coast to be stored in the vast lodges of the port houses. Two years later, they are assessed. The great majority of the wines will end up as some kind of ruby port, running the gamut from everyday ruby to vintage port. Some wines, however, will be allotted a tawny destiny.

Ordinary tawny port (without any declaration of age on the label) is a pleasant, fruity, fortified wine that changes from purple to reddish brown due to heavy filtration or the occasional addition of white port. Its low price reflects its youth. Aged tawny port, with its label boasting that it has aged ten, twenty, thirty or more years in the pipe, is far more interesting. Its color fades naturally over time and the wine develops elegance and marvelous complexity, evolving into a beautiful accompaniment to all sorts of things—from nuts and dates and dried fruits to foie gras to milk chocolate to . . . butter tarts and cupcakes.

Fast and Fresh
Finger-licking Good

Garlic Scape Vichyssoise

Spiced Shrimp and Corn Boil
with Herb Mayonnaise

Fruit Salad with Lemon Mascarpone Cream

SERVES 4

THIS MENU is for people who want to entertain but avoid the grill. It highlights summer ingredients and requires hardly any prep, but it is a messy menu, since most people like to eat the corn and shrimp with their fingers, so have lots of napkins on hand. If you wish, buy some coleslaw to round out the menu.

And to drink . . .

A crisp dry white from Bordeaux or Bergerac in France or from northern Italy will cut the richness of the vichyssoise—a refreshing contrast. For the main course, a slightly off-dry Riesling from Alsace, Ontario or Australia can handle the spicing and still enhance the flavors of shrimp and sausage.

Garlic Scape Vichyssoise

SERVES 4

Garlic scapes are a hot new vegetable in the marketplace, but they are familiar to any garlic grower. Scapes are the edible curly tops and seed pods of hard-necked garlic. They form in early summer and have to be cut off to allow the garlic cloves to mature properly. The taste is milder than garlic, and you can use them in any garlic recipe. I love them tossed with pasta or in this soup. They will keep for weeks in the refrigerator.

Serve the soup hot or cold. Float a few diced scapes on top for garnish. If scapes are not available, use ¼ cup sliced garlic and increase the leeks to 2 cups. If you like spicy soups, sprinkle with a few drops of chili oil before serving.

1 tbsp butter	4 cups chicken stock
2 cups chopped garlic scapes	¼ cup whipping cream
1 cup sliced leeks	Salt and freshly ground pepper
2 cups diced peeled Yukon Gold potatoes	2 tbsp chopped parsley

Heat butter in a pot over medium heat. Add scapes and leeks and sauté for 2 minutes. Add potatoes and sauté until slightly softened, about 2 minutes. Add stock and bring to a boil. Reduce heat to medium and simmer for 10 minutes, or until potatoes are cooked.

Puree soup. Return to pot, add cream and season with salt and pepper. Simmer for 5 minutes to blend flavors. Stir in parsley. Serve hot or cold.

Spiced Shrimp and Corn Boil with Herb Mayonnaise

SERVES 4

This terrific combination of corn, shrimp, red potatoes and smoked sausage is cooked in a seasoned broth, traditionally on the grill. The dish is served all over the southern United States, particularly in the summer, when blue crabs are added to the mix.

This recipe will serve four people very generously, but it can also be easily expanded if you are entertaining lots of people. Just keep adding shrimp, corn and sausage to the pot. Serve the herb mayonnaise on the side.

2 lbs large shrimp
1 lb Polish sausage, skin removed
4 ears corn, shucked
2 lbs small red potatoes
12 cups water
4 bay leaves
¼ cup chili powder
3 tbsp kosher salt
1 tbsp paprika

1 tbsp dried thyme
1 tbsp dried oregano
1 tbsp hot red pepper flakes
1 tbsp peppercorns
1 tbsp coriander seeds
Salt and freshly ground pepper
Garnish
Fresh oregano and parsley sprigs

Wash shrimp but leave in shells to retain more flavor. Cut sausage into 1-inch pieces. Cut corn into thirds. Cut potatoes in half.

Bring water to a boil in a large pot. Add bay leaves, chili powder, salt, paprika, thyme, oregano, hot pepper flakes, peppercorns and coriander to pot and boil for 5 minutes.

Add sausage and potatoes to pot and boil for 8 to 10 minutes, or until potatoes are crisp-tender.

Add corn to pot and boil for 4 minutes, or until nearly cooked. Add shrimp and boil for about 2 minutes longer, or just until shrimp are pink and curled.

Drain shrimp, sausage and vegetables well and pile on a large serving platter. Season with salt and pepper and sprinkle with oregano and parsley sprigs.

Fruit Salad
with Lemon Mascarpone Cream

SERVES 4

Make this lovely simple dessert using any fresh local fruit. If you use yellow fruit like peaches and apricots, make the sauce with apricot jam instead of red currant jelly. Although it is a hassle to pit cherries, it makes a huge difference to a fruit salad. Cherry pitters are available at kitchen shops.

The mascarpone cream should keep for about a week in the refrigerator.

2 cups fresh raspberries	Lemon Mascarpone Cream
2 cups pitted cherries	1 cup mascarpone
2 cups fresh blueberries	½ cup plain yogurt
2 cups fresh strawberries,	2 tbsp granulated sugar
halved if large	1 tbsp grated lemon zest
½ cup red currant jelly	2 tbsp lemon juice
¼ cup sherry, port or Madeira	

Layer raspberries, cherries, blueberries and strawberries in a glass bowl. Combine red currant jelly and sherry in a small pot. Bring to a boil, stirring. Cool slightly and pour over berries.
Whisk together mascarpone, yogurt, sugar, lemon zest and juice. Serve with fruit salad.

Herb Mayonnaise This fragrant, mildly spicy mayonnaise can also be served with poached fish or as a dip with vegetables.
Combine 2 cups mayonnaise, ¼ cup finely chopped red onions, 3 tbsp lemon juice, 2 tbsp chopped parsley, 1 tbsp chopped fresh oregano, 1 tbsp chili powder, 2 tsp finely chopped garlic and 1 tsp ground cumin. Season with salt and freshly ground pepper.
Makes about 2½ cups.

A Drop More

Rosé Wine

ARISTOCRATIC AND IMMENSELY RICH, a celebrated Chardonnay found herself quite ignored at the garden party. Beside her, a plummy old Cabernet of impeccable pedigree felt equally ostracized. Everybody was crowding around a blushing little rosé who was keeping her cool while reveling in the attention.

"No depth at all," sniffed the Chardonnay. "No breeding or character. You can't go through life relying on youth, looks and charm."

But those are precisely the qualities most in demand at casual summer gatherings, and rosés have always been summer wines. They come by their carefree character honestly. In hot Mediterranean climates, where it used to be hard to make whites that weren't sun-scorched and clumsy and where big, powerful reds were the norm, people looked for something refreshing to drink in the long, parched summers. They knew that their red wines grew darker, more tannic and more complex with every day that the newly pressed grape juice stayed in contact with the crushed skins. What if they drained off some of the juice after only a few hours—just enough time to leach a pink tint from the skins but hardly any tannins—and then fermented it like a dry white? The rosé could scarcely be expected to have much depth or complexity, but it would be bursting with the juice's own fruit flavors. It wouldn't age well, but who cared? It only had to last until the end of next summer.

For me, rosé conjures the shimmering heat of many a Mediterranean afternoon, the rasp of cicadas in the olive trees, an old table set in their shade, laden with lunch—grilled shrimp, tuna and harissa in Tunisia, rascasse and ratatouille in the south of France, bread and tomatoes and barbecued seabream on the Ionian island of Corfu. My wife and I lived there for years when we were in our twenties, farming olives and writing and having babies. Once a week we drove down out of the parched, dazzling mountains into the shady boulevards of Corfu Town to do the shopping, loading our Land Rover with supplies. The wine store by the cathedral of Aghios Spiridon was our final stop. Splashing water in the cool, damp darkness, the vintner sluiced out our old eight-liter demijohn and filled it from whichever barrel we wished—white, red, rosé or retsina. We always chose the rosé, because it was dry and fresh and tasted faintly of wild strawberries, a flavor that seemed fragile but was strangely persistent, regardless of what we found to eat that day.

Back home, we tried to make our own rosé from the two prolific vines we discovered when we bought the property, augmented with fruit purchased from Dmitri the grape seller. He appeared in the village every September with a truck laden with crates full of mushy, anonymous grapes, the ancient vehicle laboring up the mountain, haloed by a cloud of intoxicated wasps. We trod the grapes in a great wooden tub, feeling like characters from the Odyssey, and poured the must with a jug into two old oak barrels. Rosé was our goal but, the first year, our wine was brown and oxidated and we ended up turning it into exceptionally good vinegar. Subsequent vintages were an improvement—drinkable, if a tad bitter, and as pink as the dawn. There is no better way to learn about wine than to try to make it yourself. I have had a sentimental attachment to rosé ever since.

In later years there were other, more serious moments: an extraordinary coral-colored Pinot Noir crafted by a renowned German winemaker for his own amusement and brought out at the end of a long day's tasting; a matchless lunch of cold salmon and colder Lirac rosé at the home of a Parisian chef; in Épernay, a dinner of braised pheasant and strawberry tart both served with the same vintage pink Champagne.

I don't mean to meal-drop. It's just that rosé wines get so little respect in North America, their versatility undiscovered, their distinctive differences ignored. We lump them together with all the "blush" produced on this continent—white Zinfandel as sweet and one-dimensional as liquid Jell-O—and their reputation suffers. In the right time and place, when the sun is hot and the company merry, the world is an even better place when seen through a rosé-tinted glass.

Fast and Fresh
Market Special

Grilled Corn and Tomato Salad

Pan-seared Striped Bass with Salsa Verde

Mum's Smashed Potatoes

Blueberry Chocolate Clusters

SERVES 4

ROADSIDE VEGETABLE STANDS and farmers' markets brim with local produce in the summer. Corn, tomatoes, wild blueberries and lettuce are all at their peak. Here is a great menu that highlights the season's harvest.

And to drink . . .

The safe bet for both the salad and that tangy salsa verde is a vibrant Sauvignon Blanc from New Zealand. A dry Canadian or Australian Riesling would also be suitably refreshing, offering a lighter body with an intense flavor and racy acidity.

Grilled Corn and Tomato Salad

SERVES 4

When you are grilling corn on the barbecue, add a few extra ears to make this salad. It can be made with boiled corn, too, but it won't have the same smoky flavor.

3 ears corn, shucked	1 tbsp chopped fresh basil
1 jalapeño pepper	Salt and freshly ground pepper
1 tbsp vegetable oil	1 head red leaf lettuce
½ tsp chopped garlic	4 oz green beans, cooked
1 tsp maple syrup	2 tomatoes, seeded and diced
2 tbsp white wine vinegar	¾ cup chopped red onions
¼ cup olive oil	2 tbsp chopped fresh coriander

Brush corn with a little oil and place on grill over high heat. Grill, turning occasionally, for 10 to 12 minutes, or until corn is tender and kernels are golden. Grill jalapeño for 5 to 6 minutes, or until skin is blistered. Peel and seed jalapeño and chop. Slice off corn kernels, reserving any corn juices.

Place ½ cup corn and any juices in a food processor. Add garlic, maple syrup, vinegar, oil and basil. Process until smooth. Dressing should have consistency of lightly whipped cream. Season with salt and pepper.

Tear lettuce into a salad bowl or platter. Top with green beans, tomatoes, red onions, reserved corn and jalapeño.

Drizzle vinaigrette over salad and sprinkle with coriander.

Pan-seared Striped Bass with Salsa Verde

SERVES 4

This is one of my favorite summer fish dishes. You could substitute red snapper, turbot or orange roughy fillets for the bass. Salsa verde is an addictive, versatile sauce, and this is my friend Stephen Grant's recipe. He uses it with all his grilled and roasted meats.

Drape each fillet, skin side up, on a mound of potatoes.

Salsa Verde
1/3 cup coarsely chopped parsley
3 anchovy fillets
2 tbsp capers
2 tbsp fresh breadcrumbs
1 clove garlic, coarsely chopped
1/2 cup olive oil

1 tbsp lemon juice
Salt and freshly ground pepper
Fish
4 striped bass fillets (about 6 oz each)
1/4 cup all-purpose flour
Salt and freshly ground pepper
2 tbsp olive oil

Combine parsley, anchovies, capers, breadcrumbs and garlic in a food processor. Process until finely chopped. Add olive oil and lemon juice and process just until combined. Season with salt and pepper.
Dredge bass fillets lightly with flour. Season with salt and pepper.
Heat oil in a large skillet over medium heat. Add fillets flesh side down and cook for 2 minutes. Turn and cook for 3 minutes longer, or until fish is firm to the touch.
Serve fish with salsa verde.

Pan-seared Striped Bass with Salsa Verde;
Mum's Smashed Potatoes (p. 177)

Mum's Smashed Potatoes

SERVES 4

These lower-calorie mashed potatoes are cooked and mashed with stock instead of cream or milk. Use the good-quality chicken stock sold in Tetra Paks, or use diluted canned chicken stock.

2 lbs small red potatoes, unpeeled   ¼ cup butter
2 cups chicken stock   Salt and freshly ground pepper

Place potatoes in a pot with stock and bring to a boil. Reduce heat to medium-low. Cover and cook for 10 to 15 minutes, or until potatoes are soft.
Drain potatoes, reserving cooking liquid. Return pot to turned-off burner and shake to dry out potatoes slightly.
Mash potatoes lightly with enough potato cooking liquid to make a rough mash. Potatoes should still be a little lumpy. Beat in butter. Season with salt and pepper.

Blueberry Chocolate Clusters

SERVES 4

Use a bittersweet chocolate that you love to eat. I like to use wild blueberries, but regular blueberries work well, too. These clusters soften at room temperature, so eat them straight from the refrigerator. Serve alone or with ice cream.

3 oz bittersweet chocolate, coarsely chopped
1½ cups fresh blueberries

Melt chocolate in a small pot over low heat. Remove from heat as soon as chocolate melts.
Stir in blueberries. With a spoon, drop mounds of blueberries onto parchment paper. Refrigerate until firm, about 1 hour.

A Drop More

Rum

THERE ARE TWO APPROACHES TO RUM. The first involves mixing it with fruit juices and ice, padding across hot white sand to a hammock strung in the shade of a coconut palm (whisper of surf, glittering blue Caribbean), and taking the rest of the afternoon off. The second approach is to look a little more closely at the spirit in the glass—at its rich and rowdy past and its amazing range of styles, from basic white to the complexity and refinement that a great oak-aged rum can show when tasted with due care and attention.

Either way, the pleasure is guaranteed. And there is the added bonus of knowing you stand on the cutting edge of fashion, for rum's time is upon us. Granted, it may never be as popular in North America as it was in 1775, when the average per capita consumption among the colonists was a staggering four gallons a year. But rum covers all the bases—black, white, gold and amber, flavored, spiced or pure as nature intended. The spirit has come a long way since an Englishman wrote home from Barbados in the seventeenth century: "The chief fudling they make in the islands is rumbullion, alias kill-devil, and this is made of sugar canes distilled, a hot, hellish and terrible liquor."

All rums still begin with sugar. The hard canes, like giant, solid bamboo, are cut and crushed, yielding a sweet juice. On Martinique and elsewhere, this fresh liquid is sometimes turned into rum, a delectable style called *agricole*, but far more often the juice is boiled down to dark syrup. Pure sugar crystals form and are removed, leaving only a residue of thick black molasses, the raw material of rum. The molasses is diluted and allowed to ferment, sometimes with the addition of dunder, the leftovers from a previous distillation. Like the sour mash used in making American whiskey, dunder adds depth and complexity to the distilled spirit. That distillation may take place in a pot still (for rums full of flavor and personality) or a continuous still (for lighter, more neutral spirits), but whichever method is used, all rums start their lives white. Some will be tinted to gold or black with flavorless caramel; others will be aged in used oak barrels, gaining color, smoothness and complexity. Even white rums undergo some barrel aging, to emerge blinking into the sunshine after a year or so, looking decidedly yellow. Charcoal filtering restores their watery complexion.

Deluxe rums are almost always golden. These are the showcase spirits upon which a distillery lavishes time and money, cherishing them in American oak for decades. Intended to challenge similarly gifted brandies, bourbons and single malt whiskies, they repay contemplation in the bottom of a balloon glass. One could spend a very happy evening with the fifteen-year-old El Dorado from Guyana's Demerara region, for example, mulling over its amazing dimensions, its crème brûlée flavor, its divinely silky weight.

More accessible bottlings give their finest performances on the cocktail circuit—Myers's rum, dark and unforgettable in a Planter's Punch; Bacardi white, powerful in a muddled Mojito.

The Daiquiri White rum is an odd spirit, one of a very few liquors that aren't particularly palatable when served on their own. Its strength is as an ensemble player, especially with freshly squeezed fruit juice. The rum seems to intensify the fruit's personality, making it even more refreshing. Hence the pleasure of a Daiquiri.

Many Americans like to claim the Daiquiri was invented at the Daiquiri mine in Cuba by an American engineer named Jennings Cox in the summer of 1896. Perhaps it was, but its sudden burst of fame came when President Kennedy mentioned how much he enjoyed the cocktail—the happiest of his many associations with Cuba. Use a ripe Caribbean lime and you may not need to add any sugar syrup, but the classic, no-blender recipe calls for a little.

Add 2 oz white rum, 1 oz freshly squeezed lime juice and a dash of sugar syrup to a cocktail shaker half filled with cracked ice. Shake long and vigorously. Strain into a cocktail glass. A few drops of fresh grapefruit juice is a dazzling extra flourish.

autumn food

AS THE LEAVES CHANGE COLOR and slowly drift down, I feel a renewed energy after the luxury of the summer break. Friends to see, dinners to cook. I think of fall as the season for entertaining—the time for parties large and small. This urge to reconnect with others is accompanied by the wonderful fall produce bursting from the shelves—baskets of red peppers, football-sized Sicilian eggplants, pristine white cauliflower, dark-tinged broccoli and the more unusual broccoflower and romanesques that are becoming part of our vegetable vocabulary. Mountains of zucchini fight with apples, pears, blue plums and barrels of grapes for eating or making your own wine. Then the early root vegetables appear—more varieties of squash than we knew existed, baby turnips and candy-colored beets ready to be tossed into a skillet for a quick stir-fry.

What better time to produce great meals, when everything you need is fresh and locally grown?

autumn drinks

Autumn is the season of the vine. This is the time when all the hope and anxiety of the preceding year, all the sunshine and rain, the labor and patience focus down to the moment of harvest. Science, art and instinct come together in the vineyard and then in the winery—a season of inspired endeavor and pragmatic compromise.

Wine producers are ferociously busy in the fall; we wine lovers can only sit and twiddle our thumbs, waiting for crumbs of information and gossip as the leaves change color and winter looms. The objects of our affection are still in embryo, gestating in wombs of oak or steel—except for the late harvest fruit shriveling out on the vine, awaiting the winemaker's pleasure. Word percolates through. There was botrytis in a corner of the vineyard. The starlings got two rows of Riesling. Overall, the yield was low this year, but thanks to that unexpectedly balmy September, the fruit was perfectly ripe—full of extract and flavor, deep color and natural sugars. A very promising vintage. By next June we'll be enjoying the whites. In a couple of years, the reds will be starting to strut their stuff.

So long to wait! Thank goodness the wines of two years ago are finally ready to drink.

A Bistro Dinner

Salade Landaise
Crisp-skinned Salmon with Citrus Sauce
Bistro Frites
Buttered Spinach
Prune and Armagnac Tart

SERVES 4

TODAY THERE IS A MOVE BACK to more relaxed dining, whether you are eating out or dining in. The concept of the casual French bistro fits into this trend nicely. A true bistro feels like an extension of your own kitchen. It is defined by the *patron* and the regular customers who keep coming back for the good food and a warm welcome. A real bistro has a casual ambiance and serves large plates of market-based family fare. Instead of exotic preparations you'll find wine-laced stews, earthy lentils and soul-satisfying gratins, as well as fresh fish, simple grills of beef, lamb and duck, and mounds of skinny French fries.

This menu features a version of a salad often served in bistros, a plain cooked fish and wonderful frites as well as a traditional tart from the southwest of France.

Bon appétit!

The Pousse-Rapière

THE GASCON SPIRIT. For many, the words conjure images of seventeenth-century musketeers, of D'Artagnan and Cyrano de Bergerac, with their courage and swagger, their empty purses and extravagant pride, their indestructible panache. Panache is also a quality I would ascribe to that other great Gascon spirit, Armagnac—a brandy that, like Cyrano, has a unique style brimming with poetry, and an incredible nose.

Armagnac has been made for at least six hundred years. Its history is far older than that of Cognac, fifty miles to the north. Both brandies are made from the thin, acidic white wine of their regions, but while Cognac went on to worldwide fame and fortune, its Gascon cousin remained relatively obscure, cherished by discerning connoisseurs. Some traditional producers still use the *alembic armagnacais*, a pot still developed in the early nineteenth century that operates at a lower temperature than the pot stills of Cognac. The spirit that emerges is richer in flavor but considerably less potent. The lower alcoholic strength means young Armagnacs take longer to draw the benefits from the wood in which they age, but when they do reach maturity they are full of complex personality. The best of them have a most spectacular and lingering finish—what renowned producer Olivier de Montal calls "the peacock's tail."

One could spend a lifetime exploring different vintages, blends and expressions of Armagnac, proving or disproving the expert opinion that those from the Ténarèze region have violets in the aroma while those from Bas Armagnac (usually considered the finer source) suggest prunes, wet wood and caramel. Such voyages of discovery are best conducted after dinner—a dinner that ends with a prune and Armagnac tart and is preceded, perhaps, by the traditional Gascon aperitif, a swashbuckling cocktail called a Pousse-Rapière. The name refers to the skillful twist of the wrist with which a swordsman withdraws his rapier from the body of a skewered opponent.

The drink is a great deal more civilized. Pour a measure of Armagnac into a Champagne flute, top it up with sparkling white wine (if you can't find the local Gascon *vin sauvage*, Champagne will just have to do) and finish with a twist of orange zest squeezed over the drink and then hung over the rim of the glass.

Salade Landaise

SERVES 4 AS AN APPETIZER

This salad, from the Landes region of France, is quite substantial and could also be served as a light supper. Grilling the chicken livers makes them crisp on the outside but soft in the center. Traditionally this salad is made with a confit of giblets, but my version is easier and just as satisfying. You'll need a peppery green like endive or frisée to contrast with the livers.

To clean chicken livers, cut them in half and remove any bitter bits of green.

Dressing
¼ cup mayonnaise
¼ cup olive oil
2 tbsp white wine vinegar
2 tsp Dijon mustard
1 tsp minced garlic
Salt and freshly ground pepper
2 tbsp chopped chives

Salad
¼ cup all-purpose flour
1 tsp dried thyme
Salt and freshly ground pepper
8 oz chicken livers, trimmed and halved
2 tbsp olive oil
1 head endive or frisée, torn
4 slices bacon, diced and cooked
¼ cup pine nuts, toasted
½ cup croutons

Soak four small wooden skewers in water for 30 minutes.
Whisk together mayonnaise, oil, vinegar, mustard and garlic for dressing. Season with salt and pepper. Stir in chives. If dressing is too thick, whisk in a little water.
Combine flour, thyme, salt and pepper.
Pat chicken livers dry. Dust with flour mixture. Divide chicken livers among the 4 skewers, pressing them together tightly. Brush with oil.
Grill chicken livers in a grill pan or on barbecue over high heat for 2 to 3 minutes per side, or until crusty on outside but still pink in middle.
Toss endive with dressing and pile on individual plates. Sprinkle with bacon, pine nuts and croutons. Lay a skewer of chicken livers on top of each serving.

And to drink . . .

CHICKEN LIVERS ARE INTERESTING THINGS to pit against a wine. Even grilled, they are halfway to becoming a pâté—rich and pungently meaty with a smoky, bittersweet edge. Not really white wine time, you might think, but there is one that can engage in dialogue with the smoky flavors and fatty richness of the chicken livers. A dry Alsatian Gewürztraminer has the textural cojones and the exotic aromatics to do just that.

A wine snob once told me (and the rest of the dinner table) that admitting to a fondness for Gewürztraminer was like saying you enjoyed the films of Elvis Presley. As a boyhood Elvis fan, I had no problem with the remark, but it turned out he found the King's movies vulgar, shallow and obvious and was therefore trying to be rude. Combat, inevitably, followed.

Gewürztraminer, in its Alsatian apotheosis, is quite simply drop-dead gorgeous. Some offer the intense aroma of litchis with a hint of smoke and ginger. Others carry the scent of old-fashioned roses. They all have a most voluptuous body, the ideal balance of weight and perfume with just enough acidity to give vigor and tone. And yet it's a difficult wine to get right, as winemakers in other countries continue to prove. Pick too late and the acidity is gone: the wine is fragrant but flabby and dull. Pick too early and it's thin and shrill with a mute aroma.

Fortunately, there are many good dry Gewürztraminers from Alsace on the market, and they don't cost the earth. Serve this wine well chilled and buy several bottles. It's awfully easy to drink.

Croutons Combine 5 cups bread cubes, 3 tbsp olive oil and 2 tbsp melted butter. Spread on a baking sheet and bake at 350°F for 10 to 15 minutes, or until golden. Stir occasionally during baking.
Makes 5 cups.

Crisp-skinned Salmon
with Citrus Sauce

SERVES 4

Wild salmon has a stronger taste and a tighter texture than farmed, and it is not as fatty. If I can't find wild salmon, I look for organic farmed salmon as an alternative.

The sweet-tart sauce in this recipe highlights the flavors of the fish and tastes great with the frites. Serve the salmon over the buttered spinach, top with sauce and surround with fries.

1 tbsp olive oil	½ cup whipping cream
4 salmon fillets (about 6 oz each)	1 tsp honey
Salt and freshly ground pepper	1 tbsp chopped fresh tarragon
Citrus Sauce	Salt and freshly ground pepper
½ cup orange juice	2 tbsp chopped chives
¼ cup lemon juice	

Heat oil in a large skillet over medium heat.

Season salmon with salt and pepper. Place skin side down in hot skillet. Cook for 2 minutes, or until skin is crisp.

Cover skillet, reduce heat to medium-low and cook for 5 to 7 minutes longer, or until salmon is still slightly pink in center.

Prepare sauce while salmon is cooking. Combine orange juice, lemon juice, cream, honey and tarragon in a separate skillet. Bring to a boil and boil for 5 minutes, or until slightly thickened. Season with salt and pepper and stir in chives. Serve sauce with salmon.

And to drink . . .

ONCE, ALL SALMON TASTED LIKE WILD SALMON—as different from the fatty, bland farmed fish as a free-range chicken is different from a battery hen. If you make this delicious recipe with wild salmon, slice off a little from the raw fillet and taste it. Encourage your children to taste it and to remember the flavor and texture so they can bore their own kids one day about the time they experienced the real McCoy. No wonder so many people move to the Pacific coast.

Rich and intensely flavored, salmon leaps easily over the weir between red and white wines. It is gorgeous with Pinot Noir, opulently suited to a big, buttery Chardonnay and delightful with pink Champagne. Spoiled for choice, we should remember there is more on the plate than fish. The sauce, rich with cream, flavored with orange, lemon and tarragon and slightly sweetened with honey, is a scene-stealer, and it helpfully narrows the options. Yes, it's tangy; yes, it's a little sweet, but its silk-smooth weight is the first thing to consider. It may be time to splash out on a good white Burgundy (a Meursault, perhaps) or a juicy Sonoma County Chardonnay from California—nothing too oaky but with the fruity heft and suppleness to play nicely with the sauce, enhance the lean richness of the fish and cope beautifully with the buttery spinach.

As for the double-fried bistro frites, there's something appealingly democratic about popping them between sips of a regal white Burgundy.

Bistro Frites

SERVES 4

In Australia Bruce and I had lunch with Bob Oatley at Rosemont Estates in the Hunter Valley. He served us fish and chips for lunch and insisted that Champagne was the only possible accompaniment. James, who will drink Champagne at the drop of a hat, would have loved it.

Do the first frying early in the day and refry just before serving. (You do not need to refrigerate the fries after this first cooking.)

4 Yukon Gold potatoes, peeled
Vegetable oil for deep-frying
Salt

Cut potatoes into slices ¼ inch thick, and then cut again into matchsticks. Pat dry with paper towels.

Heat 2 inches of oil in a wok or deep-fryer to about 275°F. The oil should bubble gently when you add potatoes. Slide potatoes into oil in batches. Fry for about 7 minutes, or until potatoes are limp and cooked through but not colored. Drain on paper towels and reserve.

Reheat oil to 375°F, or until a bread cube browns in 15 seconds. Refry potatoes in 2 or 3 batches until golden, about 2 to 3 minutes. Drain well in a strainer placed over a bowl or on paper towels. Season with salt. Serve at once.

Buttered Spinach

SERVES 4

A simple, flavorful preparation for spinach. Steam the spinach ahead of time and sauté just before serving.

2 bunches spinach, trimmed
2 tbsp butter

3 cloves garlic, sliced
Salt and freshly ground pepper

Rinse spinach and place in a pot over medium-high heat. Cover and steam in water that clings to leaves until spinach is just wilted, about 5 minutes.
Drain spinach and refresh under cold water. Squeeze with your hands until spinach is quite dry, then chop.
Heat butter in a skillet over medium heat. Add garlic and sauté for 2 minutes, or until slices turn golden. Add spinach and sauté for 2 minutes, or until heated through. Season well with salt and pepper.

Prune and Armagnac Tart

SERVES 4 WITH LEFTOVERS

While driving through France on a road trip one year, we were constantly seduced by the wonderful tarts in the pâtisserie. This traditional tart from the Armagnac region of France is one of my favorites. Although the tart makes more than four servings, leftovers are superb for a few days. For the best flavor and texture, use moist pitted prunes.

¼ cup orange juice	3 eggs
¼ cup Armagnac or brandy	⅓ cup granulated sugar
2 cups pitted prunes, halved	2 tsp grated orange zest
1 recipe Sweet Tart Pastry (page 224)	¾ cup whipping cream

Pour orange juice and Armagnac over prunes and let soak for 30 minutes.
Preheat oven to 425°F.
Roll out pastry and fit into a 9-inch tart pan. Prick pastry with a fork, line with foil and fill with dried beans or pie weights. Bake for 15 minutes. Remove foil and beans and bake for 5 minutes longer. Reduce oven temperature to 350°F.
Beat together eggs and sugar. Stir in orange zest.
Drain prunes, reserving liquid. Stir cream and reserved liquid into egg mixture.
Arrange prunes over tart shell. Pour egg mixture over prunes. Bake for 30 to 35 minutes, or until mixture is set. Serve at room temperature.

And to drink . . .

THE TEMPTATION IS TO BRING OUT the Armagnac with dessert, and one should always give in to temptation. But what, then, to pour after dinner when the tart is finished? More Armagnac? It may be the only plausible answer. Serve anything else after such a noble spirit and you risk anticlimax. Better, perhaps, to find something different to go with the tart and save the Armagnac for a nightcap.

The nutty, dried-fruit sweetness of brandy-soaked prunes sets the tone. A good-quality medium oloroso sherry (in other words, not one of the bland commercial cream sherries) would work well, as would a Bual Madeira (page 105) or a tawny port with the sort of character that only age can bring—a twenty-year-old, for example. Any of these wines, served in tantalizing moderation, would lead naturally into the Gascon finale of a snifter of Armagnac.

The Book Club

Arugula and Gorgonzola Spread
Braised Chicken with Olives and Figs
Vegetable Couscous
Triple Chocolate Truffle Tart

SERVES 6

IN THIS INCREASINGLY IMPERSONAL WORLD filled with e-mails and voice mails, there are fewer opportunities to meet with friends face to face and exchange conversation and ideas. We all miss those interactions, and our lives are poorer for it, so it's no surprise that there has been a large rise in book clubs. Although the chosen book is the excuse for the interaction, the meetings are often part gossip and part therapy, too. I think of book clubs as the quilting bees of the twenty-first century.

James and I felt that an easy approach to the food and wine was best. This eastern Mediterranean–influenced menu is easy and make-ahead. And all you'll need is a red and a white or rosé for pouring during the evening.

This simple menu serves six but can easily be doubled.

And to drink . . .

THIS EVENING, the vino will be taking a back seat to literary conversation. The role of the wine will be to refresh and lubricate the intellect and also to get along well with the food. Nothing too distracting is required.

That favored part of the world that hugs the Mediterranean is full of simple, inexpensive, crowd-pleasing wines. Many of them are ignored because we don't recognize their names or grape varieties. All of them, naturally enough, shine when set beside the pungent, sun-drenched flavors of Mediterranean food.

Dolcetto is the everyday red wine of the Piedmontese in northwestern Italy. There are seven designated areas where the grape is most at home and one or other of them may be attached to the name (for example, Dolcetto d'Alba). Just because this red has a reputation for being pleasant and undemanding does not mean it is puny or dull. Dolcetto has enough acidity to cope with tomatoes and olives, but hides it under a soft mouthful of fruit and a pleasantly bittersweet suggestion of mulberries and almonds.

Modern rosés from France's Languedoc region can be delicious bargains. Made from Syrah, Grenache, Merlot or Cabernet Sauvignon grapes, they are dry and fruity and show surprising length (old-fashioned rosés always seemed to forget about any lingering aftertaste) and are delightfully versatile food wines. Chill them as you would a white wine.

White wines from Sicily and southern Italy used to be famously sunburned, often oxidated and highly alcoholic. These days, ambitious producers seem to have paid attention to what the rest of the world is doing, lowering yield in the vineyard to boost flavor and investing in technology in the winery to cool things down and keep fresh fruitiness to the fore. Often blends of relatively obscure local grape varieties, these delectable wines are great value. If the taste of New World whites is painted in primary colors, these are subtle pastels, more concerned with nuance and harmony.

Arugula and Gorgonzola Spread

SERVES 6

The fresh peppery flavor of the arugula provides a contrast with the pungent cheese. Gorgonzola aficionados will love this dish, and even those who claim to dislike blue cheese will be tempted.

Place the spread on a platter and surround with green onions, Belgian endive leaves, pita triangles and yellow and red peppers cut in diamond shapes for dipping.

4 cups chopped arugula

¼ cup chopped fresh basil

1 tbsp chopped garlic

2 cups mayonnaise

2 cups crumbled Gorgonzola cheese

1 cup mascarpone

1 cup grated Parmesan cheese

1 tbsp Worcestershire sauce

salt and freshly ground pepper

Combine arugula, basil and garlic in a food processor. Add mayonnaise, Gorgonzola, mascarpone, Parmesan and Worcestershire. Blend until smooth. Taste and season with salt and pepper if necessary.

Braised Chicken with Olives and Figs

SERVES 6

This sweet-tart dish can be made with any part of the chicken, but boneless, skinless chicken thighs work the best. This casserole can be completely cooked ahead. Reheat at 325°F for 20 minutes, or until the chicken is hot.

1 cup large cherry tomatoes, halved and seeded
3 tbsp olive oil
1 cup dried figs, quartered
1 cup white wine
1 tbsp paprika
2 tsp ground ginger
1 tsp dried thyme
¼ tsp cayenne
Salt and freshly ground pepper

3 lbs boneless, skinless chicken thighs, halved
1 cup chopped onions
2 tsp chopped garlic
2 cups chicken stock
2 tbsp balsamic vinegar
1 tbsp tomato paste
1 cup pitted green olives, cut in half if large
2 tbsp chopped parsley

Preheat oven to 325°F.

Toss cherry tomatoes with 1 tbsp olive oil. Place cut side up on a baking sheet and roast for about 15 to 25 minutes, or until slightly dried out. (Cooking time will depend on size of tomatoes.)

Prepare figs while tomatoes are roasting by combining figs and wine in a small pot. Bring to a boil and boil for 1 minute. Remove from heat and let sit for 20 minutes. Strain and reserve figs and soaking liquid separately.

Combine paprika, ginger, thyme, cayenne and salt and pepper. Season chicken with half the seasoning mix.

Heat remaining 2 tbsp oil in a large skillet over medium-high heat. Brown chicken in batches for 1 to 2 minutes per side, or until golden. Transfer chicken to a casserole. Drain all but 1 tbsp oil from skillet.

Add onions, garlic and remaining seasoning mix to skillet and sauté for 3 minutes, or until softened. Add reserved soaking liquid, chicken stock, vinegar and tomato paste and bring to a boil. Pour sauce over chicken and scatter with figs and olives.

Cover and bake for 10 minutes. Add tomatoes and bake, uncovered, for 10 to 15 minutes longer, or until chicken juices run clear.

Taste for seasoning and sprinkle with parsley.

Vegetable Couscous

SERVES 6

Made with instant couscous, this one-pot starch and vegetable dish takes just minutes to prepare.

2 tbsp olive oil
½ cup finely chopped carrots
½ cup finely chopped zucchini
1 tbsp chopped garlic
½ cup chopped green onions

1 tsp paprika
¼ tsp hot red pepper flakes
2 cups chicken stock or water
2 cups instant couscous
Salt to taste
2 tbsp chopped parsley

Heat oil in a pot over medium heat. Add carrots and sauté for 1 minute. Add zucchini and garlic and sauté for 2 minutes longer, or until vegetables are softened.
Stir in green onions, paprika and hot pepper flakes.
Add stock and bring to a boil. Sprinkle in couscous. Stir, cover and remove from heat. Let sit for 5 minutes.
Stir and season with salt and parsley before serving.

Triple Chocolate Truffle Tart

SERVES 8

This sensational professional-looking tart is simple to make. However, if you don't want to make the pastry, combine 2 cups crushed chocolate wafers with ⅓ cup melted butter, pat it into the tart pan and chill completely. It is not as elegant but works perfectly well.

Raspberries go wonderfully with chocolate, but you could use other fresh berries, chopped fresh peaches or even well-drained orange sections.

Chocolate Pastry
1 cup all-purpose flour
¼ cup cocoa
3 tbsp granulated sugar
Pinch salt
½ cup butter, diced
3 tbsp orange juice

Filling
8 oz bittersweet chocolate,
    coarsely chopped
4 oz white chocolate, coarsely chopped
1¼ cups whipping cream
3 tbsp butter
1 cup fresh raspberries

Combine flour, cocoa, sugar and salt in a food processor or large bowl. Add butter and cut in just until mixture is crumbly. Sprinkle orange juice over mixture and blend in, then gather dough into a ball. Flatten slightly, wrap in plastic wrap and refrigerate for 30 minutes.

Preheat oven to 400°F.

Roll out pastry on a floured board and fit into a 9-inch tart pan. Prick base with a fork. Place a sheet of parchment paper or foil over pastry and fill with dried beans or rice.

Bake pastry for 10 minutes. Remove beans and rice and bake for 10 to 15 minutes longer, or until pastry loses its sheen. Cool.

Place bittersweet chocolate and white chocolate in separate bowls. Bring cream to a boil in a pot over medium-high heat.

Add ½ cup hot cream to white chocolate and remainder to bittersweet chocolate. Stir until chocolates have melted. Stir 1 tbsp butter into white chocolate and remaining butter into bittersweet chocolate.

Scatter raspberries over bottom of baked tart shell. Pour dark chocolate cream over berries. Pour white chocolate cream over dark chocolate and swirl in using tip of a knife.

Chill for about 3 hours, or until set.

Cooking for a Crowd

Marinated Roast Pork with Sweet and Sour Onions

Coconut Shrimp Curry • Steamed Rice

Egg Noodles with Broccolini and Sesame Sauce

Red-cooked Chicken with

Mandarin Pancakes and Hoisin Ginger Sauce

Spinach and Avocado Salad with Sesame Lime Dressing

Coconut Cranberry Slices

Chocolate Passion with Mango Lime Sauce

SERVES 16

WHEN WE HAVE LOTS OF PEOPLE OVER for a buffet, I always choose a theme. Themes encourage interesting food choices and make recipe decisions easier. As a bonus, they provide great inspiration for decorating the table. The theme doesn't have to be exotic. Try comfort food, vegetarian, all wrapped up, pub night, etc. The possibilities are endless.

This buffet is a very simple Asian meal. You can decorate the table with chopsticks and strew fortune cookies over the table. Arrange mandarins, papaya and starfruit in a Chinese bowl surrounded by small teapots.

Almost all these dishes can be made ahead; only the curry and rice are served hot. If you want to pass hors d'oeuvres, serve spring rolls (page 285), or buy some of the excellent frozen dim sum available. The chicken could also be served as an hors d'oeuvre.

This complete menu will provide enough food for sixteen on a buffet. Individual dishes will serve ten to twelve. The recipes can easily be halved or doubled.

Buffet Tips

The most attractive recipes for a buffet are those that can be made ahead of time and served warm or at room temperature. Keeping food hot on a buffet is difficult unless you have copper chafing dishes or professional staff.

Use different-shaped serving dishes. Bowls are fine as long as they are fairly shallow, but I prefer platters for salads—they are much more dramatic, and it is easier for guests to serve themselves when they don't have to dig into a deep bowl.

Professional buffets are appealing to look at because the platters are placed at different heights. Pedestal dishes, for example, give focus to the table. To achieve this look at home, pile books at different heights on the table, then cover with a large tablecloth. Place a platter on top of a stack of books for instant height.

Keep flowers low and use lots of votives or dramatic candlesticks with colored candles.

For faster service, make sure the buffet table can be reached from both sides.

Set plates at one end of the table and napkins and cutlery at the other. It is difficult for guests to serve themselves if they are handling more than a plate.

Assemble the wine, drinks and glasses at a separate table to prevent the food table from becoming too congested.

Marinated Roast Pork with Sweet and Sour Onions

SERVES 12

This sensational dish is a kind of Asian sweet-hot pork heightened with sweet and sour onions. It can be served at room temperature or reheated at 350°F for 20 minutes before slicing. Make it up to three days ahead of time. Use a rib end pork loin roast for the juiciest result.

1 pork loin roast (about 3 lbs)
Salt and freshly ground pepper
½ cup ketchup
½ cup hoisin sauce
¼ cup soy sauce
¼ cup maple syrup
¼ cup vegetable oil
2 tbsp Thai red curry paste
2 tbsp finely chopped gingerroot
2 tbsp finely chopped garlic
1 tsp grated lime zest

Sweet and Sour Onions
1 tbsp vegetable oil
2 large sweet onions, thinly sliced
1 tbsp slivered gingerroot
2 tbsp soy sauce
2 tbsp rice or cider vinegar
1 tbsp granulated sugar

Season pork with salt and pepper.

Combine ketchup, hoisin sauce, soy sauce, maple syrup, oil, curry paste, chopped ginger, garlic and lime zest. Reserve ½ cup marinade. Brush remainder of mixture over roast and refrigerate overnight.

Preheat oven to 450°F.

Place roast on a rack. Cook for 15 minutes. Reduce heat to 250°F and cook for 1½ hours, or until just a hint of pink remains in pork. Baste every half hour during cooking.

Prepare onions while pork is cooking by heating oil in a large skillet over high heat. Add onions and sauté for 2 minutes, or until slightly softened. Add slivered ginger and sauté for 1 minute longer.

Reduce heat to medium-low. Add soy sauce, vinegar and sugar and cook for 10 minutes, or until onions are soft and turning golden. (Onions can be made ahead and reheated.)

Heat reserved marinade in a pot over medium heat, and simmer for 5 minutes, or until flavors are combined.

Slice pork thinly and serve warm or at room temperature surrounded by onions. Drizzle cooked marinade over pork.

The Home James

CREATING A NEW COCKTAIL FOR A PARTY is a fine way to flatter your guests. It needn't be anything theatrical or overly complicated: simplicity is a virtue in itself and a necessity if you're going to be mixing dozens of drinks in an evening. The process of invention also provides plenty of innocent pleasure, involving patient weeks of testing and much tasting of prototypes.

The Home James is essentially an elaborated Dry Martini. It's a dry cocktail that offers the refreshing fruitiness of freshly squeezed citrus juice but still allows the rich botanicals of your favorite gin (mine is Plymouth) to shine through. Orange juice tends to mask the taste of the gin, but grapefruit enhances it and adds a pleasant touch of bitterness. Ruby grapefruit also contributes a very subtle blush to the color of the drink. Using orange zest as the garnish gives a lovely aroma of orange as the glass is lifted, while the vermouth softens and rounds out the overall effect of the cocktail. Which vermouth you choose is a matter of taste—I prefer Noilly Prat. A less dry product such as Cinzano Bianco adds smoothness, weight and sweetness, slightly mitigating the flavor of the gin.

Purists insist that cocktails should be made one at a time, but shortcuts can speed up the process. You could combine large quantities of gin and vermouth in the correct proportions in a single bottle and put it in the freezer for an hour or two before guests arrive. Squeezing and straining the grapefruit juice can also be done in advance. Using bottled or frozen concentrated grapefruit juice is not an acceptable option.

To make a Home James, put some ice in a cocktail shaker. Add 1½ oz gin, ½ oz dry white vermouth and 1 oz freshly squeezed grapefruit juice. Shake or stir until well chilled and strain into a cocktail glass. Garnish with a long twist of orange zest.

Coconut Shrimp Curry

SERVES 12

An aromatic, slightly spicy curry. Replace the shrimp with cubed firm-fleshed fish fillets, scallops, mussels or a combination. The kaffir lime leaves provide a distinctive flowery, fragrant flavor, but grated lime zest can be substituted if necessary.

The sauce can be made a few days ahead, but the shrimp is best poached just before serving.

2 cups coconut milk
1 tbsp Thai red curry paste
2 cups chopped onions
1 tbsp finely chopped gingerroot
1 tbsp finely chopped garlic
1 cup fish or chicken stock
6 kaffir lime leaves, or 2 tbsp grated lime zest

2 tbsp fish sauce
1 tbsp granulated sugar
2 cups fresh or canned tomatoes, seeded and chopped
3 lbs large shrimp, shelled
¼ cup chopped fresh basil
¼ cup chopped fresh mint
1 tbsp lime juice
Salt and freshly ground pepper

Place coconut milk in a large skillet and bring to a boil over high heat. Reduce heat and simmer for 8 to 12 minutes, or until reduced by half. Stir in curry paste, onions, ginger and garlic. Continue to cook until onions are softened, about 2 minutes.

Stir in stock, 4 whole lime leaves, fish sauce, sugar and tomatoes. Cook for 8 to 10 minutes, or until sauce is thickened and fragrant. Remove lime leaves. Cut 2 remaining lime leaves into thin strips.

Salt shrimp lightly and stir into skillet. Cover and cook, stirring occasionally, for 3 to 4 minutes, or until shrimp are pink and curled.

Stir in basil, mint and lime juice. Season with salt and pepper. Scatter with shredded lime leaves.

Thai Curry Paste Thai curry pastes are the foundation of Thai curries. Red curry paste is made with red chilies; green paste uses green chilies. Yellow curry paste is usually colored with turmeric. The pastes are generally quite hot, though red paste is usually slightly milder than green.

And to drink . . .

CAREFULLY MATCHING WINES to a buffet of many different dishes is a challenge the host cannot hope to meet, especially with a large crowd and especially when the flavors and ingredients have an Asian theme. Better to think of wines that will establish a general rapport with the feast and will also be delicious in their own right.

Thai food in Thailand is a cuisine of simultaneous extremes—searing acidity, burning chili heat and sudden moments of salt or sweetness—a dangerous obstacle course for wine. Lucy's dishes are more subtle, and that makes wine a much more feasible accompaniment. With their robust fruitiness and no-nonsense acidity, Sauvignon Blancs from New Zealand or South Africa are the most obvious choice. They have the weight to handle rich sauces and the sharpness to refresh the palate. Slightly off-dry Canadian Riesling works in the same way, as does less delicate Australian Riesling. Austrian Grüner Veltliner is another white that holds up its head with honor.

Finding a red wine for this buffet is more difficult. Instinct suggests something fairly fruity and undemanding with low tannins and decent acidity—a Valpolicella, perhaps, or a good Ontario Gamay Noir—but any red may be in for a bumpy ride.

The two desserts deserve accompaniments of their own. While Ontario Icewine is usually too big, too sweet and too intense to fare particularly well as a dessert wine, it works admirably with the coconut squares, bouncing its complex fruit flavors off the coconut. The perfect accompaniment exists for desserts made with chocolate, chilies and spices. Barolo Chinato is made by infusing Barolo wine with quinine, cloves, cinnamon, ginger and dozens of other botanicals, aged in oak for many years. The result is bizarre, slightly medicinal and stunningly delicious.

Steamed Rice

SERVES 12

I like to use a rice steamer to cook rice. It takes all the tension out of cooking. However, if you have a large, heavy pot with a tight-fitting lid, it is easy to steam rice on the stove. The rice can remain in the pot, covered, for up to 30 minutes before serving.

5 cups uncooked Thai jasmine rice
5 cups water

Rinse rice in plenty of cold water until water runs clear.
Place rice and water in a large heavy pot. Bring to a boil over high heat.
Cover and reduce heat to low. Steam rice for 20 minutes without removing lid. Taste rice and steam for 5 minutes longer if necessary.

Fish Sauce Asian fish sauce is made from small fish that have been salted and fermented for a few months. The sauce is pungent and salty and usually only a little is added to dishes. The higher grade sauce (often from Vietnam) is more expensive and less raw and salty than lower grade fish sauces. Use the higher grade in dipping sauces and the less expensive version in cooked dishes.

Egg Noodles with Broccolini and Sesame Sauce

SERVES 10

This is a beautiful cold vegetarian noodle dish to serve with the chicken. If garlic chives are unavailable, use regular chives or slivered green onions. Tahini (sesame seed paste) can be found at the supermarket.

This dish should be tossed together on the day of the party, but the ingredients can be prepared a day ahead.

2 tbsp chopped garlic
1 tbsp chopped gingerroot
¼ cup tahini
¼ cup soy sauce
¼ cup mirin
2 tbsp sesame oil
2 tbsp rice wine vinegar
2 tbsp honey
2 tsp hot Asian chili sauce
½ tsp five-spice powder, optional

Noodles
1 lb fresh or dried Chinese egg noodles
2 bunches broccolini, cut in 2-inch lengths
8 oz baby bok choy
2 tbsp vegetable oil
1 lb shiitake mushrooms, trimmed and sliced
1 tsp finely chopped garlic
Salt and freshly ground pepper
2 cups garlic chives (cut in 2-inch pieces)
¼ cup toasted black or white sesame seeds

Place garlic, ginger, tahini, soy sauce, mirin, sesame oil, rice vinegar, honey, chili sauce and five-spice powder in a food processor and blend until smooth. Reserve.

Cook egg noodles in a large pot of boiling water for 2 minutes, or until tender. Remove noodles with a slotted spoon, rinse under cold running water and drain.

Add broccolini to pot and boil for 2 to 3 minutes, or until crisp-tender. Remove with a slotted spoon, refresh with cold water until cold and drain.

Add bok choy to pot and boil for 2 to 3 minutes, or until crisp-tender. Drain and refresh with cold water. Toss bok choy with 2 tbsp dressing.

Heat oil in a large skillet over high heat. Add mushrooms and sauté for 2 minutes. Add garlic and sauté until mushrooms are cooked and garlic is fragrant. Season with salt and pepper.

Toss noodles, broccolini, mushrooms and chives with remaining dressing. Place on a large serving platter and surround with bok choy. Garnish with sesame seeds.

Red-cooked Chicken

SERVES 10

This recipe was developed by my recipe tester Eshun Mott. You can set up the chicken on the buffet table before the other dishes are served or serve as part of the main meal. If I'm feeling lazy, I buy mandarin pancakes from a Chinese restaurant or use large flour tortillas cut in quarters. This is also a great dish for a casual family supper. Kids love to roll up the pancakes, or you can serve the chicken on its own over rice.

I prefer chicken thighs on the bone for this dish, but you could use a whole chicken cut up or just breasts, if desired. The chicken can sit in the broth, refrigerated, for up to two days before serving. You can also bring the finished broth to a boil and freeze to use another time.

To serve, place the chicken strips on a large platter. Surround with mandarin pancakes, slivered green onions and hoisin ginger sauce. Serve at room temperature. To eat, brush half a pancake with sauce. Add chicken strips and a slivered green onion and roll up to eat.

6 lbs chicken thighs, with skin, on bone	¼ cup granulated sugar
4 cups cold water	1 tbsp sesame oil
2 cups soy sauce	8 slices gingerroot
1 cup sherry	6 star anise
	12 green onions, slivered

Place chicken, water, soy sauce, sherry, sugar, sesame oil, ginger and star anise in a large pot. Bring to a boil. Reduce heat to medium-low and simmer for 30 to 40 minutes, or until chicken is cooked through.

Cool chicken in broth and refrigerate in broth overnight.

Remove chicken from broth, remove skin and bones and tear chicken into strips. Serve at room temperature.

Red-cooked chicken; Mandarin Pancakes (p. 209)

Mandarin Pancakes

MAKES 24 LARGE PANCAKES

These can be served at room temperature or softened and warmed in a steamer or microwave before serving. The pancakes also freeze well. Cut them in half before serving.

3½ cups all-purpose flour
1½ cups boiling water
2 tbsp sesame oil

Combine flour and water by hand or in a food processor, kneading for 3 minutes, or until dough comes together. Cover dough with a damp cloth and set aside for 30 minutes.

Form dough into 2 cylinders 12 inches long. Cut each cylinder into 1-inch segments. Brush one side of each segment with sesame oil.

Press oiled sides of two segments together. (This is so you can peel apart cooked pancakes). Repeat until you have used all dough. Flatten and roll each doubled pancake into a circle 7 inches in diameter. You should have 12 double pancakes.

Heat an ungreased griddle or nonstick skillet over medium-low heat. Add a double pancake to skillet and cook until one side has dried out and formed a few brown spots. Turn and cook second side. Pancakes should puff up a little. Remove from pan and peel apart pancakes while they are still hot (this is hard on the fingertips!). Repeat until all pancakes are cooked.

Hoisin Ginger Sauce

Combine 2 cups hoisin sauce, 2 tbsp grated gingerroot, 2 tsp finely chopped garlic and 2 tsp sesame oil.

Makes about 2 cups.

Spinach and Avocado Salad with Sesame Lime Dressing

SERVES 12

This Asian-flavored salad can be made with arugula instead of spinach, green onions instead of red and cashews instead of almonds.

1 cup sliced almonds
1 lb baby spinach
3 avocados, peeled and diced
½ red onion, thinly sliced
1 seedless cucumber,
   peeled and diced
½ cup fresh coriander sprigs

Sesame Lime Dressing
½ cup lime juice
¼ cup vegetable oil
2 tbsp soy sauce
2 tbsp brown sugar
1 tsp sesame oil

Preheat oven to 350°F.
Spread almonds on a baking sheet and bake for 10 minutes, or until browned. Stir once during baking.
Place spinach in a large bowl. Sprinkle avocados with a little lime juice and toss with spinach, onion, cucumber and coriander. Scatter almonds over salad. Whisk together lime juice, oil, soy sauce, brown sugar and sesame oil. Pour dressing over salad and toss.

Coconut Cranberry Slices

MAKES 16 SLICES

This is a rich, candy-like dessert. A small piece goes a long, delicious way. For a more intricate icing, drizzle melted red currant jelly in straight lines over the icing. Pull the point of a knife through the lines to make a pretty design.

Use about 8 oz shortbread cookies and process in a food processor to make the crumbs. Make the slices up to three days ahead of time.

½ cup butter	Icing
¼ cup whipping cream	2 tbsp butter, melted
¾ cup chopped white chocolate	4 tsp warm water
1½ cups shortbread cookie crumbs	½ tsp lemon juice
1 cup dried cranberries	1½ cups icing sugar, sifted
1 cup flaked unsweetened coconut	

Combine butter and cream in a pot over high heat. Bring to a boil, remove from heat and stir in chocolate until melted. Cool slightly.

Stir in cookie crumbs, cranberries and coconut.

Grease an 8-inch square baking dish and line with parchment paper. Pat in chocolate-cookie mixture. Refrigerate for 1 hour, or until set.

Combine melted butter, warm water and lemon juice for icing. Beat in icing sugar until smooth.

Spread icing over top of dessert with a warm palette knife. Chill. Cut into 1- by 2-inch slices before serving.

Chocolate Passion
with Mango Lime Sauce
SERVES 8

For this menu, make two of these sensational chocolate loaves developed by my former recipe tester Penny Griffiths. Use the best chocolate you can find—the darker and richer the better. The chili powder has chocolate overtones, and it will enhance the chocolate taste of the dessert, but may be omitted. Any leftover cake can be well wrapped and refrozen. I usually keep one in the freezer to bring out as a last-minute dessert.

The sauce recipe was developed by my daughter Emma Waverman.

Chocolate Passion
8 oz bittersweet chocolate,
   coarsely chopped
1/3 cup water
4 eggs
1 cup granulated sugar
1 tsp ancho chili powder or hot
   red pepper flakes, crushed
1 tbsp all-purpose flour
1 cup butter, melted

Mango Lime Sauce
1/4 cup sugar syrup (page 222)
2 tbsp chopped candied ginger
1 ripe mango, peeled and coarsely
   chopped
1/2 tsp grated lime zest
1 tbsp lime juice
1/4 cup whipping cream

Preheat oven to 350°F. Butter a nonstick loaf pan and line bottom and sides with parchment paper.

Melt chocolate and water in a heavy pot over low heat. Cool slightly.

Whisk eggs, sugar and chili powder until light. Beat in flour. Slowly whisk in chocolate and melted butter. Pour into prepared loaf pan.

Place loaf pan in a larger baking pan. Pour boiling water into larger pan until water reaches halfway up sides of loaf pan. Bake for 1 hour, or until loaf is firm on top and a cake tester comes out clean. Remove from oven, cool and refrigerate in pan until set.

Turn out loaf onto a large sheet of parchment paper. Fold paper over dessert, wrap in foil and freeze.

Prepare sauce by pureeing sugar syrup, ginger, mango, lime zest, lime juice and cream in a food processor.

Remove cake from freezer about 15 minutes before slicing. Slice and serve with sauce.

Chocolate

CHOCOLATE IS SENSUAL, MYSTERIOUS and addictive, and it is important to choose the best. The finest-quality chocolate is expensive but worth every penny; your cakes, truffles and mousses will never taste the same.

The secret to chocolate lies in the bean. Cocoa beans are grown around the world—in the Caribbean, Mexico, West Africa and South America—and the taste of the chocolate will vary greatly depending on the origin of the bean and the way it is prepared. The cocoa beans are fermented, heated and ground into a thick paste called chocolate liquor, which is the basis of all chocolate.

Unsweetened chocolate is pure chocolate liquor combined with cocoa butter, with no added flavoring or sugar. It is sometimes combined with bittersweet or semisweet chocolate to add a more intense chocolate flavor to cakes and cookies. However, if you have a good-quality bittersweet chocolate, you should not need to use unsweetened chocolate in baking.

Bittersweet chocolate is a blend of chocolate liquor, cocoa butter, sugar, lecithin and vanilla. The higher the percentage of chocolate liquor, the darker and richer the chocolate.

Semisweet chocolate contains more sugar than bittersweet, although the two can be used interchangeably. The best rule of thumb is to find a dark chocolate that you like to eat, and use that in your cooking.

Milk chocolate contains milk solids and should not be used in baking unless the recipe calls for it. It is a popular garnish, however, and can be shaved and sprinkled on cakes and pastries.

White chocolate is not chocolate at all, because it does not contain chocolate liquor. It is a mixture of sugar, vanilla, cocoa butter and milk solids. Avoid brands that contain vegetable shortening instead of cocoa butter; they are bland and boring.

Working with Chocolate

Chop chocolate using a serrated knife. The ridges will grip the chocolate and help it to split apart.

Store chocolate well wrapped in a cool, dry place. Temperature changes can cause it to develop a white coating called "bloom," though this will not affect the taste.

Food Friends for Dinner

Squid "Pasta" with Tomato Mint Sauce

Umbrian Slow-cooked Lamb with Pecorino

White Beans with Garlic and Sage

Dried Pears, Taleggio and Caramelized Walnuts

Lemon Tart with Licorice Ice Cream

SERVES 6

EVEN AN ACCOMPLISHED COOK becomes a little tense when foodie friends come for dinner. When James had us for dinner, he insisted on cooking the most complicated menu with about seven courses and ten fancy vegetables. He wanted to produce that restaurant experience, but the results were disastrous. Happily, the wines were outstanding, we had a great evening, and memories of that meal will keep us laughing for years to come.

When you entertain foodie friends, simplicity is the key. As a person who loves good food, what I really appreciate is simple foods made with superb ingredients. A perfect piece of meat, a simple lemon tart, a magnificent slice of cheese—what could be better?

Your food-loving friends will love this menu, and the cook can avoid disaster, because except for the appetizer, all the dishes can be cooked ahead.

Pineau des Charentes

I WISH WE ALL HAD ACCESS TO MACVIN, a curiously delicious aperitif produced in France's Jura region. It is made a little like port, by mixing unfer-
mented grape juice with the local eau-de-vie de marc (page 264) and then
aging the concoction in oak barrels. All the sweet fruitiness of the juice is
preserved, like a yellow jewel set in the matrix of the marc. A single well-
chilled sip fills the mouth with the flavor of peaches and pears, figs, raisins
and even a hint of anise. It is glorious, resonant stuff but very hard to find
outside the Jura since the locals enjoy it so much themselves.

Fortunately, other parts of France produce much the same drink and in
more commercial quantities. In Champagne they call it Ratafia, in Gascony
it's Floc and in the south of France you may be offered it as Mistelle. The best-
known version is from the Cognac region, where it is known as Pineau des
Charentes, an aperitif that can double as a match for foie gras, pâté or fruit
desserts. The recipe was made into law in 1935, insisting that two parts
freshly pressed red or white grape juice from local vines be mixed with one
part Cognac from the previous year with the result aged in oak for a year.
Though it lacks Macvin's intensity of flavor, a good Pineau is a fine thing,
heavy and fairly sweet, with the Cognac and the barrel aging adding depths
that are missing from wines fortified with neutral spirits. The Cognacais
have been drinking and selling it since the sixteenth century and will tell anyone who is prepared to listen that it has aphrodisiac qualities. Louis XIII, who
had stayed away from his queen for years, is said to have visited her after an
evening spent with a bottle of Pineau. Indeed, he was so inspired by the aperitif that he managed to beget Louis XIV. Something to consider as you sip a
small glass before dinner, served very cold to mitigate the sweetness a little.

Squid "Pasta" with Tomato Mint Sauce

SERVES 6 AS AN APPETIZER

In this recipe, the squid looks like fusilli once it is cooked. Sauced with tomatoes, it even has the feel of pasta.

The tomatoes should be peeled to keep the sauce smooth. To remove the skins, bring a pot of water to a boil and blanch the tomatoes for one minute. The skins will slide off easily.

6 large squid, cleaned (about 1 1/2 lbs total)	1/2 tsp hot red pepper flakes
3 tbsp olive oil	Salt and freshly ground pepper
1 tsp chopped garlic	2 tbsp slivered fresh mint
3 anchovy fillets, finely chopped	1/4 cup grated Parmesan cheese
6 tomatoes, peeled, seeded and chopped	

Slice squid lengthwise into long, thin strips (about as wide as a linguine noodle).

Heat 1 tbsp olive oil in a skillet over medium heat. Add garlic and anchovies and sauté until garlic is softened, about 2 minutes.

Add tomatoes and cook for 5 to 10 minutes, or until mixture is thickened and flavorful (the more watery the tomatoes, the longer it will take to reduce sauce). Stir in hot pepper flakes. Season with salt and pepper. Stir in mint.

Heat remaining 2 tbsp oil in a large skillet over high heat. Add squid, season with salt and lots of pepper and sauté for 1 minute, or until whitened. Immediately add to tomato sauce and stir together. Cook for 1 minute longer.

Serve sprinkled with Parmesan.

And to drink . . .

ONE OF THE PLEASURES of inviting food-savvy friends to dinner is that everyone wants to play matching games. They are keen to be introduced to wines and even grape varieties that lie slightly off the beaten track. Opening several bottles for each course is part of the fun—realizing how this wine brings out that ingredient, how the personality of another varietal seems to change with every mouthful. Lack of consensus is probable (we all taste things in our own way) and to be celebrated.

Such a dashing opening dish deserves a little effort on the part of the host. The sauce is essentially a mild-mannered puttanesca enriched by anchovies, perfumed with mint and lifted by the acid of the tomatoes. Squid and anchovies make me think of some of the new well-made Portuguese Encruzados—deliciously spicy, dry white wines that work beautifully with weighty seafood. But there is an Italian influence to the menu that it would be perverse to deny. Greco di Tufo is a white Greek grape grown since ancient times in a tiny area of southern Italy's Campania region, just inland from Naples. In the hands of the major local producer, Mastroberardino, it achieves greatness. Dry but full-bodied with an amiable lemony, almondy flavor, Greco doesn't leap out of the glass, but it's extraordinarily resilient, strolling unperturbed and debonair through the jostling, burly flavors on the plate. It will take this dish in its stride, supporting the subtle taste of the squid but equally at home with the anchovies.

For the sake of comparison, a fruity young Chianti Classico has the necessary acidity and a light enough body to work with the dish. Opinions on whether the red wine's tannins are a problem or an asset should fuel enthusiastic debate.

Sagrantino di Montefalco, in a claret jug

Umbrian Slow-cooked Lamb with Pecorino

SERVES 6

This is my interpretation of a dish I first tasted in Umbria, Italy. The sweet, succulent, slowly braised lamb is balanced by the saltiness of the Pecorino. Ask the butcher to bone out a lamb shoulder and cut it into pieces. A lamb leg works, too, but the meat will be much drier. The dish can be made ahead and reheated in the sauce at 350°F for 25 minutes before serving.

To make this dish really spectacular, borrow a restaurant concept and garnish it with one roasted lamb chop per person. Season a rack of lamb with salt, freshly ground pepper and 1 tsp chopped fresh rosemary. Roast at 425°F for 25 minutes, or until medium-rare.

3 lbs boned lamb shoulder, cut in 6-oz pieces	¼ cup olive oil
1 tbsp chopped fresh rosemary	1 cup chopped onions
2 bay leaves, crumbled	½ cup red wine
4 garlic cloves, sliced	1 cup beef or chicken stock
½ tsp hot red pepper flakes	Salt and freshly ground pepper
	1 cup grated Pecorino cheese

Toss lamb with rosemary, bay leaves, garlic, hot pepper flakes and 2 tbsp oil. Refrigerate overnight, turning occasionally. Remove garlic and reserve. Preheat oven to 300°F.

Heat remaining 2 tbsp oil in an ovenproof casserole over high heat. Brown lamb in batches for about 2 minutes per side, or until meat is a rich brown color. Remove to a plate.

Reduce heat to medium and add onions and reserved garlic slices to casserole. Sauté for 2 minutes. Pour in wine, scraping up any little pieces from bottom of pan. Bring to a boil. Add stock and combine well.

Return lamb to casserole, cover and bake for 1 hour. Uncover and continue to bake for 1 hour longer, or until meat is tender and glazed with sauce. Depending on size of your casserole, sauce may reduce too much; add more stock if necessary. Sauce should be rich and slightly thickened.

Remove lamb and keep warm. Skim any fat from sauce. Strain sauce into a pot, pressing on any solids. Reheat, and add salt and pepper if necessary.

Serve lamb with a little sauce. Liberally sprinkle lamb with cheese.

And to drink . . .

SUCH A MESMERIZINGLY DELICIOUS DISH deserves a wine of real stature. Lucy was inspired by an Umbrian recipe, so the first bottle to open might be a dry, red Sagrantino di Montefalco, a wine from the hills southeast of Perugia. No one seems to know where this grape came from or how it reached Umbria, but for most of its century or so of history it was used to make sweet sacramental wine. Now producers are turning it into big, meaty, dry reds with a refreshing tang of acidity and the sort of tannins that fall for lamb. A cult wine whose reputation has barely spread beyond Italy, Sagrantino may be hard to find but will repay the effort.

As an alternative, return to Italy's south and seek out a wine made from the Aglianico grape. Like its neighbor, Greco, Aglianico was brought to Italy by the Greeks, and it thrives in the volcanic soil of Campania and Basilicata. In the first location it produces Taurasi; in the second, Aglianico del Vulture, named for the volcano upon whose slopes it grows. Both can be fabulous, long-lived reds when conscientiously made, rivals for great barolo or brunello. But production is small and marketing diffident, which accounts for the cult status both wines enjoy. Rich, robust and full of black fruit flavors, these wines need to be a few years old before they open up and show how magnificently they can partner lamb.

White Beans with Garlic and Sage

SERVES 6

This traditional Italian recipe is a perfect foil for the lamb. Use cannellini, navy or pea beans. Cook the beans until they are very soft (older dried beans may take longer to cook), and add salt only after cooking, as salt will toughen the beans if it is added too early.

Use your best extra-virgin olive oil in the garnish.

2 cups dried white beans	2 tbsp chopped fresh sage
2 tbsp olive oil	Salt and freshly ground pepper
1 cup chopped onions	Garnish
8 cloves garlic, peeled	2 tbsp extra-virgin olive oil
	2 tbsp chopped parsley

Soak beans overnight in twice the amount of water. Drain beans and rinse.

Heat oil in a pot over medium heat. Add onions and cook, stirring occasionally, for 5 minutes, or until softened.

Stir in garlic cloves, sage and beans.

Add enough water to cover beans by 1 inch. Bring to a boil. Reduce heat to medium-low and cook, covered, for 30 minutes.

Uncover beans and cook, stirring occasionally, for 30 to 45 minutes longer, or until beans are soft and a thick sauce has formed. (You may need to add water if beans are too dry.) Stir beans vigorously to break up garlic.

Season well with salt and pepper. Before serving, drizzle each portion with extra-virgin olive oil and sprinkle with parsley.

Preparing Dried Beans I use two methods to prepare dried beans for cooking. They work equally well, though the second method is quicker.
1) Soak the beans overnight in cold water. Use twice the amount of water as beans. Drain and rinse the beans before using.
2) Place the beans in a pot with twice the amount of water and bring to a boil. Boil for 2 minutes, remove from heat, cover and let sit for 1 hour. Drain and rinse the beans before using.

Dried Pears, Taleggio and Caramelized Walnuts

SERVES 6

Composed cheese plates are all the rage in restaurants these days, and they are perfect for home dining, too. Instead of arranging several cheeses on a cheese tray, serve this cheese course on individual plates. I like to serve a little salad around this, but James insisted I remove it for the wine to work. It's your choice.

The walnuts and pears are simple to prepare, but you can also serve the fig confit (page 300).

Sugar Syrup	1 tbsp honey
1 cup water	1 tbsp water
1 cup granulated sugar	1 tsp vegetable oil
1 tbsp lemon juice	2 tbsp granulated sugar
Pears and Walnuts	½ tsp salt
4 Bartlett pears	12 oz Taleggio or Gorgonzola cheese
1 cup walnut halves	

Combine water and sugar in a pot over high heat. Bring to a boil and boil for 3 minutes, or until a light syrup forms. Add lemon juice and reduce heat to low, or until syrup is barely simmering.

Preheat oven to 200°F.

Cut pears into slices ⅛ inch thick with a mandolin or a sharp serrated knife. Add to sugar syrup and poach for 3 to 4 minutes, or until slightly translucent. Remove slices with a slotted spoon and drain any syrup back into pot. Syrup can be frozen and reserved for another use.

Arrange pear slices on a parchment-lined baking sheet. Place in center of oven and bake for 1½ to 2 hours, or until slices are firm. Cool and store in an airtight container.

Prepare walnuts by preheating oven to 325°F. Spread walnuts on a baking sheet and bake for 10 to 15 minutes, or until golden.

Combine honey, water and oil in a skillet and bring to a boil. Reduce heat to medium and stir in walnuts. Cook, stirring frequently, until all liquid has evaporated, about 1 minute.

Toss nuts with sugar and salt. Spread on a parchment-lined baking sheet to cool and dry. Arrange cheese, pear slices and nuts on individual plates to serve.

And to drink . . .

YOUR GUESTS ARE EXPECTING NOTHING LESS than a sensory epiphany with the cheese course, so merely leaving the unfinished red wines on the table and wheeling in some Parmesan or aged Cheddar simply will not do. Generalizations fly out the window when it comes to matching cheese to wine. There is so much to consider.

On the cheese side, think about saltiness, acidity and fat, about mouth-coating texture, about the age of the particular piece of cheese you have purchased. From the wine's point of view, questions of tannin, sweetness, fruitiness, acidity and viscosity all add to the complexity of the equation. And in the end the only reliable test is to try it. Why is mature amarone so great with hunks of Parmigiano Reggiano? Maybe because the undertone of raisiny berries in the dry red wine finds an affinity with the taste of sweet, nutty, super-rich milk that is part of the cheese's character. Why is vintage port superb with Stilton, Sauternes with Roquefort, Monbazillac with Bleu d'Auvergne, Alsatian Gewürztraminer with Munster? Why does dark red Cahors make Mimolette taste like caramel? The chemistry is complex, the enchanting effects much more easily appreciated.

For this menu, Lucy has chosen Taleggio, a soft, sweetish, aromatic mouthful of a cheese from a northern Italian Alpine valley. As it happens, this cheese works quite well with the southern Italian reds, but quite well is not good enough for this company. Try a Muscat de Rivesaltes from France's Roussillon region. It's a sweet, fortified, white Muscat dessert wine—not very complicated but delectably grapy, less profound than a Sauternes. Dried pears are almost embarrassingly harmonious partners with this wine. But take a bite of Taleggio, then take another sip of the Muscat . . .

Amazing.

Lemon Tart

SERVES 6 WITH LEFTOVERS

A very lemony French tart that everyone adores. Serve it with the licorice ice cream.

The basic French tart pastry is rich and shortbread-like (leftover pastry makes fine cookies). However, because of the high fat content, it can be tricky to roll out. If necessary, pat the pastry into the pan with your fingers.

Most pastries for tarts or quiche are baked blind. This means they are weighted down and partially or fully baked before filling.

Sweet Tart Pastry
1½ cups all-purpose flour
3 tbsp granulated sugar
½ tsp salt
½ cup butter, diced
1 egg yolk
2 tbsp lemon juice

Filling
3 eggs
¾ cup granulated sugar
½ cup butter, melted
1 tbsp grated lemon zest
½ cup lemon juice

Combine flour, sugar and salt in a food processor or by hand. Scatter butter over flour. Pulse until mixture resembles coarse breadcrumbs.
Beat together egg yolk and lemon juice. With machine running, pour egg mixture through feed tube. Pulse just until liquid is incorporated into flour. If dough seems dry, add a little lemon juice.
Turn mixture into a bowl and knead together gently until it forms a ball. Flatten into a disk.
Wrap pastry in plastic wrap and chill for 15 minutes before using.
Preheat oven to 425°F.
Roll out pastry on a floured board and fit into a 9-inch tart pan. Cut away excess pastry. Prick pastry base with a fork, line with foil and fill with dried beans or pie weights.
Bake for 15 minutes. Remove foil and beans and bake for 5 minutes longer or until pale gold. Cool.
Reduce oven temperature to 350°F.
Whisk together eggs and sugar. Stir in melted butter, lemon zest and juice. Pour into pastry shell.
Bake for 15 to 18 minutes, or until just set. Cool on a rack.

Lemon Tart; Licorice Ice Cream (p. 225)

And to drink . . .

THE PERFECT BALANCE OF CITRUS, acidity and sweetness in the lemon tart makes it a natural companion for a Select Late Harvest Riesling (page 37). But the world is sticky with alternatives, including the luscious, golden, vibrant Passito di Pantelleria, a little gem from the tiny island of Pantelleria, between Sicily and Tunisia. The vines there are a kind of Muscat known locally as Zibibbo, and they are grown in deep holes to protect the foliage from the fierce winds that blow across the volcanic island.

Unlike a late harvest wine, these grapes do not start to dehydrate on the vine. They are picked when ripe and then set out to dry for a while before being pressed (*passito* is the Italian term for wines made this way). Sugars and flavors are concentrated and though the intense acidity of a Riesling is missing, Zibibbo has enough to produce a satisfying tang on the tongue. The aromas and flavors are more complex than most Muscat wines, with all sorts of dried orange and lemon zest harmonics ringing behind the variety's typically grapy, honeyed sweetness. There is even a faint whisper of anise and clove to pick up the taste of the licorice ice cream.

Licorice Ice Cream

Let 2 cups vanilla ice cream sit for 30 minutes at room temperature.

Combine softened ice cream with 1 tbsp Sambuca or Pernod and ¼ cup finely chopped black licorice candy. Refreeze for at least 4 hours.

Makes about 2 cups.

Wine Tech

Botrytis

KUDOS GOES TO THE COURAGEOUS GOURMET who first tasted cheese that was veined with blue mold or a game bird that smelled of decay or the fetid ferment of cabbage kimchi. To this bold but anonymous group must be added the reckless pioneer who once gazed, lip curling, at a bunch of botrytis-affected grapes and decided to press them for wine.

Almost always, it's the last thing a grape farmer wants to see: *Botrytis cinerea*, a certain form of a fungus that goes by the unruly handle of *Botrytonia fuckelinia*. Gray bunch rot, as it is also called, spells disaster for any vineyard it hits, except under very particular conditions. In parts of the world where healthy, fully ripe white wine grapes enjoy autumn days of humid, misty mornings to spread the rot and sunny, dry afternoons to keep it in check, a benevolent form of botrytis develops. Microscopic fungal filaments pierce the grape skins and set about changing the chemistry of the juice within, adjusting the sugars and acids, altering aromas, flavors and color. Infected grapes lose a lot of their water content and they look hideous—shriveled, webbed and powdered with gray fungus. But, if picked, pressed and vinified with due care and attention, they yield the most sublime dessert wines in the world.

The winemakers of Tokaji in northeastern Hungary were probably the first to discover that grapes affected by "noble rot" were worth pressing. Legend tells of a threatened Turkish attack delaying the harvest of 1650 until rot had set in, and of a stubborn priest insisting that the seemingly ruined fruit should not be wasted. In Germany's Rheingau, a similar tale of tardiness dates from 1775. In France, the first botrytized Sauternes is said to have been the 1847 Château d'Yquem. All these wines are extraordinarily difficult to make. Pickers must work through the vineyard many times, harvesting bunches, even individual grapes, as they reach the optimum peak of infection. Crushing them is arduous, and the sticky juice that is eventually recovered is almost too sweet for yeasts to ferment. But the effects of the botrytis make it all worthwhile. The wines are unusually viscous, they age for decades in the bottle and they have a unique, deep aroma woven into their natural fruitiness, like dark honey with a faint hint of truffle.

Yeasts

YEASTS DON'T GET A LOT OF PRESS in the world of wine writing. They may be mentioned when the subject turns to sherry or Champagne or a white wine that is aged on its lees, but unless the scribe is doing a thorough piece on the biochemistry of winemaking, they rarely make headline news. Without yeasts there would be no wine, of course—and no beer or spirits, come to that—but these microscopic, airborne one-celled plants are more than just alcohol factories. They can also bring dramatic nuances to a finished wine. The extent of their influence was brought home to me once by a winemaker who had used two different strains of cultured yeast on separate batches of an otherwise identical Riesling. We tasted both from their chilled steel tanks. One was floral, perfumed, like walking into a room where summer lilies and a bowl of lemons had been set before an open window; the other was all mineral, cold as flint, like sucking a pebble. It was hard to believe the two wines came from the same vines grown in a single vineyard.

The wine most often referred to as "yeasty" is Champagne. As part of the method used to make Champagne, an extra mixture of wine, sugar and yeasts is added to the wine before bottling to induce a second fermentation in the bottle, trapping the fizz in the liquid. Aging for years in the cellars of the Champagne houses, the wine eventually picks up complex yeasty aromas and flavors from the lees in the bottle, adding all sorts of biscuity and freshly baked bread character.

The lees in question are dead yeast cells and other solids that slowly settle out of the wine. They are usually filtered out of a still white wine as it rests in a barrel or tank after fermentation, but sometimes the winemaker lets them stay until the time comes to bottle. The lees add complexity to the maturing wine, especially when they are regularly stirred up with a stick, a disturbance the French call *bâtonnage*. The effect may be an attractive bready aroma among the fruit or sometimes a sense of creaminess—but always a vibrant freshness. I can offer no justification for such a fanciful statement, but these wines always seem to me to be particularly alive. A French Muscadet sur lie, for that reason, is the perfect foil for raw seafood, sharp as a blade and as refreshing with oysters or raw scallops as sucking a lemon after a swim in the sea.

Thanksgiving

Wild Mushroom Essence with Truffle Oil

Perfect Roast Turkey with Pan Gravy

Laird's Fruit Stuffing • Chestnut Stuffing

Lemon Garlic Roasted Potatoes • Squash Brûlée

Roasted Brussels Sprouts with Pearl Onions

Cranberry Orange Chutney

Classic Apple Pie with Cinnamon Ice Cream

SERVES 8

THIS BIG THANKSGIVING MENU has a large bird as its centerpiece. I remember many years ago my mother-in-law getting up in the middle of the night to put the Christmas turkey in the oven. The bird certainly was well cooked when we ate it. My turkey, on the other hand, is cooked as quickly as possible.

I like to cook lots of side dishes at Thanksgiving so there is something for everyone (and that way I don't have to cook a separate vegetarian main course), but you can adjust this menu to suit your own family's likes and needs. Make one or both stuffings and cook any extra alongside the turkey so the vegetarians can have stuffing, too (if you are cooking for vegetarians, use vegetable stock instead of chicken stock in these recipes). The pie, chutney, soup, sprouts and squash can all be cooked ahead and reheated. The squash can be brûléed at the last minute while you are making the gravy.

Champagne

THANKSGIVING IS A TRADITIONAL OCCASION. Gathering the extended family into one overheated room and obliging them to sit and talk for many hours while wine flows like water can so easily turn into confrontation therapy or some kind of Eugene O'Neill drama of memory and revelation. At best, it is a time for breathing new life into long-dead jokes and dredging up anecdotes of embarrassment that were far better left forgotten. To mollify this cathartic ritual, mankind has been blessed with the gift of Champagne.

The great wine of solace, Champagne brings its grace and bracing elegance to our most traumatic moments—the doomed weddings of ill-matched couples, the passing of yet another year. Its very existence is a miracle of hope, coaxing exuberance and beauty from the cold chalk hills of northern France. The Chardonnay, Pinot Noir and Pinot Meunier that strive toward ripeness in that unlikely landscape become sour, thin wines. When the blenders of the Champagne houses assemble their cuvées they show as prescient an imagination as a sculptor gazing at a block of marble and seeing within it a human form. The blend is dosed with sugar and yeast to inspire a second fermentation in the bottle, trapping the fizz in the wine and leaving it for years while the yeasts impart their own biscuity aromas and flavors. It's a complex chemistry but it pays dividends, especially when you cellar a robust vintage Champagne for five or ten more years. Mature Champagne has its own mellow, nutty beauty. Its fans are truly fanatical, looking for those extra-yeasty tones even in younger wines.

So we begin this occasion by silently toasting the Champagne makers while hungry relatives mill around and disrupt the careful itinerary of the kitchen, or sit like vultures waiting to resurrect those ancient family stories.

Wild Mushroom Essence with Truffle Oil

SERVES 8

This soup is an outstanding start to a special meal. Truffle oil is olive oil mixed with truffle essence, and it gives a mysterious, delicate flavor to the soup (the more expensive the oil, the better the quality).

1 cup dried porcini or morel
   mushrooms
1½ cups boiling water
¼ cup butter
1 lb mixed fresh mushrooms, such
   as shiitake, oyster and Portobello,
   trimmed and sliced
Salt and freshly ground pepper
1 cup chopped onions

1 cup chopped carrots
1 cup chopped celery
6 cups chicken stock
1 tbsp soy sauce
¼ cup whipping cream
1 tbsp lemon juice
1 tsp truffle oil or to taste
¼ cup chopped chives

Soak dried mushrooms in boiling water for 15 minutes.

Heat 2 tbsp butter in a large pot over medium heat. Add fresh mushrooms and sauté for 3 minutes, or until wilted. Season with salt and pepper.

Add remaining 2 tbsp butter to pot. Stir in onions, carrots and celery. Sauté for 3 minutes, or until softened.

Stir in soaked mushrooms, mushroom soaking liquid, stock and soy sauce. Bring to a boil over medium heat. Reduce heat and simmer for 20 minutes, or until mushrooms are tender.

Puree soup, return to pot and add cream. Simmer for 5 minutes to amalgamate flavors. Stir in lemon juice and truffle oil. Sprinkle each serving with chives.

And to drink . . .

TRUFFLE IS THE MOST ETHEREAL OF FLAVORS. Even a trace of truffle oil in this soup fills the room with its fragrance. Its aroma seems to hover over the bowl like an invisible cloud, and the expectation is that the soup will taste no less intensely of truffle. But the flavor is more elusive than the smell, like something you see in the corner of your eye that vanishes when you turn to stare.

Down at the earthy, barnyardy bottom of the Pinot Noir range of aromas—far from the bright red berry pinnacles—is a patch where mushrooms and truffles lurk. The nuances may not be immediately apparent, but serve a good, mature Pinot with this soup and the porcini or morels will coax them out to a surprising degree. The wine can then be left on the table for the main event of the turkey.

An option—since we are firmly in traditional mode—might be a wee glass of dry amontillado sherry of as good a quality as can be found. The better the sherry, the more complex the tangy, nutty aromas that reach into the taste of the soup like tiny tentacles, curling around the buttery mushroom flavors.

Perfect Roast Turkey with Pan Gravy

SERVES 8

If a turkey weighs less than 16 pounds, I like to roast it on high heat (page 235). The high heat crisps the skin and seals in the juices, making the meat moist and flavorful.

1 brined (page 234) turkey
   (about 14 lbs)
7 cups stuffing (pages 236 and 237)
2 tbsp butter
Freshly ground pepper

Pan Gravy
3 tbsp all-purpose flour
4 cups turkey stock
¼ cup port
1 tbsp red currant jelly
Salt and freshly ground pepper

Preheat oven to 400°F. Bring bird to room temperature. Stuff turkey (page 237) and truss.

Place turkey on a rack in a roasting pan and rub skin with butter and pepper (and salt, if you are not using a brined or kosher turkey).

Roast turkey (page 235) for 1 hour. Reduce heat to 375°F and continue to roast for 2 hours or until juices run clear. Baste every half hour if you remember.

Remove turkey from oven and let sit on a carving board, loosely covered with a tea towel, for 15 minutes, to allow juices to retract while you prepare gravy. Turkey will continue to cook while it is sitting.

Drain fat and pan drippings into a measuring cup. Return 3 tbsp fat to roasting pan. Skim fat from remaining drippings.

Sprinkle flour over fat in roasting pan and cook on stovetop, over medium heat, stirring, for about 2 minutes, or until flour is browned.

Add stock, pan drippings and port to roasting pan a little at a time, stirring constantly. Bring gravy to a boil. Reduce heat and simmer for 5 minutes, or until gravy coats the back of a spoon.

Stir in red currant jelly and simmer for 5 minutes longer. Season with salt and pepper.

And to drink . . .

ANYONE WHO HAS A LARGE AND SOCIABLE FAMILY and has at least a toe rooted in Anglo–North American culture will have had their share of roast turkey gatherings. Perhaps more than their share. And with the bird and its trimmings, over the years, they will probably have run the broad gamut of wines that taste good alongside this accommodating creature—any big-bodied dry white and almost any red at all. For the easygoing host, this is an opportunity to crowd the table with bottles and let everyone drink what they like. For the traditionalist, however, it's another chance to reach for a good-quality Pinot Noir. In England, that would mean Burgundy. With this Thanksgiving menu, discreetly laced with more fruit and sweetness than the British Christmas equivalent, a North American Pinot seems an even better idea.

Carneros is a Californian region to the south of both Napa and Sonoma Counties, an area of round, bare, yellow hills with cooler weather than either. Morning fog rolls in from the ocean, to be blown away in the afternoon by relentless winds—a climate that suits the great Burgundian varieties, Chardonnay and Pinot Noir. The Pinots are naturals for this feast. The first thing you taste in them is a whack of ripe fruit like raspberries, strawberries and red plums striated with spicy American oak and smooth as silk. That fruitiness shakes hands with the fruit in the menu and smiles benignly upon the sweet natural juices of the turkey.

Pinot Noirs from Santa Barbara County, much farther south, can also be delightful. There, too, an unusual configuration of the coast allows Pacific airs to cool the valleys enough to suit this demanding grape. Oak is part of the profile of these wines, with glorious, up-front fruit like strawberries with a hint of mint.

Roasted Brussels Sprouts with Pearl Onions (p. 240);
Squash Brûlée (p. 239)

Food Tech

Brining a Turkey

BRINING IS AN IDEAL WAY to prepare a turkey, especially if it is not free-range or air-chilled. Kosher turkeys are prebrined, by Jewish laws, to remove all the blood. If you do not want to brine a turkey yourself, a kosher turkey is an excellent substitute.

Brined turkeys are soaked in a salt-water solution for up to 24 hours before cooking. Brining loosens the muscle fibers, creating a more tender, juicy and flavorful bird.

I like to use kosher salt for brining and cooking, although any coarse salt will do. Use 1 cup salt for every 4 quarts cold water. Some cooks like to flavor the brine with herbs and chilies, but I have never found that the taste is transferred to the turkey.

You will need a container that will allow the turkey to be completely immersed in the brine. You could use a very large pot or a large plastic container. Measure the volume of the pot and make up that amount of brine. You will not need it all.

Place the turkey in the pot neck side down. Add enough brine to cover the turkey. Tie a lid on the container or pot in case the turkey floats up. Place the container in a cool place for at least 6 hours or overnight.

Remove the bird from the brine, rinse it, pat dry and set it on a baking sheet in the refrigerator for another night to crisp the skin. The bird will look as though it has come straight from the spa—gleaming and shiny—and the skin will be plumped up. Because the bird absorbs about a tablespoon of the salt mixture during the process, do not salt before roasting.

When cooked, the bird will be juicy and flavorful, and it will carve easily.

Roasting a Turkey

ROAST THE TURKEY at 400°F for 15 minutes per pound for the first 10 pounds and then 7 minutes per pound for each additional pound. Reduce the heat to 375°F after one hour. A 14-pound turkey will cook for 150 minutes for the first 10 pounds (10 × 15 minutes) and 28 minutes for the last 4 pounds (4 × 7), giving a total cooking time of about 3 hours. If the bird is stuffed, add an extra 15 minutes.

This method works perfectly because the turkey starts to cook from both the outside and the inside, cutting down on the roasting time. If your bird is larger than 16 pounds, reduce the temperature to 350°F after the first hour.

Roast the bird on a rack so the air circulates, cooking the underside as well as the breast. If the skin becomes too brown, brush butter or turkey drippings on cheesecloth or parchment paper and lay it over the skin for the last hour. Never cover with foil, or you will get a steamed bird.

Take the turkey out of the oven once the juices run clear when the thickest part of the thigh is pierced. The turkey will continue to cook after it comes out of the oven.

Laird's Fruit Stuffing

MAKES ABOUT 12 CUPS

Stuffing is a personal thing. I like this recipe from my friend Laird Saunderson because I love fruit stuffing with turkey. If you are more traditional, replace the apples with a pound of crumbled sausage meat, and use chopped fresh sage instead of tarragon.

For the best results, use slightly stale bread. Challah or egg bread makes an excellent stuffing.

Place any extra stuffing in a greased baking dish and bake, covered, for an hour at 375°F.

¼ cup butter	1 cup chicken or turkey stock
2 cups chopped onions	½ cup orange juice
2 cups chopped celery root	2 tbsp chopped fresh tarragon, or 2 tsp
2 green apples, peeled and chopped	dried
8 cups fresh breadcrumbs	2 tsp ground ginger
1 cup dried prunes, cut in half	2 tsp dried marjoram
1 cup dried cranberries	Salt and freshly ground pepper

Heat butter in a large skillet over medium heat. Add onions and celery root and sauté for 5 to 8 minutes, or until softened.

Add apples and sauté for 2 minutes.

Combine onion mixture and breadcrumbs. Stir in prunes, cranberries, stock, orange juice, tarragon, ginger and marjoram. Season well with salt and pepper. (Cook a little bit of stuffing in a skillet and taste for seasoning.)

Stuff mixture into turkey cavity and sew or skewer shut.

Turkey Stock A quick turkey stock to use for gravy and stuffing.

Place turkey neck, giblets and wing tips in a large pot. Cut 1 unpeeled onion, 2 carrots and 2 celery stalks into large chunks (the onion skins will add color to the stock). Add to pot along with 3 unpeeled garlic cloves. Add 8 cups water and a 10-oz can low-salt chicken broth.

Bring to a boil, skimming off any foam that rises to surface. Reduce heat to low and simmer, covered, for 1 hour. Uncover and continue to simmer until stock has reduced to 6 cups. Strain and chill. Remove fat before using.

Makes 6 cups.

Chestnut Stuffing

MAKES ABOUT 3 CUPS

This is my favorite stuffing for the turkey neck, but you can also bake it alongside the bird. If using fresh chestnuts takes too much time, buy a can of unsweetened chestnuts or chestnut puree and use about 1 cup.

1 lb chestnuts	2 tbsp chopped chervil or parsley
2 tbsp butter	1 egg, beaten
½ cup chopped onions	Salt and freshly ground pepper
2 cups fresh breadcrumbs	

Score chestnuts with an X on rounded sides. Place in a pot, cover with cold water and bring to a boil. Boil for 5 minutes to soften skins. Remove from heat, drain and peel. Chop chestnuts finely.

Heat butter in a skillet over medium heat. Add onions and sauté for 3 minutes, or until softened.

Combine chestnuts, onions, breadcrumbs, chervil and egg. Season with salt and pepper. If stuffing is very dry, add a little stock or water. Stuff into turkey neck or bake, covered, in a greased baking dish at 375°F for 1 hour.

Stuffing Plan on ½ cup stuffing per pound of bird. The stuffing can be prepared ahead of time, but do not stuff until just before roasting to avoid any bacterial contamination. If desired, place stuffing in a greased baking dish, cover and bake alongside the bird for the final hour.

After the meal, remove any stuffing remaining in the bird and refrigerate separately.

Lemon Garlic Roasted Potatoes

SERVES 8

These crisp, golden potatoes provide a texture contrast to the other vegetables.

4 lbs Yukon Gold potatoes,
    peeled and cut in 1-inch chunks
3 tbsp olive oil
3 tbsp butter, melted
1 tbsp chopped garlic

1 tbsp grated lemon zest
¼ cup chopped fresh mint, dill or sage,
    or 1 tbsp dried
Salt and freshly ground pepper

Place potatoes in a large pot of salted water and bring to a boil. Boil for 7 to 10 minutes, or until crisp-tender. Drain.

Preheat oven to 375°F.

Combine oil, melted butter, garlic, lemon zest and mint. Pour over drained potatoes and toss together. Season well with salt and pepper. Spread over a large baking sheet.

Bake for 35 to 45 minutes, stirring occasionally, until potatoes are golden and crisp.

Squash Brûlée

SERVES 8

Sprinkling brown sugar on top of the mashed squash and then broiling gives it the look of a crème brûlée. I prefer the flavor of the drier squash such as Hubbard or buttercup, but the more popular butternut or acorn also work well in this recipe.

This can be cooked ahead and reheated in a microwave, but brûlée just before serving.

4 lbs squash, peeled and diced

4 cups chicken stock or water

2 eggs, beaten

1/2 cup whipping cream

1 cup grated Parmesan cheese

1 tsp grated nutmeg

Salt and freshly ground pepper

3 tbsp butter

1/4 cup brown sugar

Place squash and stock in a pot over high heat. Bring to a boil. Reduce heat to low, cover and cook for 10 minutes, or until squash is tender.

Preheat oven to 375°F.

Drain squash, reserving cooking liquid. Mash squash and stir in eggs, cream, Parmesan, nutmeg, salt and pepper. If mixture is very thick, add a little cooking liquid.

Transfer squash to a buttered baking dish or 8 individual ramekins. Dot with butter. Bake for 20 minutes, or until squash is hot.

Sift brown sugar over top of squash and place under broiler. Broil, watching constantly, for 1 to 2 minutes, or until sugar bubbles and turns golden.

Roasted Brussels Sprouts with Pearl Onions

SERVES 8

This recipe will even appeal to those who hate Brussels sprouts. Roasting gives the sprouts exceptional flavor, and they are never soggy. Roast the sprouts ahead and sauté quickly on the stove before serving.

Small onions such as pearl or the Italian red cipolline are great with the sprouts, or you could cut a large red onion into chunks. To peel pearl onions, place in cold water, bring to a boil, drain and then slip off the skins.

¼ cup olive oil	Salt and freshly ground pepper
2 tbsp balsamic vinegar	3 tbsp butter
1 tbsp Dijon mustard	½ cup chicken or vegetable stock,
16 pearl or cipolline onions, peeled	or water
2 lbs Brussels sprouts,	2 tbsp chopped fresh dill
trimmed and halved	

Preheat oven to 425°F.

Whisk together oil, vinegar and mustard. Toss with onions and Brussels sprouts. Season with salt and pepper.

Spread sprouts and onions in single layer on baking sheets. Roast for 20 to 25 minutes, or until sprouts and onions are tender and browned.

Heat butter in a large skillet over medium heat. Add sprouts and onions and toss until heated. Add stock and bring to a boil. Reduce heat and simmer for 5 minutes, or until stock thickens and sprouts glisten. Sprinkle with dill before serving.

Cranberry Orange Chutney

MAKES ABOUT 3 CUPS

This chutney will keep refrigerated for up to a month. It makes a good hostess gift, too.

2 cups granulated sugar
1 tbsp grated orange zest
1 tsp grated lime zest
¼ cup orange juice
2 tbsp lime juice
¼ cup cider vinegar

¼ cup red wine
1 tbsp finely chopped gingerroot
1 2-inch stick cinnamon
1½ lbs fresh cranberries
½ cup dried cranberries
¼ cup orange liqueur

Combine sugar, orange and lime zest and juice, vinegar, wine, ginger and cinnamon stick in a pot. Bring to a boil. Cook over medium-high heat, stirring constantly, for 3 minutes.

Add fresh and dried cranberries and orange liqueur. Reduce heat and simmer, stirring occasionally, for 15 minutes, or until most of fresh cranberries break open.

Classic Apple Pie
with Cinnamon Ice Cream

SERVES 8

Fruit pies are baked at two temperatures to ensure a crisp bottom crust and properly cooked fruit. Spy apples are the best apples to bake with because they hold their shape and do not turn to mush. If they are unavailable, use any tart apple.

Serve the pie with cinnamon ice cream.

1 recipe Perfect Flaky Pastry (page 165)	1 1/2 tsp grated orange zest
5 to 6 large apples	1 tbsp orange juice
1/2 cup granulated sugar	1 tsp grated lemon zest
1/2 cup brown sugar	1 tsp ground cinnamon
1 tbsp all-purpose flour	1/4 tsp grated nutmeg
	1 tbsp butter

Preheat oven to 425°F.

Roll out half of pastry on a floured surface and fit into a 9-inch pie plate or tart pan.

Peel, core and slice apples. You should have about 8 cups.

Combine apples with granulated sugar, brown sugar, flour, orange zest, orange juice, lemon zest, cinnamon and nutmeg.

Pile filling into pie shell, mounding in center. Dot with butter.

Roll out remaining pastry and fit over filling. Trim pastry and crimp edges. Make two vents in center of pie to allow steam to escape.

Bake for 15 minutes. Reduce heat to 375°F and bake for 30 to 45 minutes, or until crust turns golden and filling is bubbling.

Cinnamon Ice Cream Let 2 cups vanilla ice cream sit for 30 minutes at room temperature. Combine softened ice cream with 1 tsp ground cinnamon. Makes 2 cups.

And to drink . . .

ONE OF THE GREAT PLEASURES OF RIESLING is the array of other fruits these wines suggest in their various global manifestations—Rieslings that taste of lemon or lime or apple, that show hints of orange or grapefruit or pear. Even in a small, well-defined region like Ontario's Niagara peninsula, the spectrum of aromas and flavors can be extravagantly broad, dependent upon site and microclimate, different clones of the vine, vineyard practices and the winemaker's techniques. Sometimes pairing a wine with a certain dish brings out dormant effects that one might have missed when tasting the wine alone. I remember a couple of decidedly citric late harvest Rieslings faced with an apple tart: both suddenly produced all sorts of unexpected Granny Smith nuances.

A slightly lighter alternative might be a sweet Chenin Blanc from the Loire—a Coteaux du Layon, perhaps, or a Vouvray. These wines have thrilling acidity that lifts the sweetness of late-harvested grapes, and they are often botrytized, adding that unique honeyed depth of flavor.

Dessert Buffet

Lemon Passionfruit Meringue Roulade

Victorian Orange and Ginger Cake

Chocolate Cappuccino Torte

Spiced Pear Tart · Shortbread Cookies

Chocolate Cherry Chunk Cookies

SERVES 16

A DESSERT BUFFET is a charming way to entertain a crowd. Everyone loves desserts, and it is a treat to have them for a feast. Today you can combine homemade and store-bought desserts, as commercial dessert-making has reached new heights. However, if you are making everything yourself, choose desserts that can be made ahead. On the day of the party there should only be one thing to make and a few others to finish.

When I have a dessert buffet, I plan to have at least one chocolate, one lemon, one tart and one cake. I also like to include cookies, because that is all some people want with their coffee.

These desserts can also be served on their own as a grand finale to a dinner party. This party serves sixteen, although the individual recipes serve eight to ten.

Dessert Buffet Wines

IMAGING THIS PARTY, thinking about the array of sumptuous desserts and what drinks to serve alongside them, leaves me with a prodigious thirst. A great deal of very cold, very fizzy water with a wedge of lime sounds like a fine idea, rinsing the palate clean as we move from treat to treat. And, at the end, some exceptional coffee, as black and bitter as coal.

But what to serve in between? The true wine nerd might choose a different wine for each dessert, then line up the guests to make sure they make the appropriate match with each mouthful. I fear that would be both a logistical nightmare and a social disaster.

Better to offer two wines that will flatter every sweet on the table.

Muscat de Beaumes-de-Venise is the dessert crowd-pleaser par excellence. A fortified French white wine from the town of Beaumes-de-Venise in the southern Rhône, it shines with the fresh, grapy taste of Muscat—like someone turning on a bright, clear light in your mouth. It's sweet, it's potent, it's clean and cool, and it's as invincible as a warrior maiden in magical armor. That's why restaurant sommeliers think of it as the default dessert wine, the sticky to reach for in times of doubt. The armor is the alcohol, lifting the Muscat aromas high above whatever is happening on the plate. Pit it against fruit, caramel, pastries and cookies, even chocolate—good old B-de-V retains its integrity and triumphs like Joan of Arc.

The second suggestion is Moscato d'Asti. Some wines get no respect. Moscato d'Asti is one, the sweet sparkler from northwestern Italy that is so frothy and light it feels almost weightless in your mouth. It's a soufflé of a wine, a sweet foam that tastes of Muscat grapes, and it is a particularly charming accompaniment to cakes and meringues, allowing flavors such as lemon, orange or ginger to express themselves without heckling or interruption. Besides, it's fun to pop a few corks at a casual gathering. Eyes sparkle more brightly, talk becomes more effervescent.

Lemon Passionfruit Meringue Roulade

SERVES 8 TO 10

This cloud-like dessert is based on a recipe from the excellent Kinloch Country House in Scotland, the home of Scottish food writer Lady Clare Macdonald. Make meringue a few days ahead, and fill the day of the party.

Meringue
8 egg whites
2 cups granulated sugar
2 tbsp white vinegar
2 tbsp cornstarch
¼ cup icing sugar
Filling
½ cup whipping cream
2 passionfruit

1 cup lemon curd, homemade (page 46)
  or storebought
Sauce
1 cup apricot jam
4 passionfruit
2 tbsp orange liqueur

Preheat oven to 350°F. Line a 17- by 11-inch jellyroll pan with parchment paper. Beat egg whites with an electric mixer until frothy and doubled in bulk. Slowly beat in granulated sugar 2 tbsp at a time. Continue to beat until egg whites are thick, glossy and hold slightly drooping peaks. Beat in vinegar until egg whites form stiff peaks, then beat in cornstarch.

Spread meringue mixture over prepared pan and smooth. Bake for 20 minutes, or until top is pale gold and feels firm to the touch. Cool for 1 hour.

Turn meringue over onto a large sheet of parchment paper dusted with icing sugar. Cover with a tea towel and keep in a cool place until ready to fill.

Whip cream until it thickens.

Spoon passionfruit out of shell and beat into lemon curd. Add to whipped cream and continue to beat until cream holds a stiff peak.

Spread cream over meringue. Roll up meringue widthwise, using paper as a guide. Don't worry if meringue breaks or cracks. Trim ends.

Prepare sauce by melting jam in a small pot over medium heat. Remove from heat and combine with passionfruit pulp and liqueur.

Cut meringue into slices and place on a serving platter. Serve with sauce.

Victorian Orange and Ginger Cake

SERVES 10

This heavy, moist, English-style cake is at its best after resting for at least a few days. It's so good that I make it as a nontraditional Christmas cake.

2 tbsp grated orange zest	1 tsp baking soda
1 cup dried cranberries	1 cup plain yogurt
½ cup chopped preserved ginger	Orange Syrup
1 cup granulated sugar	½ cup orange juice
½ cup butter, at room temperature	2 tbsp granulated sugar
2 eggs	2 tbsp orange liqueur
2 cups all-purpose flour	Garnish
1 tsp salt	2 tbsp icing sugar

Preheat oven to 325°F. Grease a 9- or 10-inch springform pan. Sugar sides of pan and cut a round of parchment paper to fit bottom of pan.

Combine orange zest, cranberries, ginger and 2 tbsp granulated sugar in a food processor. Process until chopped.

Cream remaining granulated sugar and butter with an electric mixer until light and fluffy. Add eggs one at a time, beating well.

Sift together flour, salt and baking soda.

Beat one-third of flour mixture into butter mixture. Beat in half of yogurt, one-third more flour, remaining yogurt and then remaining flour, beating well after each addition. Stir in orange zest mixture.

Spoon batter into prepared pan. Bake for 1 hour, or until a skewer inserted in center comes out clean. Cool for 10 minutes. Remove sides of pan and replace while cake is still hot to make sure cake is loosened from sides so syrup can drip down.

Prepare syrup by heating orange juice, sugar and liqueur in a small pot over medium heat. Cook, stirring, for 2 minutes, or until sugar is dissolved.

Poke holes all over top of cake with a skewer. Pour syrup over cake. Let sit for 24 hours before removing sides of pan.

Dust with sifted icing sugar just before serving.

Chocolate Cappuccino Torte

SERVES 10

A dense chocolate cake decorated to look like a cup of cappuccino. It is dead easy to make, though it looks as though it has been concocted by a professional pastry chef. Your guests will be very impressed. The cake can be made up to five days ahead, but add the whipped cream just before serving. Garnish with chocolate espresso beans if desired.

1½ cups butter
¾ cup granulated sugar
¼ cup strong coffee
1 lb bittersweet chocolate, chopped
10 eggs, separated
2 tbsp all-purpose flour

Topping
2 cups whipping cream
2 tbsp granulated sugar
2 tsp ground cinnamon

Preheat oven to 325°F. Butter a 10-inch springform pan and line base with parchment paper.

Melt butter in a heavy pot over medium-low heat. Add ½ cup sugar and coffee, stirring until sugar dissolves. Add chocolate and stir until smooth.

Scrape chocolate mixture into a large bowl. Stir in egg yolks and flour.

Beat egg whites with an electric mixer until soft peaks form. Gradually beat in remaining ¼ cup sugar. When egg whites are thick, smooth and glossy, stir one-quarter of whites into chocolate mixture. Fold in remaining whites. Spoon batter into prepared pan.

Place pan on a baking sheet and bake for 25 to 30 minutes, or until edges puff and crack slightly but center is not completely set. Cake will set as it cools. Cool in pan, cover and refrigerate overnight.

Loosen sides of cake with a sharp knife. Release sides of pan.

Whip cream with sugar until cream holds its shape. Spread over top of cake.

Transfer cake to a platter and sprinkle with cinnamon. Cut into wedges, wiping knife clean between each cut.

Spiced Pear Tart

SERVES 8

Use a simple shortbread crust for this magnificent tart, or buy an unbaked pie shell and bake it, unfilled, according to the package directions. Bake the pastry and prepare the filling a day ahead and assemble the tart on the day of the party.

This dessert was a great favorite at our photo shoot. It looks spectacular baked in a rectangular tart pan. Serve it cold or at room temperature.

1 recipe Sweet Tart Pastry (page 224)

Poached Pears

2 cups water

2 cups granulated sugar

3 star anise

6 pods cardamom, crushed

4 Bartlett or Bosc pears, peeled, cored and halved

Filling

1 cup mascarpone

2 tbsp granulated sugar

2 tsp grated lemon zest

¼ cup whipping cream

2 tbsp chopped pistachio nuts, optional

Preheat oven to 425°F.

Roll out pastry on a floured board and fit into a 9-inch tart pan. Prick pastry with a fork, line with foil and fill with dried beans or pie weights.

Bake for 15 minutes. Remove foil and beans and bake for 5 minutes longer. Cool.

Bring water, sugar, star anise and cardamom to a boil in a large skillet over high heat. Boil for 5 minutes. Reduce heat to medium-low and add pears. Poach for 10 to 25 minutes, or until pears are tender. Cooking time will depend on ripeness of pears. Cool pears in poaching liquid. Remove pears to a cake rack set over a plate to drain. Reserve poaching liquid.

Prepare filling by beating mascarpone with sugar, 2 tbsp pear poaching liquid and lemon zest.

Whip cream until soft peaks form. Fold whipped cream into mascarpone. Spread filling over baked tart shell.

Transfer remaining poaching liquid to a pot and bring to a boil. Boil for 10 minutes, or until thickened and reduced by half.

Slice pears and arrange in a circle on top of filling.

Brush about 2 tbsp poaching liquid over pears. Sprinkle with pistachios.

Shortbread Cookies

MAKES ABOUT 3 DOZEN

A true Scottish shortbread uses rice flour to give it the fine, crumbly texture associated with good shortbread. This is my family's heirloom recipe.

¾ cup granulated sugar
3 cups all-purpose flour
½ cup rice flour

1 tsp salt
2 cups butter, diced

Preheat oven to 275°F.

Pour sugar into a food processor. Process sugar for about 30 seconds to give it a finer texture.

Add all-purpose flour, rice flour and salt to food processor and combine. Add butter and process until combined, but do not allow mixture to form a ball in food processor,

Scrape mixture into a bowl and knead together gently to form a ball. Divide dough into thirds and roll out each third until about ½ inch thick.

Cut dough into rounds using a 2-inch cookie cutter. Place on ungreased baking sheets and prick each cookie with a fork.

Bake in center of oven for 25 to 35 minutes, or until a creamy color. The shortbread will not be firm but it will harden as it cools.

Cool on baking sheets. Keep in airtight containers for up to a month.

Chocolate Cherry Chunk Cookies

MAKES ABOUT 4 DOZEN

This is the best chocolate chip cookie ever. The chips are chunks of chocolate and the dried cherries provide extra flavor, though you can omit them if desired. Use dark chocolate chunks instead of white if you prefer.

½ cup butter
4 oz bittersweet chocolate, coarsely chopped
1½ cups granulated sugar
2 eggs
2 tsp vanilla

1½ cups all-purpose flour
½ tsp baking powder
½ tsp salt
6 oz white chocolate, cut in small chunks
1 cup dried cherries

Preheat oven to 350°F. Line baking sheets with parchment paper.

Melt butter in a pot over low heat. Add bittersweet chocolate and stir until smooth. Remove from heat and transfer to a large bowl. Beat in sugar, eggs and vanilla.

Combine flour, baking powder and salt.

Blend flour mixture into chocolate mixture. Stir in white chocolate chunks and dried cherries.

Drop dough onto baking sheets in 1 tbsp mounds about 2 inches apart.

Bake for 10 to 11 minutes, or until cookies are glossy, cracked on surface and soft inside. Do not overbake. Remove from oven and allow cookies to set on baking sheets for 5 minutes. Transfer cookies to a wire rack to cool completely. Store in an airtight container for up to 2 weeks.

Wine Tech

Wine with Chocolate

CHOCOLATE AND CHOCOLATE DESSERTS are notorious foes to wine. The sweetness and the mouth-coating richness are simply too much for the average late harvest production. Icewine has the cojones to stay in the ring with chocolate, but they circle each other warily until the crowd starts to boo and ask for its money back.

Fortified wines offer much better sport. Muscat de Beaumes-de-Venise (page 245) retains its refreshing integrity against most chocolate manifestations. Port goes several steps further and actually starts to flirt with the chocolate. Ten-year-old tawny port and Swiss milk chocolate are delicious together; dark chocolate meets its soul mate in an LBV (late bottled vintage) port, especially if there are berries around to pick up the wine's own deep, spicy fruit. LBV is a port style designed for people who lack the patience and the budget for vintage port. It really is "bottled late," made up of ports from a single year that spend up to six years in the cask, aging far more quickly than vintage port, which is bottled after only two years and must undergo a far slower maturation in the bottle. There is no need to cellar an LBV for a decade—it's ready to drink when you buy it—and no need to decant.

Two other fortified reds are also particularly handy with desserts that have a glorious chocolate flavor but a fairly light weight and texture. Banyuls and Maury come from the French region of Roussillon, just north of the Pyrenees and on the Mediterranean side of the country—Banyuls from the coast and Maury from the mountainous hinterland. Both are red wines, made mostly from Grenache Noir vines that eke a precarious living from inhospitable soil, and both are fortified, very like port, but with a much older history.

The idea of adding grape alcohol to a fermenting wine, stopping fermentation and thereby capturing the sugars in the juice, was invented in nearby Perpignan in the thirteenth century and has been applied to these wines ever since. Production methods still seem fascinatingly old-fashioned. At Mas Amiel winery, one of the major Maury producers, the partially heat-shriveled grapes are picked by hand from the steep slopes of schist. The must is still on their skins when the alcohol is added, causing more color and flavor to be extracted. Then the sweet, alcoholic new wine is put into oversized glass demijohns (*bonbonnes*) that are left out in the sun for a year, a technique invented by the Romans. More aging follows—four to ten years in hundred-year-old casks of Austrian oak.

What finally emerges is luscious, exotic, fruity, complex, with an alcoholic content of about 17 percent and a nose full of spices, chocolate and cooked red fruit. It doesn't feel nearly as heavy as port but it shares one key characteristic: Maury, like Banyuls, is excellent with chocolate. And if berries or cherries are also part of the dish, the match is even more ambrosial.

One last chocolate suggestion is unconventional enough to seriously startle your guests. If you are serving a very dark, dense chocolate dessert—Lucy's scrumptious Triple Chocolate Truffle Tart (page 199), for example—buy a bottle of Dalwhinnie single malt Scotch and put it in the freezer for twenty-four hours. Once the tart has been served (this is a very last-minute operation), pour everyone an ounce or two of the whisky in a liqueur or shot glass. Ice-cold and viscous, it will have lost its whisky aroma—those volatile molecules are sluggish and dormant at such a low temperature—and you'll find the flavor of this elegant Speyside iteration will also have changed. The vinous perfume of the sherry casks in which it aged is most apparent, with hints of hay, sweet grass and heather—aromas that dance a fling with the dry taste of the dark chocolate. This trick doesn't work with many single malts, certainly not with a super-peaty Islay whisky, but Dalwhinnie just smiles sweetly. Whatever is left in the bottle can be put back into the liquor cabinet to return to room temperature, none the worse for its adventure.

Fast and Fresh
Simply Eclectic

Jerusalem Artichoke and White Turnip Bisque
Halibut with Mushroom Tomato Jam
Basmati Rice Pilau
Lemon Sorbet Babycakes

SERVES 4

I TASTED MY FIRST Jerusalem artichoke soup in England in the 1970s. The soup was called Crème Palestine, so I assumed that its origins were Middle Eastern. But Jerusalem artichokes have nothing to do with the Middle East. As a member of the sunflower family, they get their name from the Italian word for sunflower—*girasole*. These knotty tubers look similar to gingerroot and are grown in North America and Europe.

This simple yet unusual and elegant dinner takes very little prep time but tastes as though you spent hours in the kitchen.

And to drink . . .

The spiced tomato jam is the main course's dominant flavor and therefore dictates the choice of wine. A peppery Pinot Grigio from California or British Columbia proves a surprisingly successful match, working well with the spices and matching the acidity of the tomatoes.

Jerusalem Artichoke and White Turnip Bisque

SERVES 4

A rich soup with the slight artichoke flavor that you get from Jerusalem artichokes. The tubers must be peeled or well scrubbed before using. A small sharp knife works well.

White turnips are snowy white roots with purple tops. They are much milder than rutabagas and cook much more quickly. The combination is sensational.

Garnish each serving with a few splashes of hot chili oil, if desired.

12 oz white turnips, peeled and cut in 1-inch pieces	2 tbsp chopped fresh lemon balm, or 1 tsp grated lemon zest
1 lb Jerusalem artichokes, peeled and cut in 1-inch pieces	¼ cup whipping cream
1 cup chopped onions	Salt and freshly ground pepper
4 cups chicken stock	2 tbsp chopped chives

Combine turnips, Jerusalem artichokes, onions and stock in a pot. Bring to a boil over high heat, reduce heat and simmer for 20 minutes, or until vegetables are very tender.

Puree soup and return to pot. Add lemon balm and cream and bring to a boil. Season well with salt and pepper.

Reduce heat to low and simmer for 5 minutes to amalgamate flavors.

Sprinkle each serving with chopped chives.

Halibut
with Mushroom Tomato Jam
SERVES 4

Alaskan black cod, snapper or scallops can be used instead of the halibut. The jam is also good with grilled chicken or shrimp.

Garam masala is a fragrant blend of spices that is aromatic but not too hot. If it is unavailable, substitute a mild curry powder.

Mushroom Tomato Jam
3 tbsp butter
4 oz oyster mushrooms,
   trimmed and thickly sliced
Salt and freshly ground pepper
2 tsp finely chopped garlic
1 tsp finely chopped gingerroot
1 tbsp garam masala
2 tsp ground cumin
1 tsp ground coriander

6 plum tomatoes, seeded and diced
¼ cup tomato juice
1 tbsp balsamic vinegar
1 tsp granulated sugar
Halibut
4 halibut fillets (about 6 oz each)
1 tbsp vegetable oil
1 tsp garam masala
Salt
2 tbsp chopped fresh coriander

Heat 2 tbsp butter in a large skillet over medium-high heat. Add mushrooms and sauté for 3 minutes, or until golden. Season with salt and pepper. Remove mushrooms from skillet and reserve.

Reduce heat to medium and add remaining 1 tbsp butter to skillet. Add garlic, ginger, garam masala, cumin and ground coriander and sauté for 30 seconds.

Add tomatoes and cook for 3 minutes, or until tomatoes are softened and begin to give off juice. Add tomato juice, vinegar and sugar. Bring to a boil. Reduce heat and simmer for 12 to 15 minutes, or until sauce is thick and flavorful. Season with salt and pepper.

Preheat oven to 450°F and prepare fish while sauce is cooking.

Brush halibut fillets with oil and dust with garam masala and salt. Place fish on a lightly oiled baking sheet and bake for 10 to 12 minutes, or until white juices begin to appear.

Stir mushrooms into tomato jam and cook for 1 to 2 minutes to reheat mushrooms. Spoon onto individual plates and top with fish. Sprinkle with fresh coriander.

Basmati Rice Pilau

SERVES 4

A quick, foolproof way to cook slender, nutty basmati rice.

2 cups uncooked basmati rice
2 cups water
1 tsp ground turmeric
1 tsp cumin seeds
2 bay leaves

2 1-inch cinnamon sticks
6 whole cloves
1 cup green peas
Salt

Soak rice in cold water for 30 minutes. Rinse and drain.
Place rice in a heavy pot with water, turmeric, cumin, bay leaves, cinnamon and cloves. Bring to a boil over high heat. Cover, reduce heat to low and cook for 15 minutes, or until rice is tender.
Remove from heat and remove bay leaves and cinnamon sticks. Stir in peas and season with salt. Cover and let sit for 5 minutes before serving.

Lemon Sorbet Babycakes

SERVES 4

This is my secret dessert when I have little time to cook. It is quick, light and made with storebought ingredients. Use any fresh fruit in place of the blueberries.

¼ cup red currant jelly
2 cups fresh blueberries
½ cup whipping cream

4 individual meringue shells
1 cup lemon sorbet

Heat jelly in a pot over medium heat until liquid. Add blueberries and toss to combine. Cool.
Whip cream until it holds its shape.
Fill meringue shells with lemon sorbet. Heap fruit over sorbet and top with whipped cream.

A Drop More

Brandy

"CLARET IS THE LIQUOR FOR BOYS, port for men; but he who aspires to be a hero must drink brandy." So wrote Dr. Samuel Johnson in 1779. The great lexicographer had a habit of expressing his personal tastes as if they were laws of nature, and his tastes, like those of all bullies, were narrow. To him, brandy meant Cognac, from that broad French valley just north of Bordeaux where the Charente River winds slowly through chalky fields and peaceful woodland until it reaches the Atlantic. Centuries later, many connoisseurs still share his prejudice. To appreciate why, you have only to swirl an ounce of some princely XO Cognac in a snifter and lift it to your nose: intensity without weight, complexity without clumsiness, strength balanced by a sublime finesse.

Great Cognacs are truly great, but an average Cognac is, well, average—elegant but austere, like a conversation with a thin, clever but slightly condescending uncle. A talk with an average Armagnac (the other world-famous French brandy, from Gascony) is likely to be more full of poetry, depth and flavor (page 185). Armagnac's history goes back a hundred years earlier than Cognac's and reads like *The Three Musketeers*. But for real romance, head down to Andalucía in southwestern Spain, where brandy making began in the 1400s, and address yourself to a Brandy de Jerez. Rich, generous and precociously mature, these classic Spanish brandies share many things with the sherries that evolve alongside them, including a solera system to accelerate maturation and the fact that they offer astonishing value for money.

Turning wine into brandy may be the ultimate collaboration of science, art and nature. The science is in the actual distillation, using pot stills that have evolved little from the alembics brought to Europe by Moors in the Middle Ages. The inefficiency of the technology means that the distilled spirits are laden with beneficial impurities—the sapid, aromatic molecules from the wine. Art comes into play when the master blender sets to work with his cellar of oak-aged spirits. Nature is involved at the very beginning and at the very end of the process, for the unique qualities of the vineyard are missing from the weak, highly acidic white wines and the fiery, immature spirits. They only emerge in the brandy after years or decades in oak.

It all sounds a tad esoteric, but the evidence is irrefutable. In Cognac, for example, brandy-making methods are the same from one region to the next, but the brandies themselves vary considerably in quality and style because of differences in each region's soil. Those that are closest to the actual town of Cognac are the most highly prized. To the southeast the country is known as the Grande Champagne, with the Petite Champagne below it. Brandies made from both are notably racy, nervous, refined, needing many years in wood before they even begin to mature, but then revealing unsurpassable complexity and grace. The Borderies lies to the northwest, a small, well-defined area where the chalk in the soil is mixed with clay. Growers who farm the Borderies distill fabulous brandies that show a distinctive aroma of nuts and violets. Surrounding this heartland is the Fins Bois—source of lesser spirits but perfectly good for everyday Cognacs—then the Bons Bois and lastly the Bois Communs, best known for the brandy in which fruits are preserved.

Other factors also come into play. While Cognac is distilled twice, Armagnac only passes through the still once, giving a more aromatic but less alcoholic spirit. Barrels also make a difference. Cognac traditionally ages in casks of Limousin oak; Armagnac uses the sappier black oak of Monlezun. Brandy de Jerez grows smooth and old in oak butts previously used to age sherry.

Then there are the additives, little discussed in polite circles, but almost ubiquitous: caramel for color, an occasional drop of sugar syrup for richness, oak chips to accentuate the impression of wood. Some Greek brandies also add a dash of Muscat wine liqueur—sweet, smooth, heavy and fragrant. The effect, I am told, is just like sipping Cognac while wearing lipstick.

Napoleon Brandy   Bonaparte loved Cognac, but brandies labeled Napoleon refer to a different emperor. In the 1860s, Emperor Napoleon III's free trade agreement with England precipitated a golden age of prosperity in Cognac, soon destroyed when phylloxera wiped out the vineyards. Twenty-five years later, pre-phylloxera brandies were casually referred to as "Napoleon brandy." Inevitably, foreigners assumed a connection with the earlier, more famous Napoleon, and the Cognacais did not disillusion them, festooning their labels with Bonapartist imagery. The one house with a cast-iron connection is Courvoisier, founded in 1843 by the son of Emmanuel Courvoisier, Bonaparte's wine merchant.

Fast and Fresh
Pasta Perfect

Apple and Zucchini Soup

Oven-baked Orecchiette with Caramelized Onions and
Smoked Cheese

Roasted Pears with Pomegranate Sabayon

SERVES 4

POMEGRANATES ARE IN SEASON from late fall through January. They are sweet but with a tangy touch. They come to the market ripe and will keep for a month if they are stored in a plastic bag in the refrigerator. The seeds, which make a sensual pop in your mouth, add color, texture and flavor to salads, main courses and desserts.

And to drink . . .

Melted smoked cheese is unctuously delicious, but its weight and mouth-coating richness make it a difficult match for wine. A young Australian Shiraz has the body to cope and peppery spice behind the fruit that harmonizes with the smokiness of the cheese. If you prefer white, try an Alsatian Gewürztraminer.

Apple and Zucchini Soup

SERVES 4

A peppery, sweet combination that spikes the palate and is a good way to use all the zucchini that is available this season. Garnish the soup with extra watercress leaves and a few drops of chili oil, if desired.

2 tbsp butter	4 cups chicken stock
1 cup chopped onions	2 cups watercress leaves
1 large apple, peeled and diced	¼ cup whipping cream
4 cups chopped zucchini	Salt and freshly ground pepper

Heat butter in a pot over medium heat. Add onions and apple and sauté for 5 minutes, or until soft but not brown.

Stir in zucchini and sauté for 1 minute. Pour in chicken stock and bring to a boil. Reduce heat and simmer for 20 minutes, or until zucchini is tender.

Add watercress and simmer for 5 minutes. Cool slightly.

Puree soup and return to pot. Add cream. Bring to a boil, reduce heat and simmer for a few minutes. Season with salt and pepper.

Oven-baked Orecchiette with Caramelized Onions and Smoked Cheese

SERVES 4

Smoked cheeses are widely available, but many have smoked flavoring added. For a natural alternative, try San Simon, a superb, creamy smoked cheese from Spain.

This dish is also good made with an unsmoked cheese that melts well. Try Fontina, Taleggio or even mozzarella. You can omit the pancetta for a vegetarian version.

The dish can be prepared in advance and baked just before serving.

½ cup chopped pancetta	1 cup whipping cream
2 tbsp olive oil	⅓ cup butter
2 large sweet onions, thinly sliced	1 cup grated Parmesan cheese
Salt and freshly ground pepper	2 cups shredded smoked mozzarella or
1 lb dried orecchiette pasta	other smoked cheese

Cook pancetta in a dry skillet over medium heat for 3 minutes, or until crisped and golden. Drain on paper towels.

Heat oil in a large skillet over medium heat. Add onions and salt them immediately. (This helps to remove water.) Sauté for 3 minutes, or until softened. Reduce heat to medium-low and continue to cook, stirring occasionally, for 20 to 30 minutes, or until onions become a thick golden mass.

Preheat oven to 350°F.

Bring a large pot of salted water to a boil while onions are cooking. Add orecchiette and boil for 8 to 12 minutes, or until *al dente*. Drain and transfer to a large bowl.

Stir in cream, 4 tbsp butter, ½ cup Parmesan, onion mixture, smoked cheese and pancetta. Season well with salt and pepper.

Transfer pasta to a buttered baking dish, sprinkle with remaining ½ cup Parmesan and dot with remaining 2 tbsp butter. Bake for 15 to 20 minutes, or until pasta is hot and top is slightly browned.

Roasted Pears
with Pomegranate Sabayon

SERVES 4

Roasting pears gives them a buttery flavor and sugary crunch. For the sabayon, use any sweet wine, such as late harvest Riesling or sherry, instead of the vino santo. You can also use all pomegranate juice.

The pomegranate seeds add crunch to the sabayon. If pomegranates are unavailable, omit the seeds and use orange juice instead of pomegranate juice.

4 pears, peeled, cored and halved
2 tbsp butter
1/4 cup brown sugar

Sabayon
3 eggs
2 tbsp granulated sugar
1/4 cup vino santo or other sweet wine
1/2 cup pomegranate juice
1/4 cup pomegranate seeds

Preheat oven to 350°F.
Place pears in a baking dish in a single layer, cut side up. Dot with butter and sprinkle with brown sugar. Bake for 20 minutes, or until tender. Transfer pears to serving plates with a slotted spoon. Reserve any pan juices.
Place eggs and sugar in a heavy pot. Whisk over low heat until thickened, about 5 minutes. Whisk in vino santo, any pan juices and pomegranate juice. Continue to whisk until mixture triples in volume, about 1 to 2 minutes. Stir in pomegranate seeds.
Spoon sabayon over pears.

Pomegranates To peel a pomegranate, cut the crown off the fruit. Score the skin in quarters and bend back each quarter. Scoop the seeds into a bowl. One pomegranate yields about 3/4 cup seeds and 1/2 cup juice. The seeds can be frozen for future use. There are also new yellow pomegranates that are seedless and make superb eating.

To juice, squeeze as much out of the pomegranate as you can. Add the seeds to a blender and blend until pulpy. Press through a sieve.

Grenadine is reduced pomegranate juice. Moroccan pomegranate molasses is made by reducing the juice until it is thick and sticky.

A Drop More

Eaux-de-vie

BRANDY IS DISTILLED FROM WINE, Calvados from cider. Schnapps and liqueurs are made by steeping fruits or plants in alcohol and then sweetening the result with sugar. Those spirits most commonly called eaux-de-vie, on the other hand, are distilled directly from a mash of fermented fruit. Historically, people have used whatever crop was available—plums for slivovic, mirabelle or quetsch, raspberries for framboise, pears for poire Williams and cherries for kirsch. But in places where wine is made, the obvious fruit has always been the pomace of grape skins and stalks left in the fermentation tanks after the new wine has been removed.

The French were the first to give this eau-de-vie de marc the time to fully express itself. I remember putting my nose to the bung hole of a barrel of newly distilled marc in a damp and ancient cellar in Jura, in the foothills of the French Alps. The smell was startling—almost acrid, reeking of celery and onion. The owner of the cellar smiled knowingly and assured me that time would take care of everything. And indeed, the cask at the end of the line had held its marc for five years, and a heavenly transformation had taken place. The ethyl fires had mellowed; the colorless spirit had turned straw yellow and drawn flavors of spice and vanilla from the oak. Most strangely, the walnutty aroma of the Savagnin grapes from which it had been distilled had returned from the dead like an unlooked-for legacy.

French marc has been treasured for centuries; Italian grappa—same drink—took longer to capture the public palate, remaining a private, farmhouse solace until the 1930s. Mussolini first encouraged commercial production after the French banned exports of Cognac to Italy as a protest against Il Duce's invasion of Abyssinia. Today's grappas can be very sophisticated spirits. Refrigerating the pomace between press and still seems to give grappa a smoother body, while new stills that bathe the pomace in low-temperature steam catch more of the concentrated fruit flavors. Connoisseurs can choose from grappas made from all sorts of individual grape varieties. As with any good eau-de-vie, the sign of quality is the complete integration of fruitiness and alcohol. Pour a little into a brandy glass and sniff. The scent of the fruit should fill your head. Take a small sip and roll it around the tongue. There should be no gap between the flavor of the fruit and the heat of the alcohol. The aftertaste should linger as long as possible.

Such tests are best carried out at room temperature, where any flaws in the spirit are most apparent. Marc and wood-aged grappa should also be drunk at room temperature, I believe, for chilling can overemphasize tannins from the wood and make them seem bitter. Clear, young grappas, however, are delicious poured straight from the freezer. They become denser and smoother when cold. Sensations of sweetness are muted, while volatile elements that are released as odors at warmer temperatures also tend to calm down, so the cold spirit smells less alcoholic.

Grappa and marc are capable of great complexities of flavor. Fruit eaux-de-vie are more about length and intensity. Or raw power. Once upon a time in a restaurant in a castle in the Croatian countryside, my host and I ate our way through most of a meat-heavy menu. Between each course, at my friend's insistence, we downed a shot of the rough-and-ready local slivovic—"To relieve the weight of the food," he explained. Not so much cleansing the palate as stunning it, the plum firewater certainly knocked the jagged edge off the accompanying wines. A similar tradition in Normandy punctuates a banquet with a shot of Calvados, the famous *"trou normand."* More refined tastes observe the spirit of the occasion by bathing a spoonful of sorbet or granita in a little grappa or dry, clear eau-de-vie de framboise. A rare marc might best be saved for the end of the meal, when its fragrance will hover delightfully over the palate till bedtime.

ALTERNATIVE CHRISTMAS DINNER

•

NEW YEAR'S EVE

•

EASY COCKTAIL PARTY

•

BURNS NIGHT SUPPER

WINTER

A SENSUAL VALENTINE'S DINNER

•

SKI CHALET DINNER

•

A SPANISH DINNER

•

FAST AND FRESH
DUCK AND CHOCOLATE

•

FAST AND FRESH
SOUTHERN COMFORT

winter food

I LOOK FORWARD TO WINTER. I dream about the fires in the fireplace, the crisp white snow and snuggling down with a good book.

And, of course, the food—comforting casseroles slowly bubbling in the oven, a splendid piece of beef or lamb roasted to juicy perfection for a family gathering, a proper pudding gently baked or steamed.

Big celebrations are part of winter, too. Christmas and Hanukkah, New Year's, Burns Night and Valentine's Day—occasions that inspire fine meals.

When I was growing up in Scotland, we could not get many imported vegetables or fruits in winter. Instead we existed on local kale, chard, turnips, parsnips, potatoes and apples. Occasionally green beans would come into the stores and we would be so thrilled to see a new vegetable on the plate.

Although we can now buy produce from all over the world even in the depths of winter, it is still the seasonal roots and greens that taste the best to me. "Winter kissed," we called them in Scotland.

winter drinks

FOOD LEADS THE WAY INTO WINTERTIME. Feasts and parties offer consolation for the cold and darkness. Diets are put on hold, with promises of abstinence postponed until the New Year. And as dishes become more robust, richer and full of deep flavors, wines have to keep up. Paying attention to the body of a wine, making sure its fullness can stand up to the weight of the food, is more important than ever.

Sometimes the best part of winter starts, dare I say it, after the guests have stomped off into the blizzard, dark shapes soon lost to view in the swirling snow. Leave the dishes until tomorrow. Dim the lights, put another log on the fire, pour something purple and profound into a wineglass and think about how lucky you are to be indoors rather than out.

Alternative Christmas Dinner

Scallop and Fennel Soup
Mustard-glazed Standing Rib Roast with Pan Gravy
Potato and Mushroom Gratin • Roasted Vegetable Melange
Sautéed Sugar Snap Peas
Sticky Toffee Pudding

SERVES 8

MEAT HAS BECOME the new indulgence, and there is something especially stately and welcoming about a large roast of beef. Some of my best memories are of family dinners where we exchanged news and chatted around a table that featured a rib roast.

In Britain, a large roast used to be featured at the traditional Sunday lunch. Today it is served at celebrations like Christmas dinner. Americans eat turkey at Thanksgiving a month before Christmas, so roast beef has replaced it as the Christmas meal in many homes.

This richly textured menu also works with a roast turkey (page 232) as the centerpiece, and, as an added benefit, most of the meal can be prepared ahead. Make the soup base up to two days ahead. The potatoes and roasted vegetables can be cooked the day before and reheated in a 350°F oven for 20 to 30 minutes. Blanch the sugar snaps ahead of time and reheat in the skillet just before serving. The pudding and sauce can also be made up to two days ahead and reheated.

Blanquette de Limoux

MUCH SERIOUS EATING LIES AHEAD, so the drink of greeting should probably be a true aperitif rather than an end in itself—something light and tart and charming that will pique but not satisfy the appetite. Champagne is never far from our thoughts during the festive season, but this is an alternative Christmas and therefore an alternative bubbly is required. France is full of ethereal sparkling wines from regions other than Champagne. Most of them are called Crémant—Crémant de Bourgogne, d'Alsace, de Loire, de Bordeaux, de Die . . . The most ancient is from Limoux in Languedoc, though it has only recently been named a Crémant. Before that, it was known as Blanquette de Limoux, made in the same way as Champagne, with a second fermentation in the bottle, but with a history at least a century older.

Traditionally, Blanquette had always been made with the grapes of the area—Mauzac, which has a delicious cider-apple flavor, and a little Clairette. Changing laws in the past two decades allowed more Chardonnay and Chenin Blanc to infiltrate the blend, increasing marketability but also threatening the unique character of the ancient bubbly. Today, Crémant de Limoux stands comfortably alongside the Crémants of other regions. But some is still produced in the older style, still called Blanquette, and still with a hefty percentage of Mauzac in the blend.

How can a white wine from so far south taste so fresh and crisp and, well, northern? The vineyards are high in the southwest of Languedoc, in the foothills of the Pyrenees, influenced as much by the Atlantic as the Mediterranean. Blanquette, incidentally, just means "white" in Occitan, the old "langue d'Oc."

Frothy, lightweight and different, Blanquette or Crémant de Limoux has the anecdotal trappings to get the preprandial conversation going while fulfilling its purpose as an aperitif.

Scallop and Fennel Soup

SERVES 8

In this soup, the sweetness of the scallops is subtly balanced by the licorice-tinged fennel. Make the soup ahead and then reheat, being careful not to bring it to a boil. It will overcook the scallops, and the soup will taste grainy instead of smooth.

2 tbsp butter	1 lb scallops, trimmed
1 cup chopped onions	¼ cup whipping cream
2 cups chopped fennel	½ tsp grated orange zest
1 tsp ground fennel seed	Salt and freshly ground pepper
1 tsp chopped garlic	¼ cup chopped chives
4 cups chicken or fish stock	

Heat butter in a large pot over medium heat. Add onions and fennel and sauté for 3 to 4 minutes, or until beginning to soften.

Add fennel seed and garlic and sauté for 2 minutes, or until fragrant.

Add stock and bring to a boil. Reduce heat and simmer for 10 minutes, or until vegetables are soft.

Add scallops and simmer gently for 2 minutes, or until scallops are opaque.

Remove 4 scallops and reserve for garnish. Puree remaining soup with cream in a food processor (a hand blender does not work as well with this soup).

Return soup to pot. Add zest, salt and pepper and reheat gently over low heat just until hot.

Slice reserved scallops thinly and garnish soup with scallops and chives.

Fennel Fennel is a creamy white succulent bulb—a treat both raw and cooked. Its faint licorice taste goes well with fish and chicken. To prepare it, cut off the stalks and leafy tops. (The ferny fronds can also be used as a garnish.) Peel off any brown or bruised outer layers, cut the bulb in half and remove the thick root in the center. Cut the bulb into quarters or slice or chop.

Fennel can be roasted, cooked in broth, sautéed or grilled. To use raw fennel in a salad, shave it thinly using a mandolin or sharp knife.

And to drink . . .

THE MAIN EVENT, the big match at the heart of this meal, is the clinch of red wine and beef, but the opening bout on the card must not be neglected, especially since it offers much more of a challenge. The old books warn against serving any wine with a soup, arguing that a hot thick liquid and a cold thin one do not work well together. What's more, this is a fennel soup, and fennel contains anethole, the tongue-tingling essential oil that also adds its unique flavor to anise and licorice and is famously hostile to wine. The good news is that cooking fennel softens the perception of the anethole, while all the other wine-friendly ingredients in this subtle and delicious recipe smooth the way to some fascinating harmonies.

Think about a Pinot Blanc from Alsace, Oregon or British Columbia. Especially in their Alsatian incarnations, these delicately aromatic white wines have a voluptuous weight that won't be intimidated by the richness of butter and pureed scallops. They also have a respectable acidity to refresh the mouth and lift the soup's flavors. Lacking the intense fruit of a Riesling or Sauvignon, Pinot Blanc won't overwhelm the subtle effects in the bowl. Instead, the wine's discreet aromas complement the different sweetnesses of sautéed fennel and onions and gently simmered scallops. With so many components of the soup and the wine getting on famously, the anise taste of the fennel floats free, hovering in the foreground of the picture.

Perhaps an even better idea comes out of left field. Serve glasses of chilled dry white vermouth. The herbal and citrus flavors in the drink work brilliantly with fennel, and vermouth has ample weight to balance the pureed soup and the richness of the scallops.

Mustard-glazed Standing Rib Roast with Pan Gravy

SERVES 8

The secret to a great rib roast is to begin with great meat. Look for marbled, aged meat such as naturally raised prime beef. For easier carving, have the butcher remove the chine bone. I like to remove the meat from the rib bones before cooking and then tie the roast back together. Before serving, I cut the strings, remove the meat and slice. Then I add a bone to the bone lovers' plates.

Broiling the roast before roasting results in lots of crispy fat and makes the first few slices more well cooked than the center—good for those who don't care for rare beef. Cook the roast for 15 minutes per pound, plus an extra 15 minutes for rare; cook for 20 minutes per pound plus an extra 20 minutes for medium beef.

⅓ cup Dijon mustard	1 tbsp coarsely ground pepper
2 tbsp olive oil	1 tbsp chopped fresh rosemary or thyme,
2 tbsp soy sauce	or 1 tsp dried
1 tbsp chopped garlic	1 standing rib roast (about 7 lbs)
2 tbsp chopped parsley	Salt to taste

Combine mustard, oil, soy sauce, garlic, parsley, pepper and rosemary. Brush over roast, including bones. Let sit for 2 hours, or refrigerate overnight.

Preheat oven to 450°F. Turn on oven broiler. Place roast fat side up on a rack in a roasting pan and broil for about 4 minutes, or until fat is crispy. Turn off broiler, reheat oven to 450°F and roast for 30 minutes.

Reduce heat to 350°F and roast for about 1½ hours longer for rare.

Remove roast to a carving board and let rest for 15 minutes to allow juices to retract while you make gravy. Remove roast from bones and carve into thin slices. Serve with gravy.

And to drink . . .

THE MOST HARMONIOUS MARRIAGE of beef and wine I have ever experienced took place fifteen years ago in Argentina. The beef had been spit-grilled very slowly in the local fashion and was cooked through but still fairly moist and superbly meaty. The wine was a fine Malbec from Mendoza's Luján de Cuyo area, made in the traditional way with long aging in the barrel. Even then it was going out of fashion, as winemakers experimented with a more fruity international style, but it had the perfect qualities for that beef—a touch of spicy cherry in the bouquet but with a wealth of soft tannins from grape and wood and a subtle mineral edge. It was wonderfully smooth and sophisticated, as sleek and supple as soft, polished leather.

One of these mature Argentinian Malbecs would be great with Lucy's roast beef, but they are highly valued in their own country and finding them elsewhere can be a problem. Just as satisfactory would be a fine red from Bordeaux's Pomerol region. Unlike the Cabernet-based stars that shine forth from most areas of Bordeaux, Pomerol reds showcase Merlot as the principal variety in the blend. By local standards they are opulent and fruity, but don't expect the soft, easygoing accessibility of a Merlot from California. This is still France, and the wines show an elegance and a tannic and acidic structure that are decidedly Old World—the very characteristics that make such beautiful music with a magnificent standing rib roast.

Pan Gravy Pour all but 2 tbsp fat from roasting pan. Add ½ cup chopped shallots and cook over medium-high heat for 3 minutes, or until shallots are brown around edges. Stir in 2 tbsp all-purpose flour and cook, stirring, for 2 minutes, or until browned. Gradually stir in ¼ cup red wine, 1 tbsp balsamic vinegar, 3 cups beef stock and 1 tsp tomato paste. Bring to a boil, stirring. Reduce heat and simmer for 5 minutes, or until gravy is thick and glossy. Season with salt and pepper.

Makes about 2 cups.

Food Tech

Salt and Pepper

Salt Not all salts are equal. Forget about regular table salt, which is mined and ground down to a fine powder before being iodized and mixed with additives to keep it free running. It will do, but just in a pinch.

I use kosher salt for everyday cooking. It is an additive-free coarse-grained salt preferred by chefs and foodies for its "flake" texture that melts easily. You need less of this salt in cooking than you would regular table salt, as it has a purer flavor.

Gray sea salt comes from seawater evaporated in shallow clay basins by the heat of the Mediterranean sun. The salt is gray because it touches the clay basins and takes on the color. It is raked with wooden rakes so no metal ever comes in contact with it. It is naturally moist and high in trace mineral content.

The finest salt of all comes from the coast of Brittany in France. Specially prized by connoisseurs, fleur de sel—the flower of salt—is the topmost layer of gray salt. Fleur de sel's pristine white crystals never touch the clay basins. This special salt is very expensive and is used only for finishing a dish. Sprinkle a few grains on a juicy fresh tomato, some silky foie gras or on a beautifully barbecued steak and taste the difference. Any of the Brittany brands of fleur de sel are excellent, although each is prized for its own special flavor.

Many salt varieties are produced in other parts of the world. Other favorites include Maldon salt, which is produced in Essex, England, and Halen Mon from Wales. These salts have a light snowflake-like appearance and are made through a natural evaporation of seawater. They dissolve gently on the tongue.

Pepper At one time peppercorns were so precious that they were used as currency, but today they are relatively inexpensive. Peppercorns have a unique pungency that stimulates our gastric juices as well as cooling us down in hot weather. There are many different varieties, but to my taste the finest are Tellicherry peppercorns from Malabar in India. Left longer on the vine to develop in size and flavor, Tellicherry pepper is picked green and left in the sun to ripen into the familiar black Tellicherry color. When cracked, these peppercorns add a singular spiciness to dishes. You will find you need less pepper when you grind Tellicherry, too.

Potato and Mushroom Gratin

SERVES 8

We used dried porcini mushrooms in this recipe because they have the most flavor, but you can use any dried mushrooms. Bake this ahead and then reheat at 350°F for 20 to 30 minutes before removing the sides of the springform.

½ cup dried mushrooms

2 cups hot water or beef stock

4 lbs Yukon Gold potatoes,
   peeled and thinly sliced

1 cup milk

1 clove garlic, peeled and crushed

Salt and pepper to taste

2 tbsp butter

4 oz fresh shiitake mushrooms,
   trimmed and sliced

8 oz fresh cremini mushrooms, sliced

1 tsp chopped garlic

Salt and freshly ground pepper

¼ cup whipping cream

Soak mushrooms in hot water or stock for 15 minutes.

Combine potatoes, milk, dried mushrooms, mushroom soaking liquid and crushed garlic in a pot and bring to a boil over high heat. Reduce heat and simmer for 8 minutes, or until potatoes are slightly softened. Drain, reserving cooking liquid.

Heat butter in a large skillet over medium heat while potatoes are cooking. Add shiitake and cremini mushrooms and sauté for 2 minutes. Add chopped garlic and sauté for 2 minutes longer, or until mushrooms are limp and any liquid disappears.

Preheat oven to 375°F.

Spread one-third of potato mixture in a buttered 10-inch springform pan placed on a baking sheet. Season well with salt and pepper. Cover potatoes with half the sautéed mushrooms and one-third of reserved cooking liquid. Repeat layers, finishing with potatoes.

Combine cream and remaining potato cooking liquid. Pour over top layer of potatoes.

Bake for 35 to 45 minutes, or until potatoes are tender and top is browned. Let sit for 15 minutes before removing sides of springform. Place on a serving plate and cut into wedges.

Roasted Vegetable Melange

SERVES 8

A combination of several veggies roasted to an intense gold color makes my mouth water. The vegetables can vary as long as they are all cut to the same size. Any shape will work, but I like to cut them into long pieces.

You will need one or two large baking sheets to bake all these vegetables. Roast them ahead and reheat at 350°F for 15 to 20 minutes before serving.

1 lb parsnips	2 red onions, cut in eighths
1 lb carrots	¼ cup olive oil
1 lb sweet potatoes	1 tbsp dried rosemary
1 small rutabaga	Salt and freshly ground pepper

Preheat oven to 400°F.

Peel parsnips, carrots, sweet potatoes and rutabaga and cut into sticks about 1 inch thick and 3 inches long. Toss with onions, oil, rosemary, salt and pepper. Spread vegetables over baking sheets in a single layer. Roast, turning occasionally, for 30 to 40 minutes, or until tender and browned.

Sautéed Sugar Snap Peas

SERVES 8

These crunchy peas give texture to the plate and contrast with the other vegetables. String the peas by pulling off the tough strings from the stem ends.

1 lb sugar snap peas	2 tbsp lemon juice
2 tbsp butter	Salt and freshly ground pepper

Bring a large pot of salted water to a boil. Add peas and boil for 1 to 2 minutes, or until crisp-tender. Drain and refresh with cold water to stop cooking.

Heat butter in a large skillet over medium heat. Add peas and sauté until peas are warm but still crisp, about 3 minutes. Season with lemon juice, salt and pepper.

Sticky Toffee Pudding

SERVES 8

Scrumptious sticky puddings are a staple of British cooking, and of my dessert repertoire. This one is my particular favorite because of its rich caramel flavor. Make it as individual desserts or as one big one. Use the luscious Medjool dates for the best result.

To reheat, place the pudding in an ovenproof dish and bake at 350°F for 10 minutes. Serve warm, drizzled with sauce, with ice cream.

¾ cup boiling water	⅓ cup butter, at room temperature
1½ cups chopped pitted dates	1 cup brown sugar
1 tsp baking soda	2 eggs
1¾ cups all-purpose flour	½ cup grated peeled apple
1 tsp baking powder	2 tsp grated lime zest
½ tsp salt	

Pour boiling water over dates. Let soak for 30 minutes, or until dates soften. Stir in baking soda.

Preheat oven to 350°F. Butter a 9-inch square cake pan and line base with parchment paper. (You can also use 8 well-greased individual molds or ramekins.) Sift together flour, baking powder and salt.

Cream butter and sugar with an electric mixer until light and fluffy. Add eggs one at a time, beating well after each addition.

Add one-third of the flour and half the date mixture to butter mixture, stirring to combine after each addition. Stir in another third of flour and remainder of date mixture. Then add remaining flour and combine. Stir in grated apple and lime zest.

Spoon batter into prepared pan. Bake for 30 to 35 minutes, or until a skewer comes out clean and center of pudding feels firm to the touch. (Individual molds will take about 25 minutes.)

Cool for 5 minutes, then unmold onto a serving dish.

> **Sticky Toffee Sauce** In a pot, combine ½ cup butter, 1 cup brown sugar, 1 tbsp corn syrup and ½ cup whipping cream. Bring to a boil over high heat and boil for about 5 minutes, or until mixture thickens.
> Makes about 2 cups.

And to drink . . .

LITERATURE'S GREATEST TESTIMONIAL to Hungarian Tokay (or, more correctly, Tokaji) is a book called *My Talks with Dean Spanley*, written in 1936 by the eccentric Irish peer, Lord Dunsany. It concerns a very respectable, soft-spoken, elderly English clergyman who, after taking two glasses of Tokay after dinner, regularly enters a trance-like state and reminisces about a previous life he led as a dog on a farm in Ireland. If that isn't enough to send you out in search of this unique elixir, let me tell you the tale of Chateau Megyer, an estate whose vineyards were declared a grand cru in 1737 by imperial decree.

The grapes—Furmint, Harslevelu and Yellow Muscat—grow on a hillside in a valley sheltered on three sides by the Carpathian Mountains. In the long, warm, misty autumn days, botrytis (or *aszú*, as it is known in Hungary) goes to work in the vineyard, and the shriveled, half-rotten grapes are picked by hand in November and mashed into paste. The paste is measured into baskets (*puttonyos*) and then tipped into barrels of white wine made from healthy grapes from the same vineyards. How many basketfuls they add—three, four, five, six or more—depends on how sweet they wish the wine to be. The wine and the honey-sweet, moldy mash spend some days together, slowly refermenting. Then the mixture is gently pressed again and the new wine goes into barrels for anything from four to eight years to age in mold-covered cellars dug like tunnels into the mountains—cellars that were originally designed to hide the precious liquid from marauding Turkish soldiers.

Complex, spicy, bizarre—like dried apricots, ginger, truffled honey and autumn woods—five- or six-puttonyos Tokay has the weight and intensity to match a sticky toffee pudding. Whether or not it will unlock the secrets of the migration of souls is another matter.

New Year's Eve

Sushi Oysters

Salmon Spring Rolls with Spiced Balsamic Dipping Sauce

Scallop Ravioli with Blood Orange Sauce

Prosciutto-wrapped Veal Tenderloin

Ricotta and Olive Mashed Potatoes

Sautéed Baby Bok Choy • Roasted Tomatoes

Coffee Pots de Crème

SERVES 6

FOR THE PAST TWENTY YEARS, my husband, Bruce, and I have celebrated New Year's Eve with the same friends. We love bringing in the new year with people we have a history with. It means great conversation and a personal touch that a glitzy party never gives you. We plan good menus and switch houses from year to year. This menu, which features scallops, veal and oysters, is one of our most popular, designed to work with excellent wines. With the right pacing we usually have dessert just before midnight.

Chablis

OYSTERS ARE ENORMOUSLY VERSATILE CREATURES, perfectly at home in a wide variety of social situations. They are delighted to yack it up at the bar of a rowdy pub with a pint of Guinness close by, but they also relish more intellectual conversation with a bottle of good Chablis. And sometimes they put on their pearls and murmur seductively for Champagne.

But a pint of stout probably isn't the best way to start this elegant evening, and those who like to drown the chimes of midnight with the popping of Champagne corks may not wish to foreshadow that drama. Chablis will be perfect for guests who love their oysters as nature intended—unadorned and tasting of the ocean. However, Lucy's delicious garnishes of ginger, soy and wasabi suggest chilled sake (page 41) as a better accompaniment.

Not entirely by coincidence, Chablis and chilled sake are both fabulous with the salmon spring rolls. The innate illusion of sweetness in even the driest sake complements the sweetness of the soft, rich fish and also works beautifully with the salty, tissue-thin layer of nori that envelopes it. The Chablis, on the other hand, has a cool, refreshing edge and vigorous acidity that provides an irresistible contrast with each scrumptious bite.

Sushi Oysters

SERVES 6

When I lived in a little fishing village on the east coast of England, we would go down to the docks in the mornings and watch the oyster boats come in. These were Mersea oysters, famous in Britain for their briny taste. The oyster men told me that the most important guide to buying good oysters is to trust your fishmonger to tell you the truth about freshness. Choose oysters that have been out of the water for less than five to seven days. A good oyster feels like a solid, heavy weight in your hand. It should have a good teardrop shape and a rounded cup, or top shell.

The oyster men also advised me never to buy oysters unless there was an R in the month (colder waters produce better oysters), though with today's farmed oysters, that rule no longer holds.

Here, hot wasabi contrasts beautifully with the icy oysters. It is a brilliant combination.

24 oysters, shucked
Sliced pickled ginger

Soy sauce
Wasabi paste

Place oysters on a platter.
Surround with a heap of pickled ginger, a little jug of soy sauce and a dish of wasabi. Let guests add condiments of their choice to oysters.

Oysters If oysters are very fresh, they should last, in the shell and covered with a wet cloth, for three days in the coldest part of the refrigerator.

To open or shuck an oyster, place it cup side down on a rough cloth. Insert a short oyster knife near the hinge and work in with a twisting motion. Twist off the flat shell.

The connoisseurs recommend a squeeze of lemon on the oysters before slipping them down your throat.

Salmon Spring Rolls with Spiced Balsamic Dipping Sauce

MAKES ABOUT 20 SPRING ROLLS

Everyone loves these spring rolls because they have real taste and texture. The soft salmon contrasts with the crisp skin. They can be fried up to 5 hours ahead of time and briefly reheated on a rack in a 350°F oven.

1 lb salmon fillet	1 package 8-inch square spring roll
2 tbsp fish sauce	wrappers
2 tbsp grated gingerroot	1 egg, beaten
2 tbsp vegetable oil	Vegetable oil for deep frying
1 tsp hot Asian chili sauce	Spiced Balsamic Dipping Sauce
1/4 cup chopped green onions	1/4 cup mirin
1/4 cup chopped fresh coriander	2 tbsp soy sauce
Salt and freshly ground pepper	1/4 cup balsamic vinegar
5 sheets nori	1/2 tsp hot Asian chili sauce

Slice salmon into pieces about 3 inches long and 1/2 inch wide.

Combine fish sauce, ginger, oil and chili sauce and toss with salmon. Marinate for 1 hour. Sprinkle with green onions and coriander and season with salt and pepper.

Cut sheets of nori into quarters. Lay a spring roll wrapper on counter with corner facing you. Top with a sheet of nori. Place a piece of salmon lengthwise across center of nori.

Brush wrapper edges with beaten egg. Fold closest corner up to 1/2 inch from top point, making a triangle that encloses salmon in nori and wrapper. Fold in sides over salmon and roll tightly away from you. Seal well and place seam side down on a baking sheet. Continue with remaining rolls.

Heat about 2 inches of oil in a wok or large skillet over high heat. When oil is hot, fry rolls, two or three at a time, for 1 1/2 to 2 minutes, or until golden. Drain on paper towels.

Prepare sauce by combining mirin, soy sauce, vinegar and chili sauce.

Serve spring rolls on a platter with dipping sauce.

Scallop Ravioli with Blood Orange Sauce

SERVES 6

We chose the ingredients for our exquisite cover photograph for their beauty and their superb tastes. Then it was my job to come up with a recipe worthy of those ingredients. Grind star anise in a coffee grinder or spice mill; if you can't find it, use ground fennel seeds. These ravioli can be made ahead. Immerse in boiling water for 1 minute to reheat.

8 oz scallops	40 wonton wrappers or dumpling skins, approx.
4 oz oyster mushrooms, trimmed and sliced	1 egg yolk, beaten
¼ cup chopped shallots	Blood Orange Sauce
2 tbsp chopped Thai basil	1 cup red wine
2 tsp grated orange zest	½ cup blood orange juice
1 tsp chopped green chilies	1 tbsp granulated sugar
1 tsp chopped gingerroot	¼ cup butter, diced
1 tsp chopped garlic	2 tbsp chopped chives
½ tsp ground star anise	Garnish
1 egg white	Thai basil sprigs
Salt and freshly ground pepper	6 whole star anise

Place scallops, mushrooms, shallots, basil, orange zest, chilies, ginger, garlic and star anise in a food processor and combine. With the machine running, add egg white through feed tube and process until smooth. Season with salt and pepper. (Cook a small amount of mixture in a skillet to check seasonings.) Lay a wonton wrapper on counter. Brush egg yolk around edges. Place 1 tbsp scallop mixture in center. Place second skin on top and press together, being sure to eliminate any air pockets. Continue until all ingredients are used.

Bring a large pot of salted water to a boil. Add ravioli and boil for about 2 minutes, or until ravioli float and scallop mixture is cooked through.

Combine wine, orange juice and sugar in a pot. Boil over high heat for 6 to 8 minutes, or until syrupy. Remove from heat and whisk in butter until emulsified. Stir in chives.

Pour sauce on plates and top with 3 ravioli per person. Garnish with Thai basil and star anise.

And to drink . . .

HERE'S ONE OF THOSE FASCINATING DISHES that lies close to the cusp where white wine merges into red. Lining up most of the principal flavors—plump scallops, blood orange juice, star anise—suggests one of the zingier Californian or Chilean Sauvignon Blancs. The best of them sometimes deliver hints of orange and fennel in their smoothly tailored profiles. But Lucy has taken the sauce a step or two further, bringing in red wine, and that pushes our wine choice in the same direction. A red wine is required, but a red from the lightest end of the spectrum that won't overwhelm the scallops with heavy fruit or disrupt their flavor with tannins. Pinot Noir from one of the world's cooler regions fits the bill—from Alsace, perhaps, where a handful of producers are currently making some delicately complex Pinots. If that proves too hard to find (and the limited production does make rarities of these treats), look to Oregon: good Pinot Noir from the Pacific Northwest is full of character and elegance. Pinot from B.C.'s Okanagan Valley, Niagara, Tasmania or New Zealand could also work well. A final suggestion might be a Chinon from the Loire—as suave and lightweight an example of the Cabernet Franc grape as one could hope to find. But even that might be too red a red.

The final verdict? An elegant, cool-climate Pinot Noir.

Star Anise Powerful, licorice-flavored star anise is a beautiful spice because it has a perfect star shape, with five to ten points radiating from the center. These hard sections are the seed pods.

Star anise is traditionally added to Chinese soups and stews to provide a characteristic licorice flavor, but it is now a popular ingredient in many other cuisines. It is added to syrups, sweets and jams and is used to make the liqueur anisette. It is also an ingredient in Chinese five-spice powder.

Prosciutto-wrapped Veal Tenderloin

SERVES 6

Veal can be quite bland, but this recipe injects it with flavor, courtesy of the salty prosciutto and herbal sage leaves. Veal tenderloin comes in different sizes, so you may need two or three for this recipe.

8 to 12 thin slices prosciutto	6 cloves garlic, sliced
24 to 36 fresh sage leaves, torn	¼ cup Marsala
2½ lbs veal tenderloin	2 cups chicken or veal stock
2 tsp cracked peppercorns	2 tbsp butter, diced
2 tsp grated lemon zest	Salt and freshly ground pepper
2 tbsp olive oil	

Lay 4 slices prosciutto overlapping on a sheet of parchment paper. Scatter prosciutto with sage leaves (amount will depend on how many tenderloins you use). Place tenderloin across prosciutto slices at one end and season with cracked pepper and lemon zest. Using paper as a guide, roll prosciutto and sage leaves around tenderloin. Tie in three places with string. Repeat with remaining tenderloin.

Preheat oven to 400°F.

Heat oil in a skillet over medium-high heat. Add garlic and cook for 30 seconds, or until beginning to turn golden. Remove garlic from skillet.

Add tenderloins to skillet in batches. Cook for about 1 minute per side to crisp prosciutto. Transfer to a roasting pan. Scatter garlic over veal.

Roast veal for 20 to 25 minutes, or until tenderloins are just pink. Remove to a carving board and let rest for 5 minutes.

Add Marsala to skillet while veal is roasting. Bring to a boil over high heat and boil until Marsala has reduced to 1 tbsp. Add stock and boil for 5 minutes, or until beginning to thicken—mixture should lightly coat back of a spoon. Reduce heat to low and whisk in butter. Season with salt and pepper.

Slice tenderloins and serve with sauce.

And to drink . . .

LUCY LOVES TO SERVE BURGUNDY with this delectably upgraded version of saltimbocca, and there's no doubt that it works beautifully. Following a lighter Pinot with a mature Côte de Beaune carries its own satisfying logic and offers interesting opportunities for comparison. But many other middle-weight reds will also perform well with this course. The veal itself is almost irrelevant in the decision, politely retreating behind the stronger flavors on the plate. The herby personality of a good-quality wine from Provence's Côtes du Ventoux or Côtes du Lubéron will pick up the sage as well as the olives in the mashed potatoes. A well-made Valpolicella Classico Superiore comes at the dish from another direction, its cherry-like fruit reaching for the sweetness in the prosciutto and canoodling with the roasted tomatoes. A cru Beaujolais or one of Ontario's top-flight Gamay Noirs will behave in a similar way.

It's almost easier to list the reds that won't show their best, either because they threaten to overwhelm the delicate taste of the veal with an inky whack of fruit or because they have too much tannin that might be embittered by the salt in the prosciutto. Lucy is still recommending her Burgundy, pointing out that the wine need not always defer to the dish and that a gorgeous mature Côte de Beaune brings its own treasure trove of aromas and attributes to the table.

Ricotta and Olive Mashed Potatoes

SERVES 6

These mashed potatoes go perfectly with the veal. Use Kalamata olives if you can find them.

2 lbs Yukon Gold potatoes,
   peeled and halved
½ cup hot milk

¾ cup ricotta cheese
½ cup black olives, pitted and chopped
Salt and freshly ground pepper

Place potatoes in a pot of cold salted water. Bring to a boil over high heat. Reduce heat and boil for 10 to 15 minutes, or until tender.
Drain potatoes well, return to pot and shake pot over turned-off burner to dry potatoes.
Mash potatoes with a potato masher, potato ricer or a food mill. Beat in milk and ricotta with a wooden spoon. Fold in olives. Season with salt and pepper.

Sautéed Baby Bok Choy

SERVES 6

Larger bok choy may be substituted, but cut it into strips before sautéing.

4 cups baby bok choy
2 tbsp vegetable oil
2 tsp chopped garlic

1 tbsp soy sauce
1 tbsp water

Cut bok choy in half.
Heat oil in a large skillet over high heat. Add garlic and sauté for 30 seconds. Add bok choy and sauté for 2 minutes, or until leaves wilt.
Add soy sauce and water. Stir together and cook for 1 minute, or until bok choy is tender.

Roasted Tomatoes

SERVES 6

In winter, cherry tomatoes are the only tomatoes with any taste, and roasting intensifies their flavor. This dish adds sweetness and color to the main course.

24 cherry tomatoes, halved and seeded
2 tbsp olive oil
Salt and freshly ground pepper

Preheat oven to 400°F.
Toss tomatoes with oil, salt and pepper. Place cut side up on a baking sheet.
Bake for 20 to 30 minutes, or until tomatoes are shrunken but not dry.

Coffee Pots de Crème

SERVES 6

These delicate custards can be made in ovenproof espresso cups, topped with whipped cream and shaved chocolate or a solitary coffee bean. They should really be served with freshly fried beignets, but that is too much to do at the last minute, so buy some doughnuts and heat them in the oven if you feel the need. Ramekin sizes vary—this recipe will fill six large ramekins or eight small ones.

1½ cups milk
1 cup whipping cream
1 tbsp ground coffee (not instant)

1 tsp vanilla
5 egg yolks
⅓ cup granulated sugar

Preheat oven to 300°F.

Combine milk, cream and coffee in a small pot. Bring to a boil over medium heat. Remove from heat and stir in vanilla. Cool slightly.

Whisk egg yolks with sugar and cream mixture. Strain through a coffee filter into a large measuring cup to remove coffee granules.

Place ramekins in a large pan. Pour strained custard into ramekins, filling them three-quarters full. Pour hot water into pan until it reaches halfway up sides of ramekins.

Place a sheet of parchment paper over ramekins. Transfer pan to oven and bake for 35 to 50 minutes, depending on ramekin size, or until custards have just a slight wobble in center.

Remove ramekins from water and cool.

And to drink . . .

SHAVED CHOCOLATE, SUGGESTS LUCY, would be an appropriate garnish for these luscious custards. With or without, my first choice as an accompaniment is a ten- or twenty-year-old tawny port (page 167). But it's New Year's Eve and no time to be timid. In Australia, around the town of Rutherglen in northeastern Victoria, the noblest scion of the extended Muscat family, Muscat à petits grains, is used to produce a uniquely heavy, intense dessert wine known as Liqueur Muscat. The brown grapes are left on the vine until they are almost raisined. The supersweet, treacly juice they yield is partially fermented, then fortified with neutral brandy and left to age in wooden barrels in stiflingly hot sheds. Younger wines are sometimes added to older, a little like the solera system used to mature sherry.

What eventually emerges (and these wines can age for decades) is a viscous, heavy Muscat that can handle just about any dessert known to man. Chocolate, mocha and even ice cream present no problem at all. Given their weight, the most surprising thing about these wines is their obvious quality and finesse and the endless resonances of raisiny flavor that carom around the palate. At their heart shines that luminous Muscat grapiness, a fresh taste that seems impervious to the heat of the vineyard and the torments inflicted by the winemaker. It is a taste immune to time, and that is an attribute to be cherished as another year passes.

Wine Tech

Air

DOES OPENING A BOTTLE of young Cabernet Sauvignon an hour or two before you need it improve the wine? Does it have any effect at all? Some years ago, I set about seeking the answer and found only controversy. Half my wine books vowed that it helped the wine breathe; the others scoffed at the idea, pointing out that pulling the cork exposed no more than a dime-sized fraction of the liquid to the air. Sommeliers and wine professionals were equally argumentative, though they all agreed that a minute with the cork out lets any "bottle stink" dissipate. I did some experiments with a Chianti and a Cabernet from Idaho. In both cases the bottles that had stood open for two hours seemed fruitier and had less of a tannic grip than those that had not. A third bottle of each, decanted, was even more welcoming.

Exposure to oxygen does open up a tight young red, mellowing tannins and letting flavors unfurl. It's true, however, that the same effect is achieved if you sit and swirl the wine in its glass for five minutes before you sip.

Decanting won't make an immature wine suddenly mature, and it isn't for every wine. Whites, rosés and simple, low-tannin reds can even lose a little of their natural zip if poured and allowed to sit in the open air. Sparkling wines, obviously, fall flat on their faces. The main purpose of decanting is to separate a long-aged wine from any solid matter that may have precipitated out over time. Vintage and crusted ports require it. So do many big reds that are growing long in the tooth, but not too long. The whole process may prove too traumatic for very old, fragile reds, destroying their last precious moments of energy.

There are other minor considerations. The sight of candlelight glinting off red wine in a beautiful glass decanter is undoubtedly pleasing, and decanting assures an even playing field if the host wants to play Guess the Wine (that humbling game). Some people enjoy the ceremony and formality of passing a decanter around the table, especially if it's filled with vintage port. Tradition requires that the host fills the glass of the guest on his or her right, then his or her own, then passes the decanter to the left (clockwise). Each guest can choose whether or not to pour a little for themselves before passing the decanter on.

Terroir

A WINE IS A LANDSCAPE PAINTING captured in a bottle. The winegrower and the winemaker are the artists who put brush to canvas, and their styles and skills are part of the painting, but its subject is the landscape itself—the soil, the climate, the quality of the light and the way air and water flow above and beneath the vineyard. The French have a useful word for those elements of place that find their way through the vine into the wine: terroir.

To be sure, it's a difficult concept to pin down. So many other, more apparent influences go into the creation of a wine. Different clones of the same grape variety, different ways of training the vines, pruning fruit and foliage and managing the water that reaches the vineyard all affect the wine's intensity, flavor and body. Choices of when to pick determine its acidity, sugar and alcohol levels. Winemaking methods, from destemming machines to presses to yeasts and fermentation temperatures to decisions about aging—a thousand details—can be far more apparent than that faint but unique fingerprint that tells the aficionado where the vines grew. The vines have to be of a certain age to pick up that ever-so-local accent, but those with ears to hear—and a lifetime of tasting to draw upon—can detect it.

The matter remains controversial. A great many experts, especially in the New World, still scoff at the very idea of terroir; the French have founded their whole system of categorization upon it. I believe it exists. Over the years, certain passionate producers have sat me down with umpteen vintages from two opposite ends of a vineyard and watched as I tried to detect some nuance repeated from year to year. Sometimes I thought I did, though the power of suggestion is strong when the winemaker is staring so hard, muttering words of encouragement.

In food and wine matching, such fleeting details are outweighed by more obvious concerns, but not always. A Toronto chef with a very good palate once startled the assembled wine geeks by serving asparagus with a certain Chardonnay from St. Innocent's Seven Springs vineyard in Oregon. Against all the received wisdom, it was a fabulous match. The winemaker was at the dinner. "It's true," he mused. "Chardonnay from that particular vineyard is always great with asparagus. I have no idea why. Must be the terroir." Must be.

Easy Cocktail Party

GRAVLAX STATION

Gravlax • Mustard Sauce • Breakneck Blinis

MEDITERRANEAN STATION

Eggplant Crush • Fig Confit

Focaccia with Shaved Fennel and Taleggio

NUEVO LATINO STATION

Chilean Beef Filet • Salsa Pebre

Mojo Sauce • Avocado Salad

SERVES 20

I USED TO DREAD hosting a cocktail party. It is exhausting to make fiddly little hors d'oeuvres that guests gobble down in a flash. And finding servers to pass them around is another issue.

I knew there had to be a way to throw this kind of party without the headaches. My solution? Lay out nibblies at self-serve stations so guests can make their own hors d'oeuvres. You might want a little in-kitchen help, but you won't need any servers.

The individual dishes here serve twelve to sixteen, but the whole menu should serve twenty, and it can easily be halved or doubled. All of the dishes can be served at room temperature.

Cocktail Party Stations

FOR THIS PARTY I HAVE CHOSEN three themes (choose two for a smaller group). Look for easy-to-manage spots to display the food, and set up the stations in three places around the house. Find locations that allow people to circulate—it will put an end to crowds hovering around the kitchen door waiting for the next tray of hors d'oeuvres to appear! For example, set up one station in the kitchen, one in the dining room and one in the living room. Provide plates and forks at each station for people to use if they wish.

Gravlax Station The centerpiece of this station is the salmon. Making your own gravlax is easy to do, but if you would rather buy smoked salmon, check around to find a really good product. If your favorite restaurant smokes their own, for instance, ask if you can order from them.

Set out bowls of chopped red onions, sour cream and cream cheese. If you don't want to make your own blinis, you can buy blinis or potato pancakes or serve a good grainy or whole wheat bread cut in thin slices. (Don't use those little pumpernickel squares—they are so strong that they overwhelm the taste of the salmon.)

Mediterranean Station Place the eggplant crush on a platter surrounded by pita triangles and Belgian endive leaves. Arrange prosciutto on a platter and surround with cubes of mango or melon and roasted artichokes (available at many supermarkets). Buy puff pastry straws and serve them in a container so people can wrap them with prosciutto if they wish. To complete this station, put out several bowls of olives and a little dish for the pits. Cut the focaccia into squares and add some great breads and a hunk of Manchego or other Spanish cheese to serve with the fig confit.

Nuevo Latino Station Nuevo Latino food is herbal, intensely flavored and spicy, but not hot. This is the "heavy" hors d'oeuvre station, where guests can garnish a good piece of beef with sauce and make their own little tortilla sandwiches or wraps. Cut tortillas in half and arrange in tortilla baskets or Chinese steamer baskets. Make one or both sauces, or buy bottled hot sauces from South America to serve on the side.

Gravlax

SERVES 12 TO 16

Gravlax is salmon that has been "cooked" in a marinade for two days. Its subtle, sensuous taste is perfect for appetizers and hors d'oeuvres, and it makes an excellent first course when served with a salad. Once the herbs have been scraped off, the salmon should keep in the marinade, refrigerated, for ten days. The fresh coriander makes this version a little different, but you can substitute the more traditional dill in both the marinade and the mustard sauce.

2 center-cut salmon fillets (about
   1½ lbs each)
1 tbsp cracked peppercorns
1 tbsp cracked coriander seeds
2 tbsp kosher salt

2 tbsp granulated sugar
1 tsp dry mustard
¼ cup vodka
1 large bunch fresh coriander sprigs,
   trimmed

Place salmon fillets skin side down on a large sheet of plastic wrap.
Combine peppercorns, coriander seeds, salt, sugar and mustard. Press mixture evenly onto salmon fillets.
Place one fillet skin side down in a dish just large enough to hold it. Sprinkle with 2 tbsp vodka. Lay coriander sprigs on top. Place second fillet on top so that flesh sides meet. Spoon remaining vodka over fish.
Cover salmon with a sheet of parchment paper. Place a small tray or plate on top of salmon. Weigh down with cans or other heavy weights.
Refrigerate for 2 days. Turn salmon and baste with juices every 12 hours.
Remove salmon from marinade. Remove coriander sprigs but leave remaining seasonings. Slice salmon thinly and sprinkle with extra cracked peppercorns, coriander seeds and chopped fresh coriander if desired.

Mustard Sauce

MAKES ABOUT 1¼ CUPS

Serve this sauce with gravlax, hamburgers or sausages. It will keep for up to two weeks in the refrigerator.

⅓ cup Dijon mustard
2 tbsp granulated sugar
1 tsp dry mustard
2 tbsp white wine vinegar

¼ tsp hot red pepper sauce
⅓ cup olive oil
2 tbsp whipping cream
¼ cup finely chopped fresh coriander

Combine Dijon, sugar, dry mustard, vinegar and hot pepper sauce to form a paste.
Slowly whisk in oil until a mayonnaise-like mixture is formed. Stir in cream and coriander.

Breakneck Blinis

MAKES ABOUT 40 BLINIS

A traditional blini recipe uses yeast, but this is a quicker version. Serve warm or at room temperature. The blinis also freeze well. Place the frozen blinis in a 350°F oven for 10 minutes before serving.

1 cup all-purpose flour
⅓ cup buckwheat flour
1 tsp baking powder
½ tsp baking soda
1 egg

½ tsp salt
Pinch granulated sugar
1½ cups milk
3 tbsp plain yogurt
2 tbsp butter, approx.

Combine all-purpose and buckwheat flours, baking powder and baking soda in a large bowl.
Stir together egg, salt, sugar, milk and yogurt in a separate bowl.
Beat egg mixture into flour mixture. Let stand for 20 minutes.
Heat butter in a nonstick skillet over medium heat. Spoon batter into skillet in ½ tbsp portions. Cook for about 30 seconds, or until mixture bubbles and bottom is crisp. Turn and cook second side for 20 seconds, or until golden. Repeat with remaining batter, adding more butter to skillet if necessary.

Eggplant Crush

SERVES 12

Use the pale purple Sicilian eggplants in this recipe if you can.

2 large Sicilian eggplants
1/3 cup olive oil
Salt and freshly ground pepper
1 tbsp chopped garlic
1 tsp ground cumin
1 tsp paprika

1/2 tsp cayenne
6 fresh or canned tomatoes, chopped
2 tbsp lemon juice
1/4 cup chopped parsley
1/2 cup plain yogurt

Preheat oven to 450°F.

Peel lengthwise strips from eggplants about 1-inch apart. Cut eggplants into slices 1/2 inch thick. Brush both sides lightly with 3 tbsp olive oil and place in a single layer on a baking sheet. Bake for 15 minutes, turning once, or until browned. Sprinkle with salt and pepper and chop.

Heat remaining 3 tbsp oil in a skillet over medium heat. Add eggplant, garlic, cumin, paprika and cayenne and sauté for 2 minutes. Stir in tomatoes.

Reduce heat to low and continue to cook and stir occasionally until mixture forms a thick mass, about 20 to 30 minutes. Stir in lemon juice, parsley and yogurt.

Fig Confit

MAKES ABOUT 2½ CUPS

Serve this chutney-like condiment with cheese, ham or curries.

1 lb dried figs, coarsely chopped
1 cup yellow raisins
2 cups orange juice
1 cup water
1/4 cup granulated sugar

1/4 cup white wine vinegar
2 tsp grated lemon zest
1/2 tsp whole allspice
1/2 tsp hot red pepper flakes
Salt and freshly ground pepper

Combine figs, raisins, orange juice, water, sugar, vinegar, lemon zest, allspice, hot pepper flakes, salt and pepper in a pot over high heat.

Bring to a boil, reduce heat and simmer, stirring occasionally, for 20 minutes, or until mixture is thick but not dry.

Focaccia with Shaved Fennel and Taleggio

SERVES 12

This easy savory bread can be served hot, cold or at room temperature. The recipe works best made with a long, flat focaccia. If you have a thicker loaf, cut it in half horizontally. Make this ahead of time and warm in a 350°F oven for 5 minutes before serving. Substitute 6 chopped leeks for the fennel if desired.

2 bulbs fennel, trimmed
¼ cup olive oil
2 tbsp lemon juice
½ tsp hot red pepper flakes, or to taste

Salt and freshly ground pepper
2 large focaccia
8 oz Taleggio or Fontina cheese, diced
2 tbsp chopped parsley

Preheat oven to 400°F.

Shave fennel with a mandolin or slice thinly by hand.

Heat 2 tbsp oil in a large skillet or wok over medium heat. Add fennel, lemon juice, hot pepper flakes, salt and pepper. Sauté for 5 minutes, or until fennel is soft and liquid has evaporated. Increase heat to high and sauté for 5 minutes longer, or until fennel is browned at edges and very soft. (You may have to cook fennel in batches.)

Place focaccia on baking sheets and brush with remaining 2 tbsp oil. Scatter fennel over focaccia and top with cheese.

Bake for 15 minutes, or until cheese has melted. Sprinkle with parsley and cut into squares.

Chilean Beef Filet

SERVES 12

The often bland filet gets a burst of flavor with this herb marinade. Guests can spread tortillas with a little mojo or salsa, add a dollop of avocado salad and top with a slice of beef.

1 tbsp chopped fresh coriander	1 tbsp lime juice
1 tbsp chopped fresh basil	¼ cup olive oil
1 tbsp chopped fresh mint	1 tsp hot Asian chili sauce
2 tsp finely chopped garlic	1 beef filet (about 4 lbs)
¼ cup orange juice	Salt and freshly ground pepper

Combine coriander, basil, mint, garlic, orange juice, lime juice, olive oil and chili sauce. Pour over filet and marinate for 4 hours or refrigerate overnight. Preheat oven to 450°F.
Season filet with salt and pepper. Place on a rack in a roasting pan. Roast for 30 to 45 minutes, or until beef is rare. Remove from oven and cool. (Beef will continue to cook as it cools.) Slice beef thinly and arrange on a platter.

Salsa Pebre

MAKES ABOUT 1½ CUPS

Pebre is a fresh-tasting, herbal Chilean hot sauce that has many different forms. This one has a pesto-like texture and is not as hot as some. It is excellent with simple meats, chicken or fish. Combined with some sour cream, it also makes a great dip.

¼ cup olive oil	½ cup chopped fresh coriander
2 tbsp red wine vinegar	½ cup chopped parsley
1 tbsp lime juice	1 tbsp chopped jalapeño pepper,
1 tsp chopped garlic	or more to taste
1 cup chopped green onions	Salt and freshly ground pepper

Combine oil, vinegar, lime juice, garlic, green onions, coriander, parsley and jalapeños in a food processor or mini chop and process until ingredients are combined but sauce still has some texture. Season to taste with salt and pepper.

Mojo Sauce
MAKES ABOUT 1½ CUPS

Mojo sauce is the classic Cuban condiment that is served with almost everything. There are as many mojo recipes as there are cooks, but the essential ingredients are sour orange juice and garlic. Because sour orange juice is not available here, I use a combination of lemon juice and orange juice.

½ cup olive oil
2 tbsp finely chopped garlic
2 tbsp chopped parsley
1 tsp ground cumin

½ cup orange juice
¼ cup lemon juice
2 tsp hot red pepper sauce, or to taste
Salt

Heat oil in a skillet over low heat. Add garlic and cook for 5 minutes, or until soft but not brown. Remove from heat.
Whisk together parsley, cumin, orange juice, lemon juice and hot pepper sauce. Whisk in olive oil mixture. Season with salt. Cool.

Avocado Salad
SERVES 12

This is a take-off on guacamole. It goes beautifully with chicken, fish and meat. Buy the pebbly, dark-skinned Hass avocados if you can find them. They have a nuttier, creamier taste than the smooth-skinned Florida variety.

¼ cup lime juice
¼ cup olive oil
Salt and freshly ground pepper
4 large avocados

1 cup chopped red onions
1 head romaine lettuce, shredded
2 tbsp chopped fresh coriander

Whisk together lime juice and oil. Season with salt and pepper.
Cut avocados in half. Stick a knife into pit and twist out. With a spoon, scoop flesh out of skin. Chop flesh into ½-inch dice.
Combine avocado, chopped onions and lime juice mixture. Serve on a bed of shredded lettuce and sprinkle with coriander.

Cocktails

A COCKTAIL PARTY can be deliciously creative fun, provided the host or hostess truly enjoys mixing cocktails. Inventing new twists on classic recipes gives the evening its own indelible identity, but stick to three, ignoring all other requests, and practice each one beforehand to iron out any problems of taste or logistics.

Gravlax Station

The Rob Roy It was the era of the great millionaires, the Gilded Age in the last decades of the nineteenth century, that gave us the Manhattan. And what time in history could be more appropriate for a cocktail of such flavor and substance? Each evening, when the stock market closed, the men of power would leave their high offices and make their way to august private clubs or the bars of their favorite hotels: the Hoffman House, the Waldorf, the Continental, the Manhattan Club. Creative entrepreneurs, they demanded equal inventiveness from the bartenders who served them. The Manhattan Club alone was said to offer a different cocktail for every day of the year, and one evening in 1874, at a banquet to honor the election of New York governor Samuel Tilden, the Manhattan itself was born, of equal parts rye whiskey and sweet Italian vermouth with a dash of orange bitters.

The new drink caught on, boosted by innumerable variations devised to the specifications of individual customers. The Smithtown added fresh lemon juice. The Manhattan cocktail à la Gilbert called for whiskey, French vermouth and Amer Picon bitters. The Plimpton substituted whiskey with rum. The Manhattan fashion lasted through the turn of the century, a perpetual challenger to the dominance of the Dry Martini, until the curtain of Prohibition fell.

Today, exotic bitters are hard to find in some jurisdictions. Instead, we have Angostura. Rendered down from tropical botanicals (though not the bark of the Angostura tree), it was invented in 1824 by a Prussian army surgeon called Dr. J.G.B. Siegert, who was working as surgeon general in the military hospital in Guyana. His descendants still make it in Trinidad, following the old man's secret prescription. If you ask me, that dash of Angostura is the heart and soul of a true Manhattan, cutting the vermouth's sweetness, bringing out the taste of the rye or bourbon.

It is also essential to a Rob Roy, a particular Manhattan variant that uses Scotch as its base. The smokiness of Scotch works better than an American whiskey with gravlax or smoked salmon, and I like to dry out the drink further by using dry French vermouth instead of sweet red Italian. In a tumbler, combine 2 oz Scotch with ½ oz vermouth, a drop of Angostura bitters and some ice.

Serious wine alternative: Alsatian Pinot Gris

Mediterranean Station

The Sazerac New Orleans mixologists claim the Sazerac was the first cocktail ever made, with origins going back to the 1830s, when apothecary Antoine Peychaud set up shop in the French Quarter. There he dispensed his own formula of medicinal bitters, making them more palatable by mixing them with brandy served in an egg cup or *coquetier*, from which the word cocktail is derived. Maybe so. Cool, complex and sweetly satisfying, the modern Sazerac calls for three ingredients that are frustratingly hard to find—Wild Turkey rye whiskey, Peychaud bitters and an anise-flavored aperitif called Herbsaint. The following version uses acceptable substitutes, with apologies to Dr. Peychaud. Rinse a Martini glass with 1 tsp Pernod. To a cocktail shaker half filled with ice, add 1½ oz bourbon and two drops Angostura bitters. Shake and strain into the Martini glass. Garnish with a lemon twist.

Serious wine alternative: mature white Rioja

Nuevo Latino Station

The Palomino The delicious food at this station calls out for good tequila, which to me means a 100 percent agave reposado tequila. Mexico's national spirit exists in many forms, most of them being *mixto*—in other words, not made purely from the blue agave plant. The law permits the use of up to 49 percent of sugars from other sources—usually sugarcane or molasses—in the fermented liquid that goes into the still. You can still taste the agave in a mixto, but that strange, earthy, sappy flavor is clearer in tequilas that say "100% agave" on the label. A reposado ("rested") tequila has been allowed to relax in oak barrels for some months, smoothing the rough edges of the spirit and tinting it pale yellow without diminishing the agave identity.

At this station, I had been thinking of a tray of 2-oz shot glasses of tequila with identical glasses of sangrito alongside. Sangrito is the nonalcoholic mix of highly seasoned tomato and orange juice, often spiked with onion, that Mexicans drink as a chaser for the tequila. But Lucy has covered that base with her salsa and the mojo sauce. So we improvise. A Margarita (page 121) is one option, but in Guadalajara the cocktail of choice is a Paloma, made with tequila, lime juice, grapefruit-flavored pop and a pinch of salt. This drink— we might name it a Palomino—calls for 1½ oz 100 percent agave reposado tequila, 1 oz freshly squeezed grapefruit juice, a dash of grenadine and a slice of lime as garnish. Chill everything before mixing.

Serious wine alternative: big, oaky, acidic red wine from Spain's Ribera del Duero region

Burns Night Supper

Smoked Salmon Rosettes

Cock-a-Leekie Soup

Roast Leg of Lamb with Oatmeal Stuffing

Chappit Tatties • Green Peas

Bashed Neeps • Drambuie Cream

SERVES 8

SCOTTISH POET ROBERT BURNS was a man who lived fully and well, and along with his poems, his legacy lives on in the tradition of Burns Suppers. To celebrate his birthday on January 25, clans from Moscow to the Sault have a roaring good time drinking whisky, eating haggis, reciting Burns's poetry and singing his songs. He would have loved it.

Born in 1759, Burns was a poet of the people. Raised as a farm lad, he always remained true to his roots. He was lusty, hearty and a great eater and drinker. The Russians have a great fondness for him, and every January planeloads of whisky and haggis are shipped to Moscow to be distributed to Burns revellers.

Robert Burns is also the most-translated poet in the world—no mean feat for an eighteenth-century poet who wrote in Scottish dialect!

Countdown to the Burns Supper

TO HOST YOUR OWN BURNS NIGHT, serve the first course, then pipe in the haggis (we use a CD). The haggis is stabbed with the ceremonial dagger while the Chairman gives Burns's "Address to the Haggis," followed by the famous Selkirk Grace. Then the meal is served. A traditional Burns dinner includes cock-a-leekie soup, haggis, lamb or roast sirloin of beef, bashed neeps (mashed turnips), chappit tatties (mashed potatoes) and Scottish trifle or any creamy, liquor-laden dessert.

After dinner, toasts are given, ranging from a toast to Burns's immortal memory, a toast to the lassies, followed by a toast to anyone else worth a dram. Everyone sings "Auld Lange Syne," and then the entertainment begins with lots of participation in songs and poems.

The traditional drink to accompany a Burns feast is straight Scotch, neat, preferably malt—none of that wimpy wine! If you must dilute the Scotch, be sure to use spring water. And although James's expert claims that guests will consume no more alcohol at a whisky dinner than they would if they were drinking wine, our last Burns supper was so much fun that we rolled our guests, still singing, into waiting taxis at three in the morning!

Selkirk Grace

Some hae meat and canna eat,
And some wad eat that want it;
But we hae meat and we can eat,
And sae the Lord, be thankit.

Haggis The great old dish of Scotland (the "Great Chieftain of the pudding race," in Burns's immortal words) is more a literary than a culinary icon.

Although its origins are misty, it was traditionally made with all the less desirable parts left over after a sheep was slaughtered. Today it is often a combination of oatmeal, liver, heart and ground lamb or beef stuffed inside a sheep's stomach (a delicacy similar to sausage) and then boiled. Don't attempt to make it—buy a haggis from a Scottish butcher.

307

And to Drink . . .

I WAS INTRODUCED TO THE NOTION of whisky dinners by an Englishman named Nick Morgan, marketing director for the group of six Classic Malts of Scotland and a leading pioneer in this challenging field. Having mapped the affinities of specific single malt whiskies with innumerable dishes, including Italian and Japanese menus, he was kind enough to share his findings—the basis for these Burns Night Supper matches. He advocates serving the whiskies in large wineglasses, diluted with a little water, and assures me that guests end up consuming no more alcohol than they would if drinking wine. One of Morgan's first discoveries was the epiphanic union of smoked salmon with Talisker, the delectable single malt from the Isle of Skye. The salty-sweet, smoky flavor of the fish really pushes this whisky's buttons.

Move back to the mainland for the cock-a-leekie soup. Robbie Burns was born in Ayrshire, in the southwestern lowlands of Scotland, and it would be fitting to serve an Ayrshire whisky at a Burns Supper. Alas, the only remaining single malt from the county, Ladyburn, is rarely bottled and exceptionally hard to find. Lowland whiskies have a character of their own—pale, delicate, often with a sweetish beginning but a dry finish, and relatively free of the peaty smokiness that typifies single malts from the Highlands and Islands. If you can't get your hands on any Bladnoch or Rosebank, look for seventeen-year-old Glengoyne, a single malt from a distillery just north of Burns country, in the beautiful countryside between Glasgow and Loch Lomond. Without that aroma of peat, it has a grainy, malty sweetness that narrows to a long, dry finale, seasoned by the sherry casks in which the whisky finished its maturation.

Roast lamb is not an enthusiastic partner for whisky (large pieces of roast meat just seem to have little to say to Scotch), but the well-seasoned stuffing more than makes up for this ovine indifference. Ten-year-old Glenkinchie is another Lowland single malt. It loves nothing more than a spicy sausage or a salty, savory biscuit and will pick up the robust taste of the stuffing with great glee. A blended Scotch is also an alternative, and the most appropriate choice must be Johnnie Walker.

Like Burns, John Walker was born an Ayrshire farmer's son, but instead of taking to the pen, he opened a grocery store in 1820 in the prosperous town of Kilmarnock. Whisky was one of the items he sold, but it was his descendants who turned Johnnie Walker into the world's bestselling Scotch. The rich, twelve-year-old Black Label was introduced in 1909 and is probably the closest in style to old John Walker's original Highland blend.

Robert Burns was a tolerant man, and upon such a festive night as this he would surely have made no objection if one or more guests asked for wine with their main course. To honor "the auld alliance" between Scotland and France, and the more pertinent relationship of lamb and peppery herbs in the dish, think Syrah, the great varietal of the northern Rhône. Hermitage or Côte-Rôtie would be magnificent, but more affordable Syrahs would probably be just as warmly received at this stage of the proceedings.

And with Lucy's dessert, hammer home a Rusty Nail, a simple but deeply satisfying cocktail made by mixing equal parts of Drambuie and the Scotch of your choice, served straight up or on the rocks. Drambuie, like most of the great liqueurs, has a story of its own, and for once the legend is true. Bonnie Prince Charlie, charismatic claimant to the English throne, saw his hopes and his Highlanders cut down at the battle of Culloden in 1745 and fled in disguise over the sea to Skye. There, the loyal Mackinnon of Strathaird sheltered him until a French ship arrived to take him to Paris and safety. In gratitude, Charlie gave his protector the one thing of value left to him, the secret recipe of his personal liqueur. (Many European aristocrats had cordials privately prepared to aid digestion or warm them while hunting.) The recipe became a treasured heirloom of the clan until, in 1906, young Malcolm Mackinnon decided to see if he couldn't find a wider market. He gathered the ingredients—herbs, honey and good malt whisky—and set to work in an Edinburgh cellar, turning out half a dozen bottles a week. Needing a name, he lifted the heart from a Gaelic phrase, *an dram buidleach*, "the drink that satisfies."

Drambuie is everything a liqueur should be: sweet but not too sweet, intense but not medicinal, complex and laden with the requisite romantic past. Its versatility is perfectly demonstrated this evening in Lucy's sophisticated version of the traditional Athole Brose and in the accompanying Rusty Nail. No one, I suspect, will have trouble sleeping tonight.

Smoked Salmon Rosettes

SERVES 8 AS AN APPETIZER

The thinner the salmon slices, the prettier this dish is. If your salmon is thickly sliced, you will probably need more than 1¼ pounds.

1¼ lbs thinly sliced smoked salmon
1½ cups soft cream cheese
1 tsp grated lemon zest
1 cup packed watercress leaves
½ cup chopped green onions
Salt and freshly ground pepper

Garnish
2 tbsp rice vinegar
¼ cup olive oil
Salt and freshly ground pepper
1 bunch watercress, trimmed

Line insides of eight ½-cup glass or other small bowls with slices of smoked salmon.

Chop remaining salmon.

Combine cream cheese, lemon zest, watercress leaves and green onions in a food processor or by hand. Stir in chopped smoked salmon. Mixture should be slightly chunky. Season well with salt and pepper.

Divide mixture among prepared bowls. Bring ends of salmon up around cream cheese mixture, enclosing cheese. Refrigerate for 2 hours or overnight. Unmold onto serving plates.

Whisk together vinegar and oil and season with salt and pepper. Toss watercress with dressing. Garnish each serving of salmon with a little watercress salad.

Cock-a-Leekie Soup

SERVES 8

Traditionally this soup is made with an old fowl that is then chopped up and served with the soup. Today you can buy excellent chicken stock in Tetra Paks if you don't want to make your own. The chicken legs are added to strengthen the stock and provide the garnish. Prunes were originally added to cut the sometimes bitter taste of the leeks, but they can be omitted if you prefer.

Make this soup a day or two ahead. Any fat can easily be lifted from the chilled soup.

8 cups strong chicken stock	3 leeks, trimmed and thinly sliced
2 chicken legs, with both skin and	Salt and freshly ground pepper
visible fat removed	8 prunes

Combine stock and chicken legs in a large pot. Bring to a boil, reduce heat and simmer over medium heat for 25 to 35 minutes, or until legs are cooked through. Remove legs from stock, cool and pull meat from bones. Shred meat. Skim any fat from stock and add leeks. Simmer for 15 minutes.

Add shredded chicken and simmer for 10 minutes longer. Season with salt and pepper.

Place a prune in each bowl and pour soup on top.

Roast Leg of Lamb
with Oatmeal Stuffing

SERVES 8

This stuffing has oatmeal in it as well as vegetables, so some might consider it a version of haggis. Ask the butcher to tunnel bone the lamb by removing all the leg bones except for the shank bone, without butterflying the meat. (You can also use a butterflied lamb leg. Place the stuffing on the lamb, roll it up and tie. You will need to reduce the cooking time slightly.)

1 tbsp olive oil	2 tbsp butter
1 cup chopped onions	3 cups beef stock
½ cup quick-cooking rolled oats	Salt and freshly ground pepper
3 tbsp chopped fresh mint	1 boneless leg of lamb
2 tbsp chopped fresh rosemary	(about 4 to 5 lbs boned)
1 tbsp chopped fresh thyme	2 tbsp all-purpose flour
4 oz ground lamb or pork	

Preheat oven to 450°F.

Heat oil in a skillet over medium heat. Add onions and sauté for 3 to 4 minutes, or until softened.

Add onions, oats, mint, rosemary, thyme, ground lamb, butter and ½ cup stock to a food processor and process until combined. Season with salt and pepper.

Stuff mixture into center of lamb, pushing it into all cavities. (Place any extra stuffing in a buttered baking dish.) Season outside of lamb with plenty of salt and pepper.

Place stuffed lamb on a rack in a roasting pan and roast for 30 minutes. Reduce heat to 350°F and roast for 45 to 60 minutes longer, or until meat is pink. Bake any extra stuffing, covered, alongside lamb for last 30 minutes of roasting time.

Remove lamb from roasting pan and cover with a tea towel. Let meat rest for 15 minutes before carving (lamb will continue to cook while sitting).

Remove all but 2 tbsp fat from roasting pan. Stir in flour and cook over medium heat, scraping up all bits on bottom of pan. Add remaining 2½ cups stock a little at a time, stirring constantly. Bring to a boil over high heat, reduce heat and simmer for a few minutes, or until gravy is thick enough to coat back of a spoon. Season with salt and pepper.

Chappit Tatties

SERVES 8

An ultra-creamy and decadently rich mashed potato with the consistency of whipped cream. A little goes a long way.

3 lbs Yukon Gold potatoes, peeled
½ cup butter, melted

1 cup whipping cream
Salt and freshly ground pepper

Cut potatoes into even-sized chunks and add to a pot of cold salted water. Bring to a boil and cook for 10 to 15 minutes, or until tender. Drain well and return to pot. Shake pot over turned-off burner to dry potatoes.
Mash potatoes until smooth using a potato ricer, food mill or electric mixer. Beat in melted butter and whipping cream. Season with salt and pepper. Mixture should be very soft and creamy. Add more cream and butter if desired.

Green Peas

SERVES 8

The Scots are famous for "mushy peas"—fat canned green peas that are mashed before eating. Like deep-fried haggis, they are definitely an acquired taste. This version uses fresh or frozen green peas.

1 small head Boston lettuce, shredded
3 green onions, finely chopped
4 cups green peas

2 tbsp butter
2 tbsp chopped parsley
Salt and freshly ground pepper

Place lettuce, green onions, peas and butter in a pot. Cover and bring to a boil. Reduce heat and simmer for 3 to 4 minutes, or until lettuce is wilted.
Stir in parsley, salt and pepper and simmer, uncovered, for 2 minutes.

Bashed Neeps

SERVES 8

Rutabagas are called turnips in Scotland. The ginger and roasted garlic make this much lighter and tastier than the traditional dish. It is good with roast turkey, too.

8 cups diced rutabaga
⅓ cup butter
1 tbsp finely chopped gingerroot
3 tbsp roasted garlic

⅓ cup sour cream
Salt and freshly ground pepper
3 tbsp chopped green onions

Place rutabaga in a pot of cold salted water and bring to a boil. Reduce heat and boil for 10 to 15 minutes, or until soft. Drain well.

Mash rutabaga with a potato masher or fork. Mixture should be slightly chunky. Preheat oven to 350°F.

Heat butter in a small skillet over low heat. Add ginger and cook for 5 minutes, or until softened.

Beat butter, ginger, roasted garlic and sour cream into rutabaga. Season to taste with salt and pepper. Stir in green onions.

Transfer mixture to a buttered baking dish. Bake for 20 minutes, or until heated through.

Roasted Garlic Cut the top ends from heads of garlic to expose cloves and remove any flaky skin, but do not peel. Place on a sheet of foil. Sprinkle with 1 tbsp olive oil per head. Wrap garlic in foil and bake at 400°F for 40 minutes, or until cloves are soft and golden. Remove garlic from skins by pressing on base of cloves.

Drambuie Cream

SERVES 8

A spectacular cream that combines the taste of Scotland with the ease of North American cooking methods. You can sprinkle the dessert with untoasted shortbread cookie crumbs instead of the oats if desired. The toasted oats can also be folded into the cream, along with a few fresh raspberries.

2 cups quick-cooking rolled oats	3 tbsp lemon juice
1 cup whipping cream	¼ cup honey
2 cups drained yogurt (page 103)	½ cup Drambuie
1 tbsp grated lemon zest	

Spread oats in a skillet over medium heat. Cook, stirring, for about 2 minutes, or until toasted.

Whip cream until soft peaks form. Combine cream with drained yogurt, lemon zest and juice, honey and Drambuie.

Spoon half the Drambuie cream into wine glasses or other dessert dishes and top with half the toasted oats. Cover with remaining cream and sprinkle with remaining oats.

A Sensual Valentine's Dinner

Artichokes Vinaigrette
Roasted Veal Chops with
Mushroom Sauce and Truffle Oil
Potato Galette
Chili Chocolate Truffles

SERVES 2

AS MUCH OF THIS EASY-TO-PREPARE MENU contains foods with aphrodisiac qualities, this dinner may well be a prelude to what James calls "dancing beneath the midnight moon." Foods with heat, such as chilies, set the mood by stimulating your heartbeat, and chocolate is purported to arouse passion.

There is also something very sensual about picking up food with your fingers and feeding it to your loved one (think of the movie *Tom Jones*). Artichokes are perfect for this, as each leaf is consumed separately. At dessert, nicely relaxed from the good food and wine, use the same technique for the truffles.

Breaking the Ice

HOW TO PUT THIS DELICATELY? Beware of overindulgence after dark on February 14. One can start with the best, most romantic intentions only to find wits fuddled and feet too entangled in alcohol or overeating to dance beneath the midnight moon. This may not be the evening, in other words, to down a couple of nerve-calming Martinis before dinner. Think long-term. A single Martini will have to do.

Or maybe not a Martini. Perhaps you are more sentimental than I am and would like to mix something pretty and pink as a prelude to Valentine's night. This invention (I call it a Cover Girl) falls somewhere between a Cosmopolitan and a Woo Woo.

Into a cocktail shaker half filled with ice pour equal amounts of vanilla-flavored vodka (Stolichnaya Vanil has a slightly more convincing taste than its competitors), freshly squeezed orange juice and cranberry juice, all well chilled. Shake and strain into two chilled Martini glasses. A garnish would seem too precious.

And if you daren't risk using a cocktail shaker (worried, perhaps, that you'll look like a maracas player in a Brazilian street band), there is always Champagne, bringing its own innate and romantic sense of occasion.

Artichokes Vinaigrette

SERVES 2

Look for compact, tightly closed artichokes that are firm and heavy for their size. Once the leaves start to separate and the head opens up like a rose, the artichoke is past its prime. Bronze-tipped leaves have been "winter kissed" by frost and have a special flavor.

1 tsp Dijon mustard	½ cup olive oil
1 clove garlic, minced	Salt and freshly ground pepper
1 tbsp chopped fresh basil, or 1 tsp dried	2 large artichokes
2 tbsp red wine vinegar	½ lemon

Whisk together mustard, garlic, basil and red wine vinegar. Slowly whisk in olive oil. Vinaigrette mixture should thicken. Season with salt and pepper.

Cut off artichoke stems. Pull off small bottom leaves. With a sharp knife, cut off top quarter of artichokes. With scissors, snip pointed tops off remaining outer leaves. Rub cut edges with lemon to keep them from turning black, or place in a bowl of water laced with lemon juice.

Bring a large pot of salted water to a boil. (Do not use an aluminum pot, as it will cause artichokes to turn black.) Add lemon and artichokes to water, pushing artichokes into water if they bob up.

Reduce heat to medium and partially cover pot. Boil for 15 to 40 minutes, depending on size of artichoke. To test for doneness, pierce bottom with a knife (it should be tender) or pull off a leaf (it should come away easily).

Drain artichokes well and pour cold water over them to stop cooking. Turn upside down on a wire rack to drain off any water. With a spoon, remove feathery chokes, leaving hearts exposed.

Serve artichokes hot or cold with small bowls of vinaigrette for dipping.

Artichokes The artichoke heart is what remains after you have removed the outer leaves. The heart consists of the tender, pale green leaves, the fuzzy choke and the bottom—the fleshy area above the stalk—which makes the best eating. The hearts of young artichokes can be eaten whole, as the choke has not yet grown. Otherwise the choke must be discarded. It can be removed with a sharp knife and spoon before or after cooking. You can also scrape out the choke while you are eating.

And to drink . . .

LUCY HAS SET ME SOME FINE CHALLENGES during the course of this book, but she surpasses herself with this romantic starter. She's quite right, of course. Eating globe artichokes with one's beloved, petal by petal, until the tender heart is finally discovered, is an act charged with sensuality. And a robust vinaigrette is entirely appropriate. But the vinegar in a vinaigrette throws down the sharp gauntlet of acidity, and artichokes themselves are one of wine's most notorious disruptors. A substance in the plants called cynarin makes anything eaten or drunk alongside—wine, water, milk, anything—taste oddly sweet or even, in extreme cases, metallic. That said, a wine must be found (it's Valentine's Day, after all), but it has to be something bone dry and with enough acidity of its own to stand up to the vinaigrette. Nonvintage brut Champagne meets these demands uniquely well.

For all its fabled elegance and sophistication, Champagne is a sturdy wine with an acidic backbone. The nuances of a vintage bottling may well be lost in the struggle with vinegar and cynarin, so economize discreetly with nonvintage. The brut style is the driest offered by most Champagne houses. If the artichokes do make it taste a little sweeter, you have a long way to go before alarm bells ring. As for romance, no wine sends a more blatant billet-doux than a flute of the real thing. The rest of the bottle can be returned to the ice bucket until much later in the evening.

If you can't drink Champagne (it does give some people a headache), try a very dry rosé from the south of France. A Tavel or a Lirac will have the alcoholic muscle under their pretty red-berry smiles to handle this dish.

Roasted Veal Chops with Mushroom Sauce and Truffle Oil

SERVES 2

French-cut veal chops have had the bones cleaned of meat and gristle. They are more attractive, but other veal rib or loin chops may also be used. Serve the chops over the potatoes. The sage leaves can be fried a few hours ahead. The leftover sage-flavored oil can be reused.

1 tbsp olive oil
2 French-cut veal chops
   (about 1½ inches thick)
Salt and freshly ground pepper
Mushroom Sauce
2 tbsp olive oil
6 oz mixed wild mushrooms,
   trimmed and sliced

1 tsp finely chopped garlic
¼ cup mushroom or beef stock
½ tsp truffle oil
Garnish
¼ cup olive oil
12 fresh sage leaves

Preheat oven to 450°F.

Heat oil in a skillet over medium-high heat. Season veal with salt and pepper. Cook chops for about 2 minutes per side, or until browned. Transfer to a metal baking dish and bake for 8 to 12 minutes, or until just pink.

Prepare mushroom sauce while veal is cooking. Heat 2 tbsp olive oil in a skillet over medium-high heat. Add mushrooms and sauté for about 3 minutes, or until limp. Add garlic and sauté for 1 minute longer. Add stock and bring to a boil. Drizzle in truffle oil.

Heat oil for garnish in a small skillet over high heat. Add sage leaves and sauté for about 30 seconds, or until crisp. Drain on paper towels.

Serve chops with mushroom sauce and sprinkle with sage leaves.

320

And to drink . . .

WE ARE ON FIRMER GROUND with a beautiful veal chop, the pale meat's sweet juices and demure fringe of fat calling for a wine of some sensitivity. You could dip a toe into the ocean of big hearty reds by choosing a velvety, fruit-forward Californian Merlot, but I think that's too much wine for this dish. A mature red Burgundy from the Côte d'Or (buy the best you can afford) works on every level. These aren't heavy, tannic wines but they have marvelous intensity of flavor, elegance and complexity and a natural affinity with mushrooms.

Choosing precisely which Burgundy underlines the importance of developing a close relationship with someone patient and knowledgeable at your favorite wine store. Vintage years matter in Burgundy—1996, 1998 and 1999 were fabulous and so was 2002, though the wines need cellaring for a few years. Just as important is the reliability of the domain (if the estate vinifies and sells its own wines) or the négociant (a merchant who buys wines from growers, sometimes blends and ages them, then sells them). There are good and not-so-good examples of both, and keeping track of them all takes more time than most of us can afford.

Having found the wine, you may wish to decant it tonight, partly because red wine looks so handsome in a decanter in the candlelight and partly because a couple of hours of exposure to the air will allow the latent fruitiness to open like a rose. And wait until you taste it with the meat and the mushrooms: the rose becomes a whole bouquet.

Potato Galette

SERVES 2

Any 6- or 7-inch metal pan will work with this dish, but a small cast-iron skillet will hold the heat best. Use clarified butter for flavor and to prevent the potatoes from sticking.

⅓ cup clarified butter
1 lb Yukon Gold potatoes, peeled and thinly sliced
Salt and freshly ground pepper

Preheat oven to 425°F.

Spread 3 tbsp clarified butter over base of a small ovenproof skillet. Layer a circle of potatoes over butter. Brush potatoes with butter and season with salt and pepper. Continue to layer potatoes, brushing each layer with butter and seasoning until all potatoes are used. Pour any remaining butter over top.

Place skillet over medium heat and cook potatoes until bottom layer starts to brown, about 5 minutes. Cover potatoes with parchment paper and a lid that sits directly on paper. Press down.

Bake potatoes for 15 minutes. Remove lid and paper and press potatoes down again. Bake, uncovered, for 25 to 30 minutes longer, pressing down twice more, until potatoes are very tender.

Drain off any excess butter. Invert galette onto a serving dish and cut in half.

Clarified Butter To clarify butter, gently melt 1 cup unsalted butter in a heavy pot. Remove from heat and let sit until cool. The white milk solids will settle to the bottom and the clear butter will remain on top. Strain butter through cheesecloth and discard milk solids.

Clarified butter will keep in the refrigerator for up to a month.

Makes about ¾ cup.

Chili Chocolate Truffles

MAKES 18 TO 20 SMALL TRUFFLES

Use ancho chili powder if possible (it has a hint of chocolate in it), but any chili will bring out the chocolate flavor in these truffles.

These also freeze well and can be eaten directly out of the freezer whenever you have a chocolate moment.

½ cup whipping cream	1 tbsp honey
10 oz bittersweet chocolate, coarsely chopped	¼ tsp ancho chili powder or cayenne
	Shaved dark or white chocolate
¼ cup butter, at room temperature	Cocoa

Bring cream to a boil in a small pot over low heat. Immediately pour cream over chocolate and butter and stir until smooth. Stir in honey and chili powder. Cool and refrigerate until set, about 4 hours.

Make truffles 1 to 2 inches in diameter by scooping out balls of chocolate mixture with a melon baller or small ice cream scoop. Place balls on a parchment-lined baking sheet. If mixture is a little soft, use your hands to roll balls. Place shaved chocolate on one plate and cocoa on another. Roll half the balls in chocolate and half in cocoa and refrigerate.

And to drink . . .

CHOCOLATE hits the pleasure zones in the brain, releasing enzymes that prompt feelings of well-being and euphoria. I find that vintage port provokes a similar effect—a wine with the sweetness, vigor, grip, fruitiness, spiciness and overall machismo to play Anthony to chocolate's Cleopatra. A very young vintage port is also amazingly delicious. It will already be two years old when it is bottled and sold. Opened within a few months, it is as full of potential glory as the bud of some oversized tropical flower. A year later, the wine enters its grumpy, tannic dormancy and will not awaken for a decade. Offering more obvious gratification, dark, sweet, heavy, fortified raspberry wine (often called framboise) is a gorgeous match with dark chocolate. A little goes a long way, for subtlety plays no part in framboise's modus operandi. It's the all-or-nothing equivalent of leaning across and planting a kiss on unsuspecting lips.

Ski Chalet Dinner

Curried Sweet Potato Soup with Candied Apples
Orange Anise-spiced Short Ribs
Steamed Sticky Rice
Key Lime Squares

SERVES 6

COMFORTING CASSEROLES are the way to get through the cold of winter. I like them because they can be made ahead of time. In fact, they taste better the second day, and you can remove the fat after they are chilled. Because casserole recipes usually double easily, you can make enough to freeze for other meals. They are portable, too—ideal for toting to friends' houses or ski chalet weekends.

Soups are another great comfort in the winter, and this sweet potato soup has loads of interesting tastes. And, after all this richness, what better dessert than homey Key Lime Squares.

Glogg

GLOGG, GLOGG, GLOGG . . . In the long, dark Swedish winter, it's the sound to warm the hearts of guests who arrive at the house knocking snow off their boots and eyeing the seats by the fire. Like mulled wine in England, glogg is a warming cup with a past—one early mention (circa 1620) describes it as a fermented apple-juice drink flavored with six botanicals. Most of those spices are still used today, though every household in Sweden seems to have its own family recipe. The apples have gone by the board in favor of a blend of either red wine and vodka or port and aquavit. Yes, indeed, a modern glogg is a potent brew, for while much of the alcohol evaporates from the wine as the drink simmers, the vodka restores what was lost—and then some. This particular version comes from a Swedish friend of mine, Goran Amnegard, who has vineyards about an hour outside Stockholm. His wines are excellent (and compelling evidence of global warming). His glogg is a purple antidote to winter.

To make enough glogg for six people, take a large pot and into it put a bottle of full-bodied red wine, 1½ cups black currant juice, 5 cloves, half a cinnamon stick, 10 cracked cardamom seeds and 1 tbsp dried orange zest called pommerance (if you can't find it, use 2 tbsp fresh). Bring to a boil, reduce heat and simmer for 15 minutes. Add ¾ cup vodka, ½ cup strong black tea and ½ to 1 cup granulated sugar, stirring until the sugar has dissolved. Place a few raisins and slivered blanched almonds in small glasses and ladle in the hot glogg. Sip and let the warmth spread through your body. I can offer no tips about eating the almonds and raisins that are left in your empty glass, except to warn that they are irresistible, like glogg itself—the world's most onomatopoeic drink.

Curried Sweet Potato Soup with Candied Apples

SERVES 6

A hearty spiced soup to warm you up on a cold day. The candied apples balance the heat of the soup, but they could be omitted. Use a mild Indian curry paste so as not to overwhelm the flavors of the sweet potatoes and apples.

2 tbsp vegetable oil	Salt and freshly ground pepper
1 cup chopped onions	3 tbsp chopped fresh mint
1 tbsp finely chopped gingerroot	Candied Apples
2 tbsp mild Indian curry paste	½ cup slivered dried apples
4 cups diced peeled sweet potatoes	¼ cup water
2 cups diced peeled green apples	1 tbsp butter
6 cups chicken or vegetable stock	½ tsp granulated sugar
½ cup coconut milk	

Heat oil in a pot over medium heat. Add onions and sauté for 3 minutes, or until softened.

Stir in ginger and curry paste and sauté for 1 minute. Add sweet potatoes and green apples and sauté for 2 more minutes.

Add stock and bring to a boil. Reduce heat and simmer gently for 20 minutes, or until vegetables are very soft.

Puree soup and return to pot. Add coconut milk and bring to a boil. Reduce heat and simmer for 5 minutes to combine flavors. Season well with salt and pepper. Stir in mint.

Prepare apple slivers while soup is simmering. In a skillet, combine dried apples, water, butter and sugar. Bring to a boil. Reduce heat and simmer for 1 minute, or until liquid is absorbed. Continue to cook, stirring constantly, for 4 minutes, or until apples are soft and golden.

Serve soup topped with slivered apples.

And to drink . . .

FOR ALL ITS COME-HITHER PRICKLE OF SPICE, this is a smooth and languid soup enriched by coconut, refreshed by apples, but underneath showing a sturdy sweet potato heart. Two approaches spring to mind—to try to match all those qualities or to make a strong appeal to one specific element in the soup. The first idea calls for a white wine made from Marsanne grapes. In its northern Rhône homeland, Marsanne is treated as the sweet-natured, big-boned sister who helps around the house—placid and full-bodied with an innocent bouquet of white flowers and almonds. (Winemakers there traditionally blend Marsanne with Roussanne, a much more skittish, racy, elegant creature.) A single-varietal Marsanne has the weight to handle this soup and will not be dismayed by the spices. Examples from Victoria, Australia, are just as fat and can show more exotic fruitiness, even aromas of mango to compliment the apple in the soup.

And that suggests Plan B. Uncork a young, off-dry Riesling from Ontario or Germany's Pfalz region that would home in on the apple like a spotlight picking out one dancer in a chorus line.

Orange Anise-spiced Short Ribs

SERVES 6

Short ribs are one of the best braising meats because they are always juicy and succulent. In this recipe the miso gives the meat a richer taste. Use the stronger-tasting brown miso if you can find it, and don't worry about the heat in the chili sauce; it provides only a background taste in this dish. Serve the ribs with sticky rice, a Thai staple.

6 cloves garlic, thickly sliced	2 cups thickly sliced carrots
¼ cup brown miso	2 cups thickly sliced white turnips
¼ cup orange juice	2 cups thickly sliced zucchini
3 tbsp vegetable oil	½ cup red wine
2 tsp hot Asian chili sauce	2 cups chicken or beef stock
6 racks short ribs	3 star anise
Salt and freshly ground pepper	1 tbsp grated orange zest
8 shallots, peeled and halved	1 tbsp honey

Combine garlic, miso, orange juice, 1 tbsp oil and chili sauce. Coat ribs with marinade and refrigerate for 12 hours or overnight. Scrape marinade off ribs and reserve marinade.

Preheat oven to 300°F.

Heat remaining 2 tbsp oil in a large skillet over medium-high heat. Season ribs with salt and pepper. Brown ribs well on all sides, about 8 minutes in total. Transfer to a casserole.

Drain all but 2 tbsp oil from skillet. Reduce heat to medium. Add reserved marinade, shallots, carrots, turnips and zucchini. Cook for about 6 minutes, or until slightly colored. Remove vegetables from skillet and reserve.

Add wine, stock, star anise and orange zest to skillet. Bring to a boil, scraping up any bits on bottom of skillet and reserve.

Pour sauce over ribs. Cover and bake for 1½ hours, stirring occasionally.

Stir in reserved vegetables and honey and continue to bake for 1 hour, or until meat is tender and falls off bone.

Remove vegetables and ribs carefully, discarding bones. Skim any fat from cooking liquid. Reduce liquid on stovetop if necessary until full of flavor, adding salt and pepper. Return meat and vegetables to casserole and reheat before serving.

And to drink . . .

SPICING THESE RICH AND SUCCULENT RIBS with Lucy's delectable marinade may seem like gilding the lily, but the dish that emerges has incredible depths of flavor that call for a serious red wine. This could be the opportunity for an amarone.

Amarone della Valpolicella, to give the wine its modern name, is a being of awe-inspiring if idiosyncratic character. Italian aficionados call it a *vino di meditazione*, a wine best sipped and meditated upon late at night, by the fireside, with no distraction other than some nuts and perhaps a few morsels of Parmigiano Reggiano. It's true that the poetry in the glass is most clearly heard in such a situation, but I think it finds a place at the table alongside these ribs. It is made from the same blend of grapes as Valpolicella but the bunches are vinified after spending the winter drying on trays in breezy lofts in the hills north of Verona. The grapes lose weight, but there is more going on than mere dehydration. Enzymes dismantle certain acids and create others. Tannins and sugars are concentrated and some of the latter evolve into glycerol, adding viscosity. Pressed in springtime, the grapes yield a luscious, sweet red dessert wine called Recioto della Valpolicella. Some of this is moved into old oak casks, where it undergoes a slow second fermentation, gradually turning the residual sugar into alcohol.

That is amarone. At its best (and there are plenty of disappointing cut-price versions on the market) the result is potent, ripe, velvety and profound, but with a beguilingly bitter (*amaro*) edge.

> **Steamed Sticky Rice** To cook sticky (glutinous) rice in the traditional manner, soak 4 cups rice in warm water for an hour or two. Rinse and place in a steamer basket or sieve lined with a clean cloth or Boston lettuce leaves. Place basket over boiling water, cover and steam for 20 to 30 minutes, or until the rice is tender.
>
> For a quicker method, rinse rice well and place in a pot with an equal amount of water. Bring to a boil and boil for 1 minute. Reduce heat to low. Cover and steam for 10 to 15 minutes, or until water is absorbed and rice is sticky.
>
> Serves 6.

Key Lime Squares

MAKES ABOUT 30 SQUARES

Make a big pan of these lemon-lime squares for dessert, breakfast and snacking all weekend. They'll keep in the refrigerator for about five days.

2 cups all-purpose flour
½ cup icing sugar
½ tsp salt
1 cup butter, diced
Topping
4 eggs
2 cups granulated sugar

⅓ cup all-purpose flour
2 tbsp grated lemon zest
1 tbsp grated lime zest
3 tbsp lemon juice
3 tbsp lime juice
2 tbsp icing sugar

Preheat oven to 350°F.

Blend flour, icing sugar and salt in a food processor or by hand. Add butter and cut in until mixture resembles fine breadcrumbs. Pat into a 13- by 9-inch greased baking pan. Prick all over with a fork. Bake for 20 minutes, or until pastry is a creamy golden color.

Beat together eggs, granulated sugar, flour, lemon and lime zest and lemon and lime juice. Pour topping mixture over cooked base.

Bake for 15 to 20 minutes, or until set. Cool. Cut into squares and dust with sifted icing sugar.

And to drink . . .

A FREEZING EVENING THAT BEGAN WITH GLOGG should certainly end with Icewine. While Amarone grapes wither in Italian attics, grapes meant for Icewine wither on the vine, risking the predations of Ontario starlings, turning a cold shoulder to the worsening weather, waiting for the Canadian winter to push the temperature down to ten degrees Fahrenheit and keep it there. It might be December or it might be as late as March of the following year, but when the moment is ripe, volunteers set out in the dead of night and harvest the crop. This is finger-numbing work, transformed into an unforgettable experience by the bonhommie of all concerned and by the view of the snow-covered vineyards glistening in the moonlight. The grapes stay frozen. The water in each berry has been turned into microscopic needles of ice that pierce the cells of the skin, releasing flavor that drips, with the concentrated sugars and acids, agonizingly slowly from the press. Exaggeratedly intense (and intensely slow and difficult to ferment), the resulting wine is as heavy as syrup, a fascinating balance of sweetness and acidity and fruitiness.

Tasting dozens of Icewines in a single sitting is a tooth-dissolving ordeal, but it amplifies the difference between those made from Riesling and those made from the hybrid Vidal. The former are usually more complex and more refined. The latter often seem more vibrant, the fruit analogies more tropical.

To be honest, I find Icewines a difficult match with food—sommeliers who pair them with foie gras will never receive my vote—but the complex swirl of citrus impressions and the sugar hit of a Riesling Icewine are just dandy with Lucy's Key Lime Squares.

A Spanish Dinner

Tortilla • Garlic Shrimp

Sautéed Oyster Mushrooms

Cod with Romesco Sauce • Saffron Rice

Spanish Flan

SERVES 4

SPANISH FOOD is hot right now. Cutting-edge chef Ferran Adria from the restaurant El Bulli on Spain's Catalan coast has brought foams, hot jellies and frozen powders—innovations that seem as much science as food—to the food world. But all the attention has also revived an interest in more traditional Spanish cuisine, which is just as exciting when done with style, as in this dinner.

Having a Spanish dinner at home is easy. Start with tapas, small dishes of savory foods that are traditionally served with sherry. Include dishes of Spanish olives, and serve the tapas while everyone is sitting around having drinks. Supply small plates and forks and let guests help themselves. Let the drinks period run for about an hour and a half, then serve the main course and dessert at the table.

Tapas Drinks

WE BEGAN THIS BOOK with sherry and we end the same way. Tapas and chilled fino sherry were literally made for each other—each salty, piquant mouthful a dazzling match for a wine as thin and intense as an unemployed poet. Sherry fortifies itself against such aggressive flavors with a shield of acid and alcohol, while its freshness and its swirling, multi-faceted, yeasty bouquet befriend them.

Fino sherry or manzanilla may be the classic accompaniment (and also Montilla, a fino look-alike from Andalucia's high plateaux, inland from Jerez), but there are other choices. Similar before-dinner dishes in Portugal would merit a vinho verde, the light, tart, slightly sparkling wine from the north of the country. Most ordinary vinho verde is ordinary indeed, but in recent years some producers near the Spanish border have been making far more interesting versions using the Alvarinho grape—still acidic, but tangy and intense with a citrus and almond aftertaste that lingers most impressively. North of the border, in Spain's Galicia region, the same grape is called Albariño. These wines seem more delicate but are still lively and tongue-tingling with subtle fruit impressions that range from apricot through apple to lemon. If nothing mentioned so far has set your imagination racing, Cava from Catalonia may be the answer (page 39)—cold, dry, refreshing, tasting of apples and as sparkling as Champagne.

Tortilla

SERVES 4

A Spanish tortilla is a special omelet—a mass of softly cooked potatoes and onions bound by egg. It can be served warm or cold. The large amount of oil used to cook the potatoes is drained off and can be re-used, but you will need it to poach the potato slices; it is this oil that gives the tortilla its authentic taste and texture.

In Spain the potatoes are shaved with a small knife to get the right texture. A mandolin is a time saver, but you can also hand slice them if you're feeling energetic. This dish needs lots of salt to give it flavor.

If flipping the tortilla worries you, use an ovenproof skillet and place under the broiler until the top is browned. Not as authentic, but good nonetheless.

1 cup olive oil	1 tbsp chopped garlic
1 lb Yukon Gold potatoes, peeled and very thinly sliced	6 eggs
1 cup diced Spanish onions	Salt and freshly ground pepper

Heat oil in a 9-inch nonstick skillet over medium heat. When a potato slice dropped into oil sizzles gently on edges, add all potatoes. Cook, stirring occasionally, for 3 minutes. Add onions and garlic. Continue to cook, adjusting heat if necessary, for 6 to 8 minutes, or until potatoes are soft but not browned.

Drain potatoes and onions through a sieve, being careful not to break up potatoes. Reserve strained oil.

Beat eggs, salt and pepper. Gently add potatoes and onions.

Wipe out skillet. Increase heat to high, add 1 tbsp reserved oil and slide in egg and potato mixture. Reduce heat to medium-low and cook slowly for 5 minutes, or until base is browned and eggs are nearly set.

Loosen base with a spatula and flip tortilla onto a large plate. Slide back into pan and cook for 2 to 3 minutes, or until bottom is light gold and eggs are set. Slide tortilla onto a serving plate and cut into wedges.

Garlic Shrimp

SERVES 4

A simple dish that can be served as a first course, as a tapas or as a main course for two with rice. Use large shrimp—the white ones are sweeter than the black tigers.

¼ cup olive oil
Pinch hot red pepper flakes
1 lb shrimp, shelled
1 tbsp chopped garlic

Salt to taste
2 tbsp lemon juice
1 tsp chopped parsley

Heat oil in a skillet over high heat. Add hot pepper flakes, shrimp, half the garlic and salt. Sauté for 2 minutes.

Add remaining garlic and cook for 2 minutes longer, or until shrimp are pink and curled and garlic is golden. Sprinkle with lemon juice and parsley. Serve immediately.

Sautéed Oyster Mushrooms

SERVES 4

You can also serve this easy tapas with a green salad as a first course at an elegant dinner. The dish may be made with shiitake or regular mushrooms, too. If the oyster mushrooms are large, remove the base of the stems, as they will be tough.

3 tbsp olive oil
12 oz oyster mushrooms, trimmed
2 tsp finely chopped garlic
¼ cup chicken stock

1 tbsp lemon juice
Salt and freshly ground pepper
2 tbsp finely chopped parsley

Heat oil in a skillet over medium heat. Add mushrooms and sauté for about 3 minutes, or until slightly softened. Sprinkle in garlic and sauté for 1 minute longer.

Add chicken stock and lemon juice and cook for 1 minute, or until mushrooms are cooked through. Season well with salt and pepper and sprinkle with parsley.

Cod with Romesco Sauce

SERVES 4

My favorite Spanish dishes are the fish dishes. The Spanish are such enthusiastic fish eaters that they cannot supply their own tables and must import much of their fish from Scotland! If you wish, use halibut or grouper instead of cod.

Use smoked Spanish paprika if you can find it. It is intense and smoky, but regular paprika will do in a pinch. For authenticity, you can use a mortar and pestle to pound all the ingredients for the sauce, as the almonds need to be very finely ground, but I use a food processor. The roasted peppers can be homemade or storebought.

Serve the cod over saffron rice.

¼ cup olive oil	½ tsp hot red pepper flakes,
½ cup sliced almonds	or more to taste
¼ cup fresh breadcrumbs	½ tsp paprika
½ cup chopped seeded tomatoes	1 tbsp sherry vinegar
½ cup chopped roasted red peppers	Salt
1 tsp chopped garlic	4 cod fillets (about 6 oz each)
	1 cup fish or chicken stock

Preheat oven to 450°F.

Heat 2 tbsp oil in a skillet over medium heat. Add almonds and sauté for 1 to 2 minutes, or until lightly browned. Add breadcrumbs and sauté for 1 minute, or until golden. Remove from heat and stir in tomatoes.

Place skillet ingredients in a food processor along with remaining 2 tbsp oil, red peppers, garlic, hot pepper flakes and paprika. Process until smooth, then blend in vinegar and salt. If puree is too thick, thin with a little water.

Spread 1 tbsp sauce over each cod fillet. Place remaining sauce in a baking dish just large enough to hold fish in a single layer. Stir in fish stock. Place fish on top of sauce.

Bake for 12 to 15 minutes, or until fish juices are just appearing and cod flakes slightly.

And to drink . . .

SPANISH WINES ARE surprisingly poorly represented in North America, with the exception of the intense, concentrated reds from the Ribera del Duero region in Castille. Plummy, dark, with serious machismo, they are based on the Tempranillo grape and have become fashionable in America and northern Europe in recent years. They are too big for this dish, but a case could be made for a mature Rioja, another wine that stars Tempranillo, though the dominant flavor is more often the spicy vanilla of the American oak barrels in which Riojas are aged. Maturity smooths and soothes these wines, making them perfectly suitable for hearty fish dishes. I tried a six-year-old Rioja Gran Reserva (a deeper, more self-involved wine than a rowdy regular Rioja) with this cod, and it wasn't a bad match at all. But it paled beside a dry rosado from Navarra.

Grenache (or, in Spanish, Garnacha) is one of the workhorse reds of southern France and northern Spain and can claim to be the world's second most widely planted grape variety (after Airén, a fairly banal white grape that is the backbone of Spain's brandy industry). Made as a rosado (rosé) in Navarra, its pretty pinky violet color conceals an impressive alcoholic strength and gorgeous, lingering red-berry fruitiness. Famously good with paella, it works in a similar way with this dish, the fruitiness embracing the sweetness of the roasted red peppers and almonds in the sauce. It may seem odd to serve a rosado as the principal wine at a dinner party, particularly in the winter, but the harmonies you'll experience justify the experiment.

Saffron Rice Heat 2 tbsp butter in a pot over medium heat. Add 1 cup chopped onions, 1 tsp chopped garlic and 1 tsp smoked Spanish paprika. Sauté for 2 to 3 minutes, or until soft. Add 2 cups uncooked short-grain rice and stir until coated with butter.

Stir 1 tsp saffron threads into 5 cups hot chicken stock. Pour stock over rice. Bring to a boil, reduce heat to medium-low and let rice cook, uncovered, for 15 to 20 minutes, or until stock is absorbed and rice is tender. Stir occasionally during cooking.

Season well with salt and freshly ground pepper and sprinkle with 2 tbsp chopped parsley.

Serves 4.

Tapas: Sautéed Oyster Mushrooms (p. 335);
Garlic Shrimp (p. 335)

Spanish Flan

SERVES 4

Although similar to crème caramel, this is a firmer-textured custard that works like a charm. Serve the flan with fresh figs or orange slices, if desired.

2 cups milk
1 cup whipping cream
½ cup granulated sugar
8 eggs
1 tbsp vanilla

Caramel
½ cup granulated sugar
3 tbsp water
1 tbsp corn syrup

Combine milk, cream and sugar in a large pot over medium-high heat. Bring to a boil. Remove from heat and cool for 10 minutes.

Whisk eggs and vanilla in a bowl until well combined. Slowly pour tepid milk mixture into eggs, whisking constantly. Pour mixture through a sieve into a bowl.

Preheat oven to 325°F.

Prepare caramel by combining sugar, water and corn syrup in a heavy pot. Stir to dissolve. Bring to a boil over high heat and boil for 6 to 8 minutes, or until pale gold. (Watch carefully to make sure it doesn't burn.) Remove from heat. Immediately swirl caramel over bottom and sides of a 6-cup round soufflé or baking dish.

Pour custard into baking dish and place dish in a larger baking pan. Pour hot water into baking pan until water comes halfway up sides of flan dish. Cover dish with a sheet of parchment paper. Bake for 50 to 55 minutes, or until custard is set and pale gold on top but still wiggles slightly in center. Chill.

Place baking dish in hot water for 2 minutes and run a knife around sides to loosen custard. Unmold onto a rimmed serving plate.

And to drink . . .

SPAIN'S BEST-KNOWN DESSERT WINE is a sherry—the dark, syrupy elixir at the farthest, heaviest end of the broad sherry spectrum that is usually referred to simply as PX. The initials stand for Pedro Ximénez, a white grape variety that was once the mainstay (with Palomino) of the sherry industry. Today the variety's fame rests on the super-sweet wines pressed from the grapes after they have been dried to raisins—a wine that is a fascinating curiosity but, frankly, too sweet for a delicate custard like Lucy's flan.

Many other Spanish dessert wines exist—Moscatel de Valencia is a fortified white Muscat not unlike Muscat de Beaumes-de-Venise—but the vanilla and caramel flavors of this pudding lead me across the border into Portugal in search of a ten-year-old tawny port. Older tawnies tend to be too complex, and expensive enough that they merit sipping on their own. Tawnies without any declaration of age are often too lacking in character, particularly if they have been created by blending immature wine with white port. But a ten-year-old is just right, resonating when set beside caramel. Love at first sip.

Fast and Fresh
Duck and Chocolate

Winter Salad of Hardy Greens and Bacon

Duck Breasts with Dried Cherries

Crisp-roasted Fingerling Potatoes

Rich Chocolate Mousse with Raspberry Sauce

SERVES 4

WHEN ASKED what she would like to be served for her last meal, Julia Child said, "Duck and chocolate mousse!" It would be my choice, too. This robust winter menu is one of my favorites.

And to drink . . .

A juicy Californian Pinot Noir will be ideal with this delectable duck dish—big enough for the rich meat and making merry with the cherries. Use the same wine in the sauce to further enhance compatibility.

Winter Salad of Hardy Greens and Bacon

SERVES 4

In winter, most lettuce is of debatable quality. But radicchio, Belgian endive and escarole are usually excellent. This dressing is strongly flavored to stand up to the robust taste of the lettuces.

1 small head escarole or romaine
1 small head radicchio
1 Belgian endive
1 cup packed watercress leaves
4 oz bacon, diced and cooked
   until crisp
½ cup toasted pecans

Mustard and Lemon Dressing
1 tbsp Dijon mustard
2 tbsp white wine vinegar
2 tsp lemon juice
1 tsp cracked peppercorns
½ cup olive oil
Salt

Tear escarole and radicchio into bite-sized pieces. Slice Belgian endive into rounds and add to lettuce. Add watercress, bacon and pecans and toss to combine.

Whisk together mustard, vinegar, lemon juice and pepper. Slowly whisk in oil until mixture thickens. Season with salt.

Toss salad greens with dressing just before serving.

Duck Breasts with Dried Cherries

SERVES 4

Buy the big and meaty Moulard duck breasts if you can find them. Some boneless breasts weigh more than 1½ pounds—at that size one breast between two people is enough.

Crack the peppercorns and coriander seeds by placing them in a plastic bag and whacking them with the bottom of a pot.

4 single boneless duck breasts (about 10 oz each)	1 tbsp balsamic vinegar
2 tsp finely chopped gingerroot	½ tsp granulated sugar
1 tsp finely chopped garlic	¼ cup red wine
2 tsp cracked peppercorns	1½ cups chicken stock
2 tsp cracked coriander seeds	¼ cup dried cherries
	2 tbsp butter, diced

Score duck skin at ½-inch intervals. Combine ginger, garlic, peppercorns and coriander seeds. Rub into duck.

Place breasts skin side down in a large cold skillet. Turn heat to medium and cook for 2 minutes. Reduce heat to low and cook for 15 minutes, or until fat is rendered. Drain fat as it accumulates in pan. Turn duck breasts and cook for 2 minutes longer.

Preheat oven to 450°F.

Place breasts skin side up on a rack in a baking pan. Roast for 7 to 10 minutes, or until pink (smaller Peking duck breasts will take only 5 minutes in the oven).

Discard fat from skillet while breasts are roasting. Increase heat to high and add vinegar and sugar. Cook for about 30 seconds, or until sticky.

Add wine and cook for 2 minutes longer. Add stock, bring to a boil and boil for 3 to 4 minutes, or until sauce is thickened and reduced. Add cherries and simmer for a few minutes.

Remove skillet from heat and stir in butter.

Slice duck and serve with sauce.

Crisp-roasted Fingerling Potatoes

SERVES 4

These potatoes look like fat little fingers. They are great roasted or steamed. If fingerlings are not available, use small red potatoes.

1 lb fingerling potatoes, cut in half lengthwise	2 tbsp olive oil
	2 tsp chopped fresh thyme, or ½ tsp dried
4 shallots, peeled and halved	
8 cloves garlic, peeled	Salt and freshly ground pepper

Preheat oven to 450°F.

Toss together potatoes, shallots, garlic and oil. Spread on a baking sheet. Sprinkle with thyme, salt and pepper.

Bake for 25 minutes, or until potatoes are tender. Turn once during baking.

Rich Chocolate Mousse with Raspberry Sauce

SERVES 4

Canadian framboise (raspberry) fruit wine is excellent in this dessert. The mascarpone cheese takes the place of eggs in the mousse.

Garnish the dessert with fresh raspberries, if desired.

2 tbsp butter	2 tbsp framboise
4 oz bittersweet chocolate, coarsely chopped	Raspberry Sauce
	12 oz frozen raspberries in syrup, defrosted
⅓ cup mascarpone	
½ cup whipping cream	¼ cup framboise
½ cup icing sugar	

Melt butter and chocolate in a pot over low heat.

Beat chocolate mixture slowly into mascarpone.

Whip cream with icing sugar until soft peaks form. Fold cream into mascarpone and stir in framboise. Spoon into a glass serving dish.

Puree raspberries and syrup in a food processor or blender. Rub through a sieve to remove seeds. Stir in framboise.

Serve mousse with raspberry sauce on the side.

A Drop More

Single Malt Whisky

"SINGLE MALT WHISKY," frowned The David, chewing the words as if they were a toffee he did not enjoy. "You wish me to teach you to understand single malt whisky . . ." The great bushy eyebrows descended farther toward the nose. The shoulders rose up behind his head, a mountain range of weather-beaten tweed. "Aye, I could do it." Then one pale blue eye fixed me like a moth on a pin. "But who's paying for the teaching aids?"

And so we began.

"Do ye ken how whisky is made?" asked The David.

"Oh, I think so. Barley is malted by soaking it and then drying it over peat fires. Hence the smokiness. It's milled and mixed with warm water and yeast to begin fermentation, then the fermented wort is double-distilled in a copper pot still, the spirits aged in oak barrels, then diluted—"

"Whisky," interrupted The David, "is made when the great principal elements of life conspire together. The good grain of the earth embraced by the pure clean water off the hills and by fire to release its majestic spirit. But the earth is always with it, in the black peat that smolders in the maltings, in the granite that blesses the rills and streams as they pass over its face." He jabbed a finger down onto the table. "Man's ingenuity plays a role, I grant you that! But the birth of a whisky is an elemental mystery. The evidence is plain to see. There are near a hundred distilleries in Scotland making a single malt whisky, and each is unique."

"That's what I wanted to ask you about," I explained. "How does one find one's way through so many, without having to taste them all?"

"And why shouldn't you taste them all?" asked The David incredulously.

"They say you can categorize them by region?"

"There's something in that," he grudgingly agreed.

"I mean, the whiskies of Islay all have that medicinal, iodine flavor, don't they?"

"And so would you," roared The David, "if your water had trickled over the peat moors and you had been confined in a sherry cask for a generation, with the wood spreading and shrinking with each passing season, and the sea knee-deep at the walls of the warehouse when the wind is high, and the brown kelp scenting the air you breathe! Aye, you can feel the ocean in a whisky from Islay's south shore—Laphroaig or Lagavulin, Ardbeg most of all."

"And what of the other islands? Talisker from Skye, Highland Park from the Orkneys? Are they as peaty?"

"Talisker is a king, high and civil and deep. But Highland Park . . ." The David allowed himself a rare chuckle. "There's the honey of the heather in her and the sweetness of smoke, and sherry from the butts if you find the twenty-four-year-old."

"The older the better, eh?"

"Pach!" grunted The David. "Didn't I say each whisky was unique? Some are best at ten or twelve, some at twenty, though there's more of the oak in them. And it matters where the barrels are from. Have they held sherry, or bourbon from America? Glenmorangie is finishing some of its whisky in port wood, or claret or Madeira—"

"I tried the port wood! It's magnificent! The color of copper and you smell butterscotch, mint and bitter chocolate, sandalwood, citrus and—"

"With a drop or two of water, you do. But add a little more and you'll smell hazelnuts and the hay of summertime. And before you add any, take a sip of it neat, to judge its body and texture."

"Glenmorangie's a Highland malt. But what about Speyside?"

"The heartland. Half of all Scotland's distilleries are there. You know The Macallan? Was there ever such a big, bold self, full of malt and sherry tones? The older the better with The Macallan for my money. Or for yours, I should say. There's sherry on the nose of The Glenlivet as well, when it's been long in the wood."

"And which of them all would you like to drink now?" I asked. The David's eyes narrowed. He seemed to be staring deep into the past.

"Lagavulin," he muttered at last.

"With ice and soda?" It was a joke, but The David did not take it well. Barbarous was the kindest epithet he bestowed upon the suggestion. I had to buy him more than one wee dram before the dust could be said to have settled.

Fast and Fresh
Southern Comfort

Southern Peanut Soup
Baked Grouper with Barbecue Sauce and Wilted Greens
Grits
Caramel Bourbon Bread Pudding
SERVES 4

THIS MENU takes its inspiration from the American South. Peanuts, fish, barbecue sauce, grits and greens are all southern specialties, but they'll provide plenty of warmth on a cold night. Serve the grouper with grits (made from ground dried corn kernels), polenta or hash browns.

And to drink . . .

Refreshing, medium-bodied, tangily acidic Barbera from northern Italy is renowned as a red that can cope with tomatoes, a principal ingredient in Lucy's tangy barbecue sauce. If you prefer white, try a zingy New Zealand or South African Sauvignon Blanc.

Southern Peanut Soup

SERVES 4

For peanut lovers, this zesty soup is a knockout, but when you serve it, always check to make sure your guests have no nut allergies.

2 tbsp vegetable oil
1 cup chopped onions
1 red pepper, seeded and chopped
2 tsp chopped garlic
¼ cup uncooked white rice
4 cups chicken stock

1 cup chopped canned tomatoes, with juice
½ tsp hot red pepper flakes, or to taste
½ cup chunky peanut butter
Salt and freshly ground pepper
1 tsp chopped fresh thyme, or ¼ tsp dried

Heat oil in a pot over medium heat. Add onions, red pepper and garlic and sauté for 5 minutes, or until soft.

Stir in rice, stock, tomatoes with juice and hot pepper flakes. Bring to a boil, reduce heat and simmer for 45 minutes, or until rice is soft.

Whisk in peanut butter until well blended. Simmer for 5 minutes. Season well with salt and pepper.

Serve soup sprinkled with thyme.

Baked Grouper with Barbecue Sauce and Wilted Greens

SERVES 4

Although this dish may seem strange—barbecue sauce with fish—it makes a magnificent centerpiece for a winter dinner.

Barbecue Sauce	2 tbsp granulated sugar
1 tbsp olive oil	1 tsp hot red pepper sauce, or to taste
2 slices bacon, chopped	Salt
1 cup chopped onions	Fish and Greens
2 tsp chopped garlic	4 grouper fillets (about 6 oz each)
2 tsp chopped jalapeño pepper	1 tbsp olive oil
2 tbsp chili powder	½ cup chopped onions
2 tsp ground cumin	1 tsp sliced garlic
2 cups chopped canned or	1 bunch Swiss chard, trimmed
fresh tomatoes	and thinly sliced

Heat oil in a skillet over medium-high heat. Add bacon and sauté for 2 minutes, or until limp. Add onions, garlic and jalapeño and sauté for 2 more minutes, or until softened. Stir in chili powder, cumin, tomatoes and sugar and bring to a boil. Reduce heat and simmer for 20 minutes, or until sauce has thickened. Stir in hot pepper sauce and salt.

Preheat oven to 450°F.

Place grouper in an oiled baking dish just large enough to hold fish in a single layer. Spoon barbecue sauce over fillets. Bake for 10 minutes, or just until white juices begin to appear.

Prepare greens while fish is cooking by heating oil in a large skillet over medium-high heat. Add onions and garlic and sauté for 2 minutes. Add chard and sauté for 5 minutes, until just wilted. Serve fish and sauce topped with Swiss chard.

> Grits Combine 3 cups water, 2 tbsp butter and ½ cup chopped onion in a pot and bring to a boil. Stir in 1 cup grits and return to a boil, stirring. Reduce heat to low and cook, covered, stirring occasionally, for 20 minutes, or until all liquid has been absorbed. Stir in 1 cup shredded Cheddar cheese and ¼ cup whipping cream. Season with salt and freshly ground pepper.
>
> Serves 4.

Caramel Bourbon Bread Pudding

SERVES 4

This feather-light bread pudding has a texture similar to crème caramel. Use any dried fruit, but dice so that all the fruit is the same size. I like a mix of dried cherries, cranberries and apricots.

Baking this in a water bath gives the pudding a delicate, creamy texture. If croissants are not available, use egg bread. You can make the caramel glaze ahead and warm it up just before serving.

1 cup milk	Caramel Glaze
1 cup whipping cream	2 tbsp butter
1 tsp vanilla	¼ cup brown sugar
3 eggs	2 tsp corn syrup
⅓ cup granulated sugar	¼ cup bourbon
2 croissants	2 tbsp whipping cream
1 cup mixed dried fruit	

Preheat oven to 325°F.

Combine milk and cream in a pot and bring to a boil over high heat. Remove from heat and add vanilla.

Beat eggs and granulated sugar with an electric mixer until thick and fluffy. Slowly beat in cream mixture.

Cut croissants into slices ½ inch thick and press into bottom of a buttered medium baking dish in a single layer, slightly overlapping slices. Sprinkle fruit over croissants. Pour egg mixture over fruit.

Place baking dish in a large roasting pan and pour hot water into pan until it reaches halfway up sides of baking dish.

Bake pudding for 45 to 50 minutes, or until set.

Combine butter, brown sugar, corn syrup and bourbon in a heavy pot while pudding is baking. Bring to a boil and boil for 2 to 3 minutes, or until mixture is golden brown and thickened. Remove from heat and stir in cream.

Serve pudding warm or cold with caramel glaze.

A Drop More

Bourbon

SMOOTH AS A RIVERBOAT GAMBLER, rich as a Manhattan millionaire, old-fashioned as a Kentucky colonel—bourbon is quintessential Americana. The word conjures images of gangsters and gumshoes, southern plantations and troubled families in Tennessee Williams plays. But in the past ten years a new layer of association has been superimposed on the old: bourbon as a most sophisticated spirit to be revered as highly as any Cognac or rare single malt Scotch—bourbon in a tuxedo instead of a T-shirt.

It was the enthusiastic welcome given to premium single malts in Asia and North America in the 1980s that brought about the bourbon renaissance. Kentucky producers scratched their heads in consternation and wondered how to compete. Altering their whiskeys was not an option—the very idea was a heresy—but it might be possible to optimize what they already had. The master distillers knew that each barrel aging in their warehouses was subtly different. They selected the best, sometimes filling bottles from a single barrel, sometimes blending the contents of a bunch of barrels and calling it "small batch." In 1984, Blanton's Single Barrel was the first "super-premium" bourbon to appear on the market, and it was greeted with delight—huge, heavy and full of spice and honey. Other distilleries have been following suit ever since.

Tradition (a living, breathing force in Kentucky) is on their side. Visit a bar today in Bardstown or Louisville and you soon learn that a southern gentle-man bought his bourbon by the barrel in the glory days between the American Civil War and Prohibition. Sit a little longer and the whole tale unfolds. How the German, Dutch or "Scotch-Irish" pioneers of western Pennsylvania finally rose up in arms in 1794 after the federal government taxed the rye whiskey they made. How President Washington (a distiller himself) snuffed out the Whiskey Rebellion with 13,000 militiamen—a larger force, incidentally, than he ever commanded against the British. How the pioneers packed up their stills and moved west of the Blue Ridge Mountains to the lands that are now Kentucky. This was corn country, so corn whiskey they made, spicing the mash with a little rye and some malted barley to set the fermentation going.

That was the seed, the proto-bourbon: religion and science completed the recipe. A Baptist minister, the Reverend Elijah Craig, may have been the first to char the insides of the new oak barrels he used to store his whiskey—a key to bourbon's character. In the 1830s, a Scottish physician, Dr. James Crow, added the finishing touch by using some of the "sour mash" liquid left from one fermentation to lend a consistent personality to the next. Loaded onto rafts at the Limestone depot in Bourbon County, Kentucky, and shipped down the Ohio and Mississippi Rivers, these whiskeys found favor with the sophisticated drinkers of New Orleans, who soon learned to ask for "bourbon."

But while the basic method is the same, every bourbon has its own style. Venerable whiskey men such as Jim Beam's master distiller emeritus, Booker Noe (grandson of the original Jim Beam), and Jimmy Russell of Wild Turkey talk of spring water, unique yeasts, different grain combinations, equipment and warehouse temperatures. For the connoisseur, the proof is in the glass. And where Booker's True Barrel is concerned, the proof is overwhelming. Most everyday bourbons clock in at under 50 percent alcohol by volume. Booker's is 63.15 percent. About seven years old, unfiltered (the only unfiltered bourbon I know) and undiluted from the barrel, it's a dark monster that scorches the palate. But add a few drops of water to your glass and the massive body reveals a complexity of vanilla, orange, caramel and spice, leading to a long, rich finish. Baker's small batch is another seven-year-old special from Jim Beam, bottled at 53 percent alcohol. The nose is full of tangy fruit, but sip the smooth liquid and the impressions are more like the smell of leather and cigar boxes. Overriding all else, however, is the sweet vanilla spice of American oak, bourbon's unmistakable signature. Because the barrels have never been filled before, the maturing whiskey draws massive amounts of color and flavor from the wood, which is why one rarely sees a bourbon much more than twelve years old. After that, it becomes too woody. Once emptied, the barrels are sold to distillers in Scotland or Ireland and used to age whiskies there—a longer if less passionate second marriage.

What is the optimum bourbon experience? That's the beauty of the beast: there are many. For me it might be a Manhattan made with Jim Beam Black Label, my favorite everyday bourbon. It could be a slug of dark, well-knit twelve-year-old Elijah Craig poured over ice. On evenings when I want to hang out with a true aristocrat, I'll pour some Four Roses Single Barrel Reserve into a brandy snifter and revel in the sweet nose and dry finish, the debonair balance of flavors. As American as apple pie, but so much more enjoyable.

Acknowledgments

A BOOK WITH TWO AUTHORS, a book about finding harmony in the midst of good company, is itself a celebration of the collaborative act. We must start by thanking Shelley Tanaka for her gently assertive editing and vision of what our book should be. Bruce Westwood and Natasha Daneman fanned the embers of the idea and found us our publisher. David Kent at HarperCollins Canada felt the moment was right and brought together a talented team to turn our notions into reality: Iris Tupholme, Kevin Hanson, Felicia Quon, Noelle Zitzer, Roy Nicol and Kirsten Hanson, tireless point person for the entire project. Alison Fryer of The Cookbook Store in Toronto gave us invaluable advice and encouragement.

Choosing a photographer was easy: for years, we had both been dazzled by the way Rob Fiocca brought his genius to bear on edible and drinkable subjects. His contribution to our book— and those of his assistant Jim Norton, and stylists Lasha Andrushko and Catherine MacFadyen— is immeasurable. Rob's talents first came to our attention through his images for *Food & Drink* magazine where we have worked side by side for more than a decade. Our sincere thanks are owed to *Food & Drink*'s Nancy Cardinal and Jody Dunn for giving us the freedom to roam the world of food, wine and spirits.

Each of us drew on a lifetime of experience in creating this book—of cooking in Lucy's case, of drinking in James's. Lucy thanks Cecily Ross of the *Globe and Mail* for ruthlessly editing her copy; Eshun Mott, her chief recipe tester, food stylist and all-time calming kitchen influence; Blake Eligh, who typed, organized, tasted and even washed dishes when needed; and Melanie Stuparyk, who followed Blake. James thanks Michelle Hunt, Laura Panter and Michael Cook of The Martini Club, who helped perfect, test and style the Home James cocktail and brought gorgeous stemware to the studio; wine experts Margaret Swaine and David Lawrason, his co-hosts of *Toronto Life* magazine's wine and food experiences, for years of fascinating insights; Nick Morgan, who opened his eyes to single malt whisky's affinity with food; Andrea Lowen of Robert Mondavi, who generously allowed him to make guinea pigs of prized California varietal wines; and Brenda Lowes of Ultra Supper Club, who came through at the eleventh hour with a much-needed Martini shaker.

Most importantly, we would like to acknowledge those who stood by us in the long watches of the night when the words were slow in coming. James thanks his wife, Wendy Martin, for her unfailing support in this and every other endeavor. Above all, he raises a glass (of her favorite Central Otago New Zealand Pinot Noir) to Lucy Waverman, whose energy, valor, friendship and infallible recipes were a bottomless pitcher of inspiration. Lucy wishes to thank her husband, Bruce, for all his support and devotion; her children, Emma and Micah, Katie and Shane, Alex and Natalie, for being loving and loyal through everything; her brother, David Geneen, for his generosity and insight; her mother, Pearl Geneen, who is still the best cook she knows; her late father, Ben Geneen, who taught her to appreciate the joys of the table; and her slew of tiny grandchildren, Zak, Josh, Noah, Liam and Ella, who make her heart melt. And finally Lucy raises her Plymouth gin Martini to James, who, apart from his constant support, helped her develop an appreciation for fine writing, wry wit and very dry Martinis.

Index

An italic page number preceded by "op" (for example, *op272*) indicates an illustration.